Advance Praise for SLEEPWOKING

"A sharp-edged takedown of the contemporary fallacies about history that plague Canada. Based on comprehensive research, and written in the engaging style of a professional journalist and novelist." —**TOM FLANAGAN**

Professor Emeritus of Political Science and Distinguished Fellow, the School of Public Policy, University of Calgary

Co-author of *Grave Error: How the Media Misled Us (and the Truth about Residential Schools)*, and author of *First Nations? Second Thoughts* and other books.

"A compelling read and a lively eyewitness account of the Canadian self-flagellation in the Justin Trudeau era." —**PATRICE DUTIL**

Professor, Department of Politics and Public Administration, Toronto Metropolitan University

Author of *Sir John A. Macdonald & the Apocalyptic Year 1885*

"This is a cogent critique of the scandalous treatment of the great heroes of Canada who worked so hard to deliver us one of the greatest countries in the world. Jerry Amernic has done a great service to our country in his clearheaded assessment of the state of the dominant ideology of our time. His book will surely play a vital role in bringing about its end." —**SAM SULLIVAN**

Former Mayor of Vancouver and member of the Cabinet of British Columbia

President of the Global Civic Policy Society and adjunct professor at the UBC School of Architecture and Landscape Architecture

"We are living at a time in Canada where anything to do with settler and Indigenous relationships seems to be decided in the court of public opinion, often communicated by activists who call themselves journalists, or worse, teachers who call themselves educators. On a number of these troubling issues, Jerry Amernic tells it like it is in a direct communicative style interwoven with personal reflections and related to the overall narrative theme."
—**Leo J. Deveau**

Journalist and Nova Scotia historian

Author of *400 Years in 365 Days, A Day by Day Calendar of Nova Scotia History*

"Jerry Amernic, well armed with wit, humour, and a sharp eye for the hypocritical, the improbable and the just plain wrong, takes a close look at the sad state of public discourse in Canada today. In particular, when it comes to the public's knowledge (or lack thereof) of history and its application to issues of politics, culture and race. After reading Jerry's critique of recent examples of the use and abuse of history by politicians, academics and the media, readers will sadly be reminded that 'Those who cannot remember the past are condemned to repeat it.'—**Greg Piasetzki**

Intellectual property lawyer and citizen of the Métis Nation of Ontario

Researcher and writer on Canadian history

"A must read! SLEEPWOKING is a well researched and meticulously documented overview of the ill-founded degradation of Canadian values, our institutions and our history. Jerry Amernic has exposed the sinister woke movement which intends to distort, discredit and malign the contribution and reputation of our nation's builders."—**Julian Fantino**

Former Chief of Toronto Police Service and Commissioner of Ontario Provincial Police

Former Member of Parliament

"Jerry Amernic's passion for Canadian history shines through in this book. He shows how misinformation, along with the lack of a strong education in Canadian history, has led to a diminished and often inaccurate sense of the country's past."—**J. D. M. Stewart**

History teacher for more than 30 years and writer

Author of *Being Prime Minister*

"Jerry Amernic has confronted the elephant in the room, the desire of some people to find individuals in the past responsible for the ills of modern society. In so doing, there has been a trend to play fast and loose with the truth. Those who question this rewriting of history are dismissed as settler-colonials who have no sympathy for the oppressed. With an engaging style, the author examines the new interpretations of history and finds them wanting, and those behind the reinterpretations in need of learning some real history."—**Ron Stagg**

Recently retired professor and former Chair of History at Toronto Metropolitan University, with a particular specialty in 18th- and 19th-century Ontario

"Novelist Milan Kundera wrote, 'The first step in liquidating a people is to erase its memory. Destroy its books, its culture, its history.' Jerry Amernic's SLEEPWOKING details the destruction of Canada's history, specifically focusing on the attacks against Edward Cornwallis, Henry Dundas, Egerton Ryerson, John A. Macdonald and Matthew Begbie. His book brings hope, however, by providing facts that will overcome narrative and misinformation. SLEEPWOKING is a wake-up call to all Canadians to study, debate and ultimately protect their history."—**DON CRANSTON**

Director, The Canadian Institute for Historical Education

SLEEPWOKING

JERRY AMERNIC

SLEEPWOKING

Copyright © 2025 Jerry Amernic

No generative artificial intelligence (AI)
was used in the writing of this work.

All rights reserved.

No part of this book may be reproduced or transmitted
in any form or by any means, electronic or mechanical,
including photocopying and recording, or by any information
storage or retrieval systems, or in training of AI technologies,
without written permission from the publisher, except for brief
passages quoted by a reviewer in a newspaper or magazine.
To perform any of the above is an infringement of copyright law.

Published by Wordcraft Communications
www.jerryamernic.com

ISBN: 978-1-7752399-4-9 (softcover)

This book was published without the
support of the Canada Council for the Arts.

There are few things in the world as dangerous as sleepwalkers.

—Ralph Ellison

Contents

LOCATIONS WHERE MONUMENTS WERE
VANDALIZED AND PLACES RENAMED   x

Part I—The New Racism

Chapter 1: Call me Emmanuel   3

Chapter 2: They don't know what they don't know   19

Chapter 3: We've been Aunt Jemima-ed   29

Chapter 4: How we got here   49

Part II—The Lynching of the Innocent

Chapter 5: The trashing of John A. Macdonald   63

Chapter 6: A paragon of education and an institution of lower learning   91

Chapter 7: The slaver who wasn't   111

Chapter 8: Cancel culture in Atlantic Canada   131

Chapter 9: An honoured judge rewritten, renounced and removed   155

Part III—The Hijacking of Our History

Chapter 10: Was Winston Churchillian   175

Chapter 11: Truth and reconciliation, falsehood and deception   191

Chapter 12: A return to pride in country   217

ENDNOTES   229
INDEX   237
ACKNOWLEDGEMENTS   247
ABOUT THE AUTHOR   249

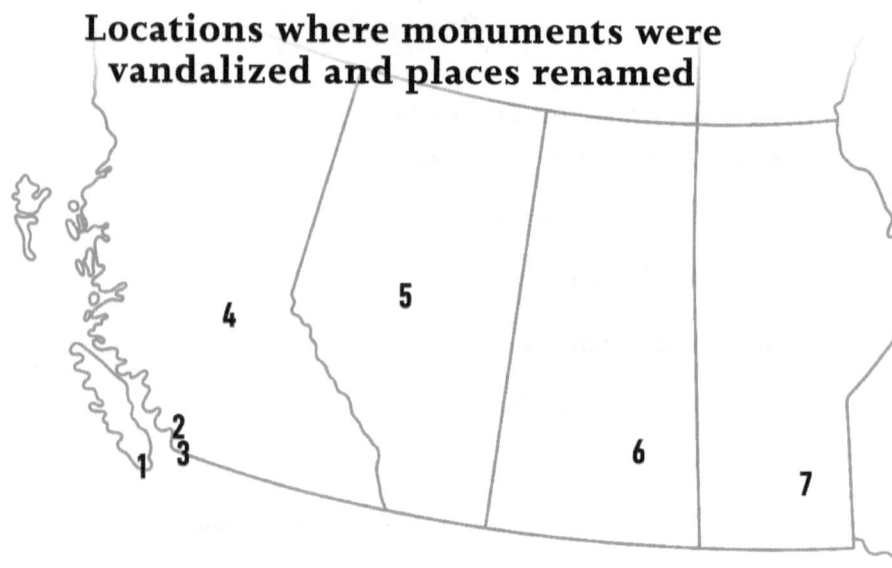

Locations where monuments were vandalized and places renamed

1. 1.1 Name Matthew Begbie removed from law school building at University of Victoria.

    1.2 Statue of John A. Macdonald removed from Victoria City Hall.
2. Statue of Matthew Begbie removed from Law Society of BC building in Vancouver.
3. 3.1 Statue of Matthew Begbie removed in New Westminster, BC.

    3.2 Statue of Winston Churchill vandalized in New Westminster, BC.

    3.3 Matthew Begbie Secondary School renamed in New Westminster, BC.
4. Plaque about Chilton chiefs unveiled in Quesnel, BC.
5. Statue of Winston Churchill defaced in Edmonton.
6. Statue of John A. Macdonald removed in Regina.
7. 7.1 Statue of Queen Elizabeth II toppled and removed in Winnipeg.

    7.2 Statue of Queen Victoria toppled and beheaded in Winnipeg.
8. Statue of John A. Macdonald removed in Baden, Ontario.
9. Statue of John A. Macdonald toppled in Hamilton.
10. Sir John A. Macdonald Public School renamed in Brampton, Ontario.
11. 11.1 Plaque unveiled about Egerton Ryerson at Ryerson University in Toronto.

    11.2 Statue of Egerton Ryerson toppled and destroyed in Toronto.

    11.3 Statue of John A. Macdonald boarded up at Ontario Legislature in Toronto.

    11.4 Ryerson University changed its name in Toronto.

    11.5 Toronto City Council renames Yonge-Dundas Square.

    11.6 Toronto Transit Commission renames Dundas subway station.

11.7 Jane-Dundas Library renamed in Toronto.
12. Statue of John A. Macdonald removed in Picton, Ontario.
13. 13.1 Statue of John A. Macdonald removed in Kingston, Ontario.
   13.2 Queen's University removed Macdonald from name of its law school in Kingston, Ontario.
   13.3 Kingston pub Sir John's Public House renamed Public House.
14. 14.1 Sir John A. Macdonald Parkway renamed in Ottawa.
   14.2 Tomb of the Unknown Soldier at National War Memorial vandalized in Ottawa.
15. Statue of John A. Macdonald toppled and decapitated in Montreal.
16. Sir John A. Macdonald High School renamed in Upper Tantallon, Nova Scotia.
17. 17.1 Statue of Edward Cornwallis removed in Halifax.
   17.2 Cornwallis Park renamed in Halifax.
   17.3 Cornwallis Street renamed in Halifax.
   17.4 Cornwallis coast guard ship renamed in Halifax.
18. Statue of John A. Macdonald removed in Charlottetown.
19. Bust of Winston Churchill vandalized in St. John's, Newfoundland.

PART 1

The New Racism

CHAPTER 1

Call me Emmanuel

LET'S IMAGINE THAT my name is Emmanuel and my grandparents came to Canada as immigrants from our family's ancestral homeland in east Africa, which means in the greater scheme of things I am what you call racialized. At least, in this country. These then are my roots and this is my story.

Now when I was little we were homeless. It's true. Funny, but I never thought of it that way before, but what else do you call it when a four-year-old boy, namely me, and his older brother Julius are living with their parents in a drabby motel, eking out their existence in a seedy part of town by the lake? And that's how it was. The street was Lake Shore Boulevard and right on the water—that would be Lake Ontario in the west end of Toronto—and what I remember most about the experience were the streetcars constantly whizzing by on the tracks. They seemed to be going at all hours of night and day.

One afternoon we were there and Julius, who at eleven was seven years older than me, got both of us into a rowboat. No lifejackets. We were out on the lake, my mother Lydia screaming her lungs at us from the shoreline. "Oh my God! Emmanuel! Julius!" Alas, we couldn't swim and neither could she. I can only imagine what she was going through, envisioning her two sons drowning like that and not being able to help. But as luck would have it we somehow made it back no worse for wear. Not long after that adventure our family wound up in a low-rent, apartment unit—the basement level of a triplex as they called such buildings in those days—and we returned to the only existence we ever knew.

Hand-to-mouth. No money. Mountains of unpaid bills and piling debt. And a perpetual state of tension between my mother and father.

This is how I grew up. My parents were not well educated, but that's just the way it was. They never made it out of high school and when you get older you can discern things about people pretty quickly by how well they read and write. For the two of them, it wasn't very well. As far as my father is concerned—his name was Benson—he didn't read anything and certainly not books although I do recall he made it through Mario Puzo's *The Godfather* after the movie came out. But that's the only book I ever remember him reading. I suppose he was attracted to all the drama associated with the criminal underworld of the Mafia. On those rare occasions when he had to read something out loud his words would be halting, slow and unsure. It was easy to tell he didn't have much schooling.

My older brother Julius always snickered with embarrassment when our Dad did that—read out loud—as if trying to hide himself from public view. My mother Lydia? She didn't read either. Not a thing. In fact, in my entire life I cannot remember a single book she ever read. As for writing, she would sit down and pen letters to her sisters—she was one of four and had six brothers as well, which meant she came from a family of ten children—and the thing that sticks in my mind is how she would scribble *mebbe* for the word 'maybe' as if that is how you spell it.

My father Benson was a likeable but simple man. For sure, rough around the edges and sometimes short-tempered, but always the first person to lend a hand. To anyone. Even if they were a stranger. When he was younger he had worked in a factory and there was the time he got his hand tangled in this printing machine which left one of his fingers disfigured. It was always like that. Later he drove a cab and liked to tell the story about two men he picked up and one of them had this long knife tied around his leg, so my father put the pedal to the metal and told them he wasn't slowing down the car until that knife got tossed out the window. And they tossed it. He said he always kept a baseball bat in the trunk of his taxi just in case and later when I was old enough to remember things it had to be true. You see, there was always a baseball bat in the trunk of our family car.

He wound up working as a salesman but on the road which I guess was his calling since he wasn't the type to sit around an office all day. What he might have done in an office I have no idea because he couldn't stay still at the best of times. So, all in all he dabbled in various things, none of which amounted to much, and unfortunately for us providing for his family wasn't something he was terribly good at. My mother I don't ever remember being employed at all, but she did relate stories about working at Tip Top Tailors, the big retailer of her day, before getting married.

Now and then we went on holidays, but not on a regular basis. There was nothing regular about our home and family since everything was done spur of the moment. Once we rented a cottage way up north in Algonquin Park for a week. Another time we took a drive all the way to Florida to sample the heat and the ocean in December, and there were also a couple trips to New York City. It was always by car. Airplanes? No. Never. That would have been unthinkable. The closest we ever got to airplanes was going out to Malton—the forerunner of Toronto's Pearson International Airport—and watch them land and take off on the runway. We actually used to do that on Friday evenings. It was a family outing. But that was the extent of air travel for us. The first time I made it onto an actual plane was when I got married and flew to Europe with my new wife on our honeymoon.

It was her first time in a plane as well.

It would be a stretch to call my father an alcoholic, but he did like to drink. I remember like yesterday when he would come home late—he always came home late—after signing up a customer. He would be singing and dancing with my mother in the middle of the kitchen floor, both of them in a state of happy delirium. He had made a sale—he got himself a *deal* as he called it—and now things were going to be better. Little did I know he had visited a bar on the way home and that, combined with the deal, was the reason for the sudden ecstasy. This sort of thing happened a lot.

However, he also had a propensity for gambling which is what ultimately did him in. Not to mention us. As the story goes, when I was a toddler we were living in this small bungalow in the north end of town and during one memorable card game he bet everything he had on his hand. Everything. But he lost and we lost the house as well. Just how much equity my parents had in that place I have no idea—probably not much—but there is this sticky issue of title and ownership and whatever the details it led to my mother packing up her two boys and the three of us shuffling off to the west coast and Vancouver. By train, of course. Why Vancouver? She had a brother who lived there and we stayed with him for the summer, my father remaining on his own back east. Later my parents reconciled and when we got back to Toronto the four of us were living in that motel on Lake Shore Boulevard.

And so, we were homeless.

My mother once told me how despite all the problems and turmoil that seemed to follow us around, we never went hungry, as if this was some great accomplishment in a country like Canada. Both she and my father were born here, she in Newmarket, Ontario just north of Toronto, and he in the nation's capital. Ottawa. But it was in Toronto where they met and two months after that meeting they were married.

Their parents—my grandparents—were bona fide immigrants who had come from across the pond. I knew only one of them and that would be my father's mother Fatima who died when I was 19. She was a short, rotund woman with a kind heart and everyone adored her, but she never mastered English and I use the word 'mastered' diplomatically, so my conversations with her were rather limited. Both my grandfathers had passed away long before I was born and the other grandmother I had met only once because of family troubles.

What was all that about? It sounds crazy when I tell people but it's the truth. When my brother Julius was five, which means this happened before I came around, he and my mother were visiting *her* mother, my grandmother Grace. She had her own house and lived with her one remaining son still at home. The son, that would be our uncle, took exception to a little boy getting in his way when he was trying to shave and decided to whack him. Later, when my Dad found out about it, he was ready to kill his brother-in-law. Now it's true my father did a bit of boxing in his time and while he wasn't a big man—five-nine and 165 pounds—he was a scrappy sort with thick hands and wide wrists, much wider than mine and those of my brother Julius, and I'm sure he could have done some damage if so inclined. Anyway, one thing led to another and the whole matter wound up in family court.

When my grandmother Grace took the witness stand she testified that her grandson Julius had tripped on the ice outside on the street—it was winter—and this was how he got banged up. It wasn't true, but that was what she said. She didn't want anything to happen to her son who was living with her. Anyway, from his vantage point in the courtroom my father stood up and called her a lying bitch which won the wrath of another brother on my mother's side—as I say there were six brothers in the family—and he took a swing at my Dad. Right there in the courtroom. My Dad turned and tried to hit him back but instead struck a court officer. The long and short of it was that both my father and his brother-in-law spent the night in jail and the judge threw the case out.

At the time there was a weekly newspaper called *The Flash*, a tabloid of course, and there is a clipping that survives to this day relating the whole episode. I have seen it many times. Nevertheless, that little escapade led to my mother becoming estranged from her mother and because of that incident I never got to know my grandmother Grace. The sad part for me was that she spoke English, so my one and only chance to have a legitimate conversation with a grandparent—someone who could have told me first-hand how things were in the old country—got nipped in the bud before I was even born.

When you add it all up it doesn't sound like a life of privilege and believe me it wasn't. Truth be told it was always a matter of scrimping and saving, but never with any saving. I find it incredible thinking about this now but when my father died his balance sheet showed a man who had never accumulated any capital or had any assets to speak of. But those are the facts.

He died at the age of 70 and even then it wasn't old, but he smoked two packs a day and sooner or later that kind of lifestyle catches up to you. At first it was diagnosed as lung cancer and he had part of a lung removed and then it metastasized into inoperable brain cancer and his last year was a terrible ordeal for all of us. My mother? She would go on to live—no, exist is a better word for how it was—another 19 years as a widow with precious little to show in a monetary sense. Her only source of income was her old age pension and during all that time it was never easy, each and every day a struggle, but then nothing ever came easy in our household.

Just how much did my mother rely on my father? Well, after his death she had to learn how to write a cheque because she didn't know. She had never done that before. She also had to learn how to put her key into the door of their apartment because she hadn't done that before either. You see, before he got sick with his cancer she didn't go anywhere without him—she never drove a car—and he was the one with the key.

Life was always hard.

If all this was due to the customs of a family whose roots are from across the ocean on another continent where things are done differently, so be it. But it seemed to me that most if not all my friends—even those of similar background—were from families better off than we were, and even those who weren't well off were probably better off than we were.

Was our misfortune attributable in any way to the kind of people we are and where we are from? After all, we were *different* from the mainstream folks, many of whom could trace their roots back multiple generations to England, Scotland or Ireland. We didn't have anybody—not a single person—who hailed from that part of the world. But if that was the case, how come none of my friends ever lived in a motel on Lake Shore Boulevard? They were pretty much from the same stock as us. Mind you, my father would often come out with these claims of prejudice against us by the WASP ruling class, but in this regard he was no different than anyone else from his ilk.

Now my wife shares the same complexion as me, but aside from that is of a completely different culture. She herself was an immigrant who arrived in Canada at the tender age of three and right off the boat at Pier 21 in Halifax, also from across the pond and from the same continent as my grandparents. Her own parents had virtually no education and I don't exaggerate when I say this. Her father's total education encompassed all of four years and her mother two years. That was it. How is that possible? Easy. There were wars—wars against other countries and a civil war in their own country—and when her parents were kids the schools were shut down.

In spite of all that her parents got married and brought their fledgling family over here and scraped by until they were able to run a small diner in the city. They never had a great deal in the material sense, but at least there would be a foundation for something—a structure, a sense of responsibility—that was sadly lacking in my family.

When my wife started school she remembers to this day being hounded by other kids because she was, well, *different*. She dressed differently. She spoke differently. For lunch she brought sandwiches to school that were different, too, because the bread was homemade which was unheard of. All this antagonism against her would last many years. Throughout her entire childhood. When she was little she would be called a DP for Displaced Person. Funny, but I distinctly remember my father joking about his mother being called by that same designation. And so, my wife and her family were part of a culture and ethnicity that was reflective of where they had come from, and likewise for me and my family.

Alas, my name is not Emmanuel and my family did not hail from east Africa. But aside from that minor tidbit and the names of those aforementioned family members, everything I just told you about my life is true. All of it. One hundred per cent. Losing the house and living in the motel on Lake Shore Boulevard. The temporary break-up of the family. The turmoil with relatives. The hand-to-mouth existence. The lack of education on the part of my parents and absolutely no guidance for my brother and me on the most vital aspects of how to get by in this world.

In fact, my grandparents were Jews who came to Canada from Europe. Two from Romania. One from Belarus. And one from Poland. Money? Nobody arrived here with any money. Now it's true some of my relatives wound up doing pretty well for themselves, but that certainly wasn't the case with my immediate family. They started with nothing and ended up the same way. My wife's family is from Greece and of Macedonian ethnicity. And, believe me, nothing ever came easy for them either.

And so, we come to this business of *white privilege*. I have to tell you my wife and I both do a double-take whenever we hear it and these days one hears it all the time. When I look up the term in the dictionary it says:

> *Inherent advantages possessed by a white person on the basis of their race in a society characterized by racial inequality and injustice.*

Let's parse that down. Have I enjoyed inherent advantages bestowed upon me for being white? Perhaps, although I never recognized it. But I have recognized inequities—no let's call it prejudice because that's what it is—for being seen as a Jew. I have recognized inequities being from a family that had little education and not as much as other families, but when that is all you know you get used to it.

Nowadays, however, I find I'm supposed to apologize to all and sundry for being white. As if I myself were the cause of the slave trade, the American Civil War, tribalism in Africa and other parts of the world, and any and all forms of discrimination against people because of the colour of their skin. But here's the thing. I am *not* responsible for any of that, any more than I am responsible for the death of Jesus, and yes I have heard that one, too.

A society characterized by racial inequality and injustice.

I have lived in Canada my whole life and the older I get the more I realize how lucky I am for this accident of birth. Indeed, what if I had been a Jew from Germany or Poland or anywhere else in Europe one generation before my time? Chances are good, very good, that I never would have survived. But I don't make it my business pointing that out every day to every person I meet. I don't think it should qualify me for anything in particular, be it a job opportunity, a grant application, or somehow being moved up the line because of all the terrible things that have happened to my people over the years and there is no question that some very terrible things have happened to my people over the years.

But you adapt and move on.

Not moving on is living a life devoted to victimhood, which is another way of saying that if not for such-and-such I could have been like prizefighter Terry Molloy (Marlon Brando) sitting in the back seat of that car with his big brother Charley (Rod Steiger) in the film classic On the Waterfront, "I coulda bin a contendah ... You wuz my brother, Charley. You shoulda looked out for me a little bit. You shoulda taken care of me just a little bit so I wouldn't hafta take them dives for the short-end money."

If only ... if only ...

Lesson no. 1. You can't live your life based on 'if only.'

This country isn't perfect but I defy anyone to point out a country where equality and tolerance are what they are in Canada. Or this was the case until recently when our standing on the tolerance scale has dropped a few notches. This has happened for a number of reasons and I'll get into it later. How about the United States? Even before the current administration took office no one would have called the US more tolerant than Canada. Indeed, all you have to do is watch the news on any given night. Great Britain? No. Maybe Australia and New Zealand are closer but even they have issues, as do places like Sweden and Norway. When we get into Central and South America, eastern Europe, Asia, the far east and Middle East, I'm sorry but no.

Is Canadian society really *characterized by racial inequality and injustice*? Not where I live. Hop onto the subway and take it downtown and on the way you come across every type of person imaginable. White people. Black people. East Indians. Asians. Arabs. What have you. You listen and hear so many different languages you would think it's a United Nations conference convening right there in the subway car and it's like that all over the city and beyond. You have millions of people cohabitating—yes, in the more densely populated areas it is cheek to jowl—and yet, by every standard of measurement and living index out there it is considered one of the most liveable cities on earth. Indeed, *National Geographic* once called Toronto the most multicultural city in the world for good reason.

As of this writing my provincial Member of Parliament—an MPP as we call it in Ontario—is a man of colour. A Tamil from

Sri Lanka. He is the Associate Minister of Mental Health and Addictions for the Province of Ontario. Our previous MPP was a woman of colour, a native of Jamaica, and she was Ontario's Minister of Education. Our current federal Member of Parliament is, just like our MPP, a Tamil from Sri Lanka. In fact, he has won the riding in the last four federal elections and is a member of the federal Cabinet.

My grandchildren go to public schools where the classes are as racially mixed as can be. In my work I deal with professional people and consultants—lawyers, accountants, financial advisors, what have you—and if what we have today is a white paradise *characterized by racial inequality and injustice* someone must have sabotaged the script because from my vantage point it just ain't so. Which is not to say things have always been like that. No, they haven't. There was a time when things were different. Just as there was a time when Jews were not admitted to the better universities, never mind the Toronto Granite Club, Royal Canadian Yacht Club, or Rideau Club in Ottawa. But they are members of these places now. Past wrongs were corrected and society evolved. Unfortunately, antisemitism is again on the rise.

I would be naïve to think the rest of Canada is as diverse as where I live. But is Canadian society *characterized* by racial inequality and injustice? Is this a core tenet of the land we call home? I can name a few societies where this is, or has been, the case. If we delve into the past Nazi Germany comes to mind. So does the past apartheid state of South Africa. But Germany and South Africa progressed and moved on.

In current times we can look at India which today has more people than any country in the world and still retains its caste system, which pure and simple is a form of open and widely accepted discrimination. It goes back to 1500 BC People were divided into hereditary classes with *Brahmins* (priests and teachers) at the top, followed in order by *Kshatriyas* (warriors and rulers), *Vaishyas* (farmers, traders, and merchants), and *Shudras* (labourers). But even the *Shudras* were not at the bottom of the totem pole. That spot was, and still is, reserved for the lowly *Dalits* or 'Untouchables.' They are called that because of the work they do—cleaning toilets, removing garbage, what have you—which renders them in India's greater scheme of things as *impure*. Indeed, in India today some 200 million people find themselves in this category and are considered sub-human. (In the community where I live city workers who collect the garbage earn about $45,000 a year and belong to a union that offers them a wide assortment of benefits.)

Thus, it's fair to say India is a society *characterized* by racial inequality and injustice. So is Saudi Arabia, especially if you are a woman. According to the World Economic Forum's Global Gender Gap Report of 2022, Saudi Arabia ranked number 127 out of 153 countries in this category. A woman in Saudi Arabia today is only a fraction of a man's worth in terms of rights concerning marriage, family, divorce, guardianship, what have you. Without getting into details I would hazard a guess that the rights of women in virtually all Muslim-majority countries are severely lacking by our standards.

I could go on, but you get the point.

This is not to say that racial inequality and injustice don't exist here. Of course, they do. They exist everywhere and always have, but if things are so bad why do people keep coming to this country from every corner of the earth? Put another way, is racial inequality and injustice the sum total of our present reality and, more than that, where we come from? Aye, there's the rub. At heart Canada is a racist society. We must be. That is why statues of the people who put this country together are statues of white Christian men. Everyone else was persecuted and if they weren't *Untouchables*, they were pretty damn close. Sub-human. So, of course, those statues should come down and all those street names should be changed, too. The statues should come down and the street names should be changed to reflect our core values of today because we are morally superior.

But there is a fatal flaw with this argument. In literary criticism the word *hamartia* refers to the fatal flaw of a hero or protagonist and we have a case of hamartia here as well. In fact, what this is all about is rewriting history through the prism of modern times and you can't do that.

Let's look at this another way. The 1936 Olympics were held in Berlin and the man presiding over those games was none other than Adolf Hitler. Jesse Owens was an American track and field star. A black man, the youngest of ten children, and the son of an Alabama sharecropper, Owens won four gold medals at those Olympics. In the process he set three world records and tied another, and did this in less than an hour which has to be one of the most incredible feats in all the annals of sport.

Owens won gold in the men's 100-meter final—much to the dismay of the Führer who wanted his Olympics to demonstrate Aryan supremacy—in a time of 10.3 seconds. But where would that rank today?

In the 2020 Olympics in Tokyo an Italian runner won gold in the men's 100-meter final with a time of 9.80 seconds. Another runner who didn't make that final—Silvan Wicki of Switzerland—finished his heat in 10.28 seconds and got cut from the competition. His time can be rounded off to what Owens accomplished—10.3 seconds—back in 1936 when they measured in tenths of seconds, not hundredths. If we look at all the sprinters who raced in those qualifying heats in the men's 100-meter event, Wicki finished 39th.

The current world record for the men's 100 meters was set by Jamaica's Usain Bolt in 2009 in a time of 9.58 seconds. Let's compare the 1936 Jesse Owens to the 2009 Usain Bolt. With AI (Artificial Intelligence) it would be easy to create a video showing the two running against each other. What would that race look like? Owens would finish more than seven-tenths of a second behind Bolt, which in this event is light years, and be so far behind it's no contest. But does that in any way diminish what Owens accomplished in Berlin?

No.

Times—for how long it took a sprinter to cover 100 meters *and* for the era we are discussing—were different. In 1936 there were no starting blocks. Runners' shoes were made of heavy leather and the track was composed of cinder which gets uneven and messy in rain, and for the week prior to the men's 100-meter final in the 1936 Olympics it had been raining in Berlin. Never mind modern dietary regimens and elite training programs of today.

In short, nothing was the same as before and history is like that, too. This is why we can't examine history from a hundred years ago or two hundred years ago or a thousand years ago through the lens of today. But that is what we do and especially what we do when we condemn everything from our past. Put another way, calling Sir John A. Macdonald—Canada's first prime minister—a racist and bigot who deserves our disdain makes as much sense as calling Jesse Owens a lousy runner.

So, where did all this nonsense begin anyway?

Well, if it didn't start it certainly got a push with George Floyd and the emergence of the Black Lives Matter movement in the United States. Floyd was a black man murdered by a white police officer, the whole thing captured on video. Now Floyd was no angel. In 2009 he got a five-year sentence for assault and robbery, and before that he had been convicted of theft with a firearm and drug possession, not to mention a slew of other things. But on May 25, 2020 he was caught trying to pass a phony $20 bill and in the ensuing interaction with police one of the officers, Derek Chauvin, held his knee on Floyd's neck—the man was already down and handcuffed—for a full nine minutes. Floyd couldn't breathe and said as much, and then he died for all the world to see. Chauvin was later convicted of murder and sentenced to 22 and a half years. Three other officers were each sentenced to several years in prison.

Floyd's death led to widespread protests across America and beyond, including Canada. Black Lives Matter, which had gotten its start earlier, became more than a movement. It became a mantra. A *social* mantra. And while it was supposed to be about highlighting racism, discrimination, and the racial inequality experienced by blacks in America, it had a strong anti-police bent attached to it with Defund the Police the rallying call, and the word *woke* front and centre. *Woke* is what it was all about and that meant everything from white privilege and white supremacy to sexism and LGBT rights.

In other words, if you weren't *woke* you were a racist and if you were *woke*—at least, in Canada—you would tear down statues of Sir John A. Macdonald, not to mention Queen Elizabeth II and Queen Victoria, because they represented our colonial and racist past. If you were *woke* you would change the names of schools and streets that honoured those from that same colonial, racist past.

By the same token, and I doubt anyone has suggested this yet but here goes, we should march down to the Toronto Granite Club which began way back in 1875 as a gentleman's curling club and remove those pictures of the first presidents and board members because they didn't allow women or Jews or people of colour as members. Same thing with the Royal Canadian Yacht Club and Rideau Club of Ottawa. Off with their heads! For that matter, how about the Boy Scouts which according to its original name in London, England in 1908 was clearly a sexist organization which means that nice portrait of founder Robert Baden-Powell should be removed immediately? Never mind that two years later the same Baden-Powell co-founded the Girl Guides which only rubbed salt into the wound.

But here's the thing. Is this really what our history is all about? Colonialism? Racism? Slavery? Are those the building blocks that made Canada what it is today? According to just about everything you read and hear, it is. This is why when school boards have Professional Development days a big priority concerns the plight of blacks, Indigenous people, and others who are deemed to be racialized. It's about pointing out how racist our history is so all these groups can feel good about themselves. This is why the Human Resources departments of companies and pretty much any organization today, big or small, tend to do the same thing. Point out our racist past.

Well, I have news for the Woke community. You people are misnamed because you are asleep. If not comatose. You see, you have things wrong. Dead wrong. And that's because you're a generation that doesn't know a damn thing about history.

Our history.

CHAPTER 2

They don't know what they don't know

HER NAME WAS ALEX and she was a candidate in the 2015 federal election for the NDP. She was already an elected official—school trustee for 12 years with the Hamilton-Wentworth District School Board. At the time she was Vice-Chairman of the Board, but prior to that she had been Chair which means being entrusted with no minor level of responsibility for the educational system in Hamilton, one of Canada's biggest cities. And for over a decade yet. The Hamilton-Wentworth District School Board administers some 14 secondary schools and 88 elementary schools. That's more than a hundred schools which is nothing to sneeze at.

What's more, Alex was a social worker with a Master's Degree from McMaster University. Her thesis topic for that degree was 'Beyond Professional Affiliation: Race, Class & Gender Dynamics in Interdisciplinary Teams.' She also had a Bachelor of Social Work from the University of British Columbia where her area of specialization was 'Social Justice and Peace Studies.' In addition to that she had her Bachelor of Arts from King's University College in London, Ontario.

When running in the 2015 election, in the federal riding of Hamilton West-Ancaster Dundas, her LinkedIn profile singled out that she was 'passionate about public education.' By all accounts, education was very much her thing.

Three degrees. Professional social worker. Long-time trustee with one of Canada's largest school boards. And back in 2015 a candidate for the federal House of Commons in Ottawa. Alas, Alex didn't win that election, finishing third beyond the Liberal and Conservative candidates, but despite the showing she did manage to attract a fair bit of national attention during the campaign.

A local newspaper, *The True North Times*, discovered something she had said seven years earlier on Facebook. A friend had posted a photo of the electric fence surrounding the Nazi death camp at Auschwitz in Poland and Alex had responded with a sexual comment: "Ahhh, the infamous Pollish (sic), phallic, hydro posts ... of course you took pictures of this! It expresses ... how the curve is normal, natural, and healthy right!"

The incorrect spelling of 'Polish' could have been attributed to a lazy finger on the keyboard, but a spelling mistake is more likely. But that wasn't what garnered all the attention. When a reporter confronted her with the Facebook posting at an all-candidates meeting, Alex was forced to admit the truth. She had never heard of Auschwitz. She had no idea what it was, where it was, or what happened there.

"Well, I didn't know what Auschwitz was, or I didn't up until today," she confided when the reporter made a point of asking.

I have no idea what Alex the social worker and long-time school trustee has been doing in the years since the 2015 election. But in November of 2022 she tried again for public office, this time in Hamilton's municipal election where she ran for councillor in Ward 4. She wound up finishing third out of 11 candidates, which is a respectable showing, and for that she deserves credit for perseverance. But the point with Alex is that a professional woman in her thirties—a graduate from an Ontario high school with three university degrees to her name, who had served as Chair of one of the biggest school boards in the country, a school board responsible for more than one hundred schools, who then ran as a candidate for office in the House of Commons in our nation's capital—had never heard of Auschwitz.

I wasn't surprised.

In the 1990s I was an instructor and lecturer at Humber College, the largest community college in Ontario. The area of study was a four-year program in Public Relations or Media Studies as it was called then. In my first year teaching I was immediately taken aback with the revelation that most of these young people had either poor or non-existent grammar skills. They didn't know a verb from an adverb. When I asked them about this they told me they had never studied grammar before, but that isn't totally true. One of them had. She was a mature student, which meant she was older than the others, and a relative newcomer to Canada from Jamaica. Yes, she was a black woman and the only person of colour in that class. She had grammar drilled into her throughout elementary school. In Jamaica. I found this sort of thing would turn out to be a common theme. Students who had been educated in other countries knew their grammar. There was a girl from Russia. She knew grammar. And so did a mature student from Nigeria. Yes Nigeria. In fact, this fellow told me himself how surprised he was to learn that all these Canadians he went to school with at Humber didn't know the parts of speech.

My own children were in high school when I taught at Humber and their school, a big one in eastern Toronto, had set up this Parents Advisory Council. The idea was that parents could *advise* the school, and so, I decided to become a member. The meetings were always held in the afternoons which meant that for many, if not most working people, attending and being a member of that body would have been impossible which, I suppose, was why there were no doctors, lawyers, accountants or business people on it. But being self-employed I could manage it.

This group encompassed a dozen individuals, including the Principal of the school. All of them were women save for me and one other man, and it quickly became apparent that all but one member of the Parents Advisory Council—yours truly—were coming to those meetings from way off in left field. At one meeting talk turned to the instruction of English language in the school system and I made a comment about what I was learning concerning the abilities, or lack thereof, from my Humber College students, almost all Ontario high school graduates. I don't remember the exact words of the Principal, but she said something like this: "At no time in history have graduates of Ontario high schools been more proficient in English and grammar than they are right now."

I was dumbfounded. Absolutely gobsmacked. But I do remember how I responded. "What planet are you living on? Because it sure as hell isn't this one."

Needless to say, we didn't get along very well after that. You see, one is not to question the Principal of an Ontario secondary school. It just isn't done.

I got a glimmer of how things were in the schools a few years later when I met Harry Giles. I wrote a feature profile on him for *The National Post* and the story ran a full page and then some. Giles was well known as an educator and critic of the public school system. This was February, 2000 and the piece began like this: "Harry Giles has little time for Ontario's education system. At his school, a private operation that he runs in the back of a Toronto church, students complete the equivalent of a high school degree in Grade 8—five years ahead of their public school counterparts. The government can only blink and stare."

Giles passed away in 2021 at the age of 91, but when I knew him he would have been 69 and still very much out there throwing darts at the Ontario Ministry of Education. He and his wife Anna Por had founded The Toronto French School in 1962, stemming from their desire to educate children in both English and French.

Now, a personal aside. I attended public school, junior high, and high school in Toronto, and had seven years of French instruction, beginning in Grade 7 and going right through Grade 13. The schools had Grade 13 back then. And while I did relatively well in French class I never really learned to speak it because when school was over nobody spoke French. Not in Toronto. And with the exception of one outstanding French teacher in Grade 10—Monsieur Potvin, God bless him—none of the teaching I had was particularly good or effective.

In the more than four decades I've been working as a writer, journalist, and communications consultant, I have never had to use French. Never. The only time was when doing contract work for the Government of Ontario where everything that came out of any ministry had to be translated and we had a translation service for that task.

Giles' wife died at a young age, but he continued on and TFS, as it was known, continued to flourish. Later, at the time I did the article on him, he was busy running his own school—The Giles School—and the big thing with his approach was emphasizing bilingualism, studies in a third language, small classes, and the highest international standards possible. He made a name for himself as an authority in neuroscience, cognitive psychology, and early childhood development, as all those things apply to education. In 1973 Giles was honoured for his work and named a member of the Order of Canada. His TFS became the forerunner of all immersion programs and would become the largest private educational facility in the country.

Giles travelled the world studying educational systems. What was his assessment back then of Ontario's school system?

"If the public was informed about what's going on in our schools, they'd burn down the Ministry of Education and shoot everybody in it," he told me.

Needless to say, Giles was not one to mince his words. He went on.

"The public shouldn't be taken in by all the BS they hear that we've got the best educational system in the world. It isn't true."

What he said, and keep in mind this was the year 2000, was that Singapore had the best educational system in the world, followed by the Koreans and then, in order, the Japanese, the Europeans—he lumped the Swiss, Germans, Poles, and Czechs altogether in that category—and then the British. The Americans, like us, were nowhere to be found. He said all these groups had much higher standards than we did.

We are now a quarter-century beyond that time and what has changed? If the latest math scores on a test administered by the International Education Association are any indication, not much. According to that organization's test for students attending grades 4 and 8 in the year 2023, Canadian students finished 32nd out of 64 countries that took this international benchmark; the IEA conducts the test every four years. Canada even finished below the United States which came in 27th. For science scores the results were similar. Who was at the top of these lists? Five Asian states—Singapore, Chinese Taipei, South Korea, Hong Kong, and Japan—in that order.

Harry Giles is no longer with us, but his observations from 25 years ago were prescient indeed.

I mentioned the Parents Advisory Council that I sat on when my kids were in high school. Here is another personal aside, this regarding my son. When he was in Grade 12 he wasn't getting particularly good marks in English class. He attributed this to the fact that, according to him, his English teacher, a woman with many years of teaching experience, had it in for the school's hockey team. In fact, hockey was a big deal at this school and it was a very good hockey team; that year the squad won the OFSAA (Ontario Federation of School Athletic Associations) championship which meant they were the best high school hockey team in the entire province. Alas, hockey players were allowed out of English class early in order to attend practice and my son was in this group.

He managed to obtain for me the paper of another student, a girl in his class, who had received an 'A' while, for the exact same assignment, he had barely passed. I scrutinized both papers and while I admit the other student's was better, it was obvious to me that the teacher was coming down hard on my son while letting a lot go with his classmate; the teacher had missed a number of errors in grammar, spelling, what have you, in the girl's paper. And so, I wanted to meet with my son's English teacher.

But when she found out I was a writer—a published author in fiction and non-fiction, a former newspaper reporter and columnist, correspondent for major dailies, and a freelancer who had written countless feature articles in Canadian and American magazines—she wouldn't see me. I was dumbstruck. She wouldn't see me? Nope. I wound up meeting with the head of the school's English department.

As I said earlier, my involvement with Harry Giles occurred a few years after my teaching at Humber College and during my years there—it wasn't full-time, only a few hours a week—I taught students in the first, second and third year of the program. Almost all were graduates of Ontario high schools. I taught them courses in corporate communications, journalism and writing. Suffice to say that anyone who wanted to pursue a career in such areas with virtually no knowledge of English grammar would have a challenge ahead of them. But that wasn't the only thing I found out. I also learned that young people in this country appear to know nothing about history.

Nothing.

It started with Methuselah, the biblical character and grandfather of Noah who according to the Book of Genesis lived a life that lasted some 969 years, which no matter how you look at it is quite a stretch. I once made a comment about him in class saying that "so-and-so is as old as Methusaleh," but there wasn't a single student who knew what I was talking about. They had never heard of Methusaleh and the same was true when I offered an analogy with David and Goliath. Yes those guys. Who are they? As it turned out, apart from the odd student who may have attended

Sunday school as a child, none of them had any knowledge of biblical history at all and it soon became apparent that this was also the case with history in general.

Later I did some teaching at Seneca at York. Seneca College, another large community college in Toronto, had joined forces with York University with a separate faculty dedicated to that union. All the students there needed a university degree to get into the course I taught, and there were stints at other community colleges as well. Over and over again I would find that when it comes to history young people in this country were in the dark to such a degree that, in this respect, we can certify them as legally blind.

In 2014, which was one year before Alex's gaffe about Auschwitz in that federal election campaign, my novel *The Last Witness* was published. Keep in mind this is fiction. The book is about a 100-year-old man who is the last living survivor of the Holocaust, but the story takes place in a near-future world—in 2039—when knowledge of the Holocaust is dim. When my Los Angeles-based literary agent was shopping the manuscript around, one of the big New York publishers turned it down because their senior editor didn't buy my story about people being so ignorant of the Holocaust a generation from now.

And so, I decided to make a video. Accompanied by a videographer who worked in the movie industry, I interviewed university students in Toronto—we didn't specify which university it was—and asked them questions about the Holocaust and World War II. As it turned out, they didn't know much. By and large, they had no idea how many Jews were killed in the Holocaust or when it happened. Joseph Mengele? Who was he? The Final Solution? Never heard of it. As far as the war itself was concerned, most students I talked to didn't know who FDR was, or for that matter, Winston Churchill. Yes him. When I asked who the Allies were they were stumped and it was pretty much the same reaction when I asked them what happened on the Beaches of Normandy on D-Day.

When making that video I had a poppy on my lapel because it was shot a few days before Remembrance Day and during Holocaust Education Week. The video ran just over nine minutes and wound up going viral all over the world. It was shown to kick off a conference about the Holocaust for educators and academics in Poland, and was later added to the film library at Yad Vashem, the World Holocaust Remembrance Center in Jerusalem.

In September, 2023 the province of Ontario introduced a section on the Holocaust in its Grade 6 Social Studies curriculum after a group called Liberation75 surveyed Ontario teenagers and found just how little they knew. British Columbia introduced something similar, but for Grade 10. The irony is that after the Israel-Hamas War broke out in October, 2023, a definite anti-Israel bent took hold on college and university campuses right across the country. One man I know, a Holocaust survivor who spent four years in concentration camps, had been doing talks about his wartime experience throughout Canada and the United States. He went to schools. But all of a sudden those talks were getting cancelled. It went against the narrative on college and university campuses.

That narrative has since continued.

Nevertheless, in the years since my novel was published I have often shown the video in presentations about how we have spawned a generation that doesn't know history. In fact, it might be two generations now and that means some schoolteachers might be suspect, too. For the most part, people are shocked when they see those student interviews. But you know what? They shouldn't be. The rot has been setting in for a long time.

CHAPTER 3

We've been Aunt Jemima-ed

AFTER TEACHING AT community college, albeit part-time, I took a break but a few years later decided to try it again. In fact, I taught at four colleges over the years and my courses included journalism, writing and corporation communications. And so, I approached the last college where I had been because the people knew me. I wound up on the phone with an administrator and there was no issue with professional and teaching experience—none at all—but then came this question: Are you a person of colour? I said no and was told not to apply.

"There is no point," the administrator said.

Case closed. I thought this was nuts and said as much. It didn't matter. But another experience, far more recent, was even more disturbing. I came across this article by an American college professor who wrote about sports. His piece was about segregated baseball in the days of the old Negro leagues and he made a comment about Babe Ruth. He said Ruth was "wildly representative of white masculinity on the baseball diamond."

The writer was black.

Now I happen to know a thing or two about Babe Ruth. My first novel *Gift of the Bambino* was about a young boy and his grandfather, and how the two are bound by baseball and their love of the Babe. The story begins with a 19-year-old Ruth hitting his first professional home run in Toronto, of all places, when he was a minor leaguer playing AAA ball for the Providence Grays. This is historical fact. In 2006 I was involved in a ceremony at Hanlan's Point on the Toronto Islands commemorating that home run with a plaque. The New York Yankees were in town and there was representation from both the Yankees and Toronto Blue Jays at the event. That day I met Ruth's grandson Tom Stevens and we have kept in touch.

Fast forward to 2018 and my non-fiction book BABE RUTH—A *Superstar's Legacy* which examines that legacy on many fronts that go far beyond baseball. It includes film, literature, culture, and a heavy dose of business, branding and marketing. Ruth has been called the first marketing superstar and he was. Tom wrote the Foreword to the book. Through him, other members of the Ruth family, and at least one notable baseball historian who has spent years researching this subject, I learned that the reason Ruth never became a manager after his playing days were over may well have been because he was dead-set *against* segregation and would have advocated for black ballplayers in the majors. The fact is Ruth played with and against Latino and black ballplayers on his barnstorming tours throughout his entire career, much to the chagrin of Major League Baseball, which was segregated until 1947. He was even fined for doing this! But he kept right on doing it.

So I took exception to that description of Ruth in the article and suggested that the writer read my book. Well, he got back to me. He said he needs no further study on "white supremacy" to understand the narrative of Ruth or "the perspective of white men today who exercise their paternalism by suggesting that his point as a black man is ignorant."

Huh? That had to be one of the most upsetting emails I ever received. I didn't write my note to him as *a white man*, but as a writer who had done extensive research on Ruth and knew that his description was unfair. But he apparently saw all this—and me personally—through the lens of race, as did that college and its college administrator who were practicing what can only be described as discriminatory hiring practices. But try taking that one to the Ontario Human Rights Commission.

Today, this sort of thing has gone into overdrive with identity politics everywhere you look. Here's another example, and more recent still. For many years I was a member of The Writers' Union of Canada, but after awhile didn't see any value there and eventually chose not to renew my membership. And out of the blue came a letter—yes, a letter in the mail—from the newly ensconced Chair of The Writers' Union of Canada. They wanted me to come back and this is how the person introduced himself.

> My name is _____ and I am proud to be the Union's first queer person of colour to take on Chair duties.

Allow me to emit another huh? Why should I care that the new Chair of The Writers' Union of Canada is a person of colour? Or that he, as he refers to himself, is queer? Well, I don't. It makes no difference to me if he is black or white or anything else and I couldn't care less about whom he sleeps with, just as I'm sure he must have more important things on his mind than whom I sleep with. And what business would it be of his anyway? The only reason for his letter stemmed from his new position with the organization and trying to get former members to come back. Race, gender and sexuality *should* have nothing to do with it, but this new approach puts race, gender and sexuality right up there with a big label on your forehead so everyone can see and judge accordingly. It flies in the face of what Martin Luther King said in his famous 'I have a dream' speech in Washington, DC in 1965.

> I have a dream that my four little children will one day live in a nation where they will not be judged by the color of their skin but by the content of their character.

Indeed. What I'm trying to say is all this *woke* business is racist and I'm not the only one who thinks so. Coleman Hughes is a black American writer and podcast host, and his book 'The End of Race Politics: Arguments for a Colorblind America' tackled this head-on. Hughes coined the term 'neoracist' to describe anti-racists whom he calls "racists in disguise."[1] He said neoracism is "the latest form of socially approved bigotry" and that's exactly what it is. What's more, he also took a quote from Martin Luther King.

Our aim must never be to defeat or humiliate the white man.

Try selling that one on Black Lives Matter, but a lot of this does go back to George Floyd. In his book Hughes cited the 2016 murder of an unarmed *white* man who had been killed by police in Dallas, Texas. It garnered absolutely no publicity. None. He then referred to a poll which showed that 54 percent of 'very liberal' Americans believed that over 1,000 unarmed black men had been killed by police in 2019 when the actual figure was 12. Says Hughes: "Social media isn't educating us. It's miseducating us."
Touché.
Two more lines from his book are noteworthy. "Neoracism takes grains of truth and builds them into a powerfully seductive narrative."[2] And this one: "White supremacist ideas have been widely shamed and tabooed. Few people are even tempted to defend them. Yet, neoracists continue depicting white supremacy as a powerful movement that threatens our democracy."[3]
So, why is this chapter called *We've Been Aunt Jemima-ed?* Here's why. Many Canadians are familiar with the name Nancy Greene. She is widely known as an Olympic ski champion and our top female athlete of the 20th century who later became a senator. But to Americans that name means something else. Nancy Green—no 'e' at the end—was Aunt Jemima. She was born as a slave in 1834 in Kentucky and died at the age of 89 in 1923 when she was struck by

a car. In between she became famous as, quite literally, the face of a brand of pancake syrup.

Nancy Green has been called "one of America's most enduring living trademarks"[4] and "the advertising world's first living trademark."[5] She toured America and by all accounts was very good at promotion. The Aunt Jemima character, prominently displayed on those pancake jars, wound up outliving her for almost a century—some 97 years to be exact. But in 2020 the company Quaker Oats, which had brought the brand in 1926 and was itself acquired by PepsiCo in 2001, effectively killed her off due to America's newfound racial reckoning in the wake of George Floyd and the burgeoning Black Lives Matter movement. Never mind that Nancy Green was a leading advocate against poverty and a champion of civil rights at a time when this sort of thing just wasn't done. Never mind that her descendants were outraged and claimed that her history was being erased which led them to raise funds to install a headstone at her grave that read 'The original Aunt Jemima.'

Said Sherry Williams, president of The Bronzeville Historical Society which preserves African-American culture in Chicago, as quoted in *The New York Times*: "History does not simply disappear when you remove the Aunt Jemima image and brand name... Aunt Jemima is more than a character. She is Nancy Green and this is her recipe and her legacy must be told."[6]

This is what happens when history is rewritten to fit a narrative pushed by certain elements in society—often extreme elements—and it can be especially effective when applied to a generation that is knowledge-deficient about the past. The most blatant illustration I can think of is support, especially on college and university campuses, of the terrorist group Hamas after the massacre of Israeli civilians on October 7, 2023. Believe it or not, there was even support expressed on social media for Osama bin Laden and what he stood for.

As I wrote in an article published by *The Hub* two months after the attack, it had become *fashionable* on university and college campuses to be anti-Israel, pro-Palestinian, and pro-Hamas. And I believe it still is. This has been true on campuses across the United States and Canada as well. Suddenly, all these young people were experts on Middle East history.

Not long after October 7 I was watching CNN interview students from UCLA who were taking part in pro-Israel and pro-Palestinian rallies. A Jewish student with his Israeli flag had to be interviewed off-campus because he said he wouldn't be able to display the flag for fear of retribution. However, a student involved in a pro-Palestinian rally was on campus and when asked about the massacre this is what he said: "We have to conceptualize it with the entirety of a 75-year occupation."

But what is there to conceptualize about a terrorist who murders babies with a machine gun?

These kids have been brainwashed, and what's happening in the schools and on our university and college campuses is frightening. As mentioned earlier, it got so bad that someone I know—a Holocaust survivor who spent four years in a concentration camp—had to stop giving talks at schools about his wartime experience. His story went against the new narrative.

Later, in the fall of 2023, the issue got even bigger and we can thank Claudine Gay for that. Outside of those connected to Harvard University, I imagine few people knew who she was before that infamous day when she, along with other university presidents, appeared before a congressional committee in Washington, DC. The topic was the rising incidence of antisemitism on their campuses in the wake of the war in Gaza. An exchange between Gay and Elise M. Stefanik, a Republican member of congress, went viral.

STEFANIK: "At Harvard, does calling for the genocide of Jews violate Harvard's rules of bullying and harassment?"
GAY: "It can be, depending on the context."

Stefanik then pressed Gay to give a yes or no answer as to whether calls for the genocide of Jews was a violation of Harvard's policies.

GAY: "Antisemitic speech when it crosses into conduct that amounts to bullying, harassment, intimidation . . . that is actionable conduct and we do take action."

Stefanik wasn't satisfied.

STEFANIK: "So the answer is yes, that calling for the genocide of Jews violates Harvard code of conduct, correct?"
GAY: "Again, it depends on the context."
STEFANIK: "It does not depend on the context. The answer is yes and this is why you should resign."

Not long after that—in January, 2024—Claudine Gay did just that. After only six months as president. In the 389-year history of Harvard she was its first black president and only the second woman to occupy the position. It was later found that Gay, the child of immigrants from Haiti, had plagiarized some of her academic work. Hers was the shortest tenure of any president of Harvard.

Now here is an interesting question. How do my roots compare with Claudine Gay's? Let's see. In Haiti her family owned a big concrete plant, so it would appear that in terms of money and wealth she is one up on me. Her parents met in university and were both professional people. Make that two up on me. She attended a private boarding school and then went on to Princeton and Stanford. There is no way on earth my family could have afforded such an education or anything even remotely close to that for my brother and me. In fact, the one year I attended university out of town—at what was then the University of Western Ontario in London, Ontario—I had to take out a student loan. So make that three up on me.

Nevertheless, in the current context of what passes as race-based truth these days, Gay is seen as a black woman who has succeeded despite the suffering and inequities experienced by the colour of her skin, while I am only a privileged white male.

An actor I admire is Morgan Freeman. I admire him both for his talent and for the stand he takes which, one might say, rubs some people the wrong way. Back in 2005 he was interviewed by Mike Wallace on *60 Minutes* and asked about Black History Month. Freeman thought it was ridiculous.

"You're going to relegate my history to a month?" he said before asking Wallace which month is White History Month. Wallace acknowledged that he is Jewish.

"Okay. Which month is Jewish History Month?" Freeman asked him and Wallace said there isn't one.

"Do you want one?" asked Freeman and Wallace said no. "I don't want a Black History Month," Freeman went on. "Black history is American history." Wallace then asked Freeman how to get rid of racism and Freeman's answer was simple.

"Stop talking about it. I'm going to stop calling you a white man and I'm going to ask you to stop calling me a black man."[7]

But the far left, Wokers, DEI community, what have you, won't do that. They can't. For racism is central to their narrative. The same Morgan Freeman took this to another level on June 3, 2014 when he was interviewed by Don Lemon, who is also black, on CNN. The topic was whether or not race plays a part in wealth inequality in America. Freeman said no which appeared to stymie Lemon.

"You and I, we're proof," said Freeman. "Why would race have anything to do with it? Put your mind to what you want to do and go from there. It's kind of like religion to me. It's a good excuse for not getting there . . . Making it a bigger issue than it needs to be is the problem here."

That is not to dismiss the history of slavery in America nor the current plight of many in Canada's Indigenous community. But it does go back to the film On the Waterfront and the character Terry Molloy, played by Marlon Brando, when he tells his older brother "I coulda bin a contendah."

You can't live your life on 'if only' because that is a life devoted to victimhood and, as Morgan Freeman said, "It's a good excuse for not getting there."

Another person worth noting is Ayaan Hirsi Ali. If you take the easy route and look her up on Wikipedia, this is what it says: 'A Somali-born Dutch-American writer, activist and former politician. She is a critic of Islam and advocate for the rights and self-determination of Muslim women, opposing forced marriage, honour killing, child marriage, and female genital mutilation.'

While I'm no advocate of Wikipedia as a source, that is a mouthful. Ali came to international attention in 2007 with her bestselling book 'Infidel' which described her life as an Islamic woman and her arranged marriage to a Canadian. She fled from her family to escape the marriage and wound up in the Netherlands where she later became a member of that country's parliament. Dutch filmmaker Theo van Gogh made a documentary about her called Submission which in 2004 got him murdered by a Moroccan-Dutch nutcase.

I mention Ali because for many years I used a clip from an interview she once did on CBC for a media-training program. The interview took place on June 13, 2007 and the idea was to show

how to stay in control of an interview. In the segment she appears with host Avi Lewis, son of former Ontario politician Stephen Lewis, on his television show *On The Map*. Lewis introduced her as a "controversial author, politician and born-again America-booster" which sounds to me like a person who might have an agenda. Note—whenever the far left labels someone *controversial* chances are good the individual advocates a view they don't share.

Ali raised the ire of Lewis because she said there was no such thing as Islamophobia in America at the time and cited the fact that Muslims in America don't tend to leave the country and go back where they came from. Instead, she said, they stay. She then proceeded to mop him up with this statement: "I don't find myself in the same luxury as you do. You grew up in freedom and you can spit on freedom because you don't know what it is not to have freedom."

She has lived in the US for many years and in the spring of 2024 gave an interview on ILTV Israel. This is an independent English-language media company based in Tel Aviv, but the interview took place in the United Kingdom and the topic was the Israel-Hamas war. Ali talked about how she was always taught to view Jews as "demons" and "monsters" when growing up in Somalia and later in Saudi Arabia, Ethiopia and Kenya. In the interview she also had a few things to say about the woke phenomenon and what she called an "unholy alliance" between antisemitism and far-left antisemitism.

"The woke narrative... the woke takeover of our institutions through diversity, equity and inclusion... they enable and empower the Islamists in their advance of antisemitism. They make antisemitism okay again. They make antisemitism even glamourous in some circles and they use this combination of playing the victim and whatever they choose out of the woke lexicon to help advance their agenda. They have infiltrated the major centre-left parties of all Western countries. The Democratic party in the United States. The Labour party in the United Kingdom. The

Social Democrats and the Greens in places like the Netherlands and Germany."[8]

Kenneth Green is a professor at the University of Toronto who teaches in the Department of the Study of Religion. He is Jewish and wears a kippah. In 2024 he dared to approach the pro-Palestinian encampment at King's College Circle in the middle of the UofT campus. Green, who had been teaching at the university for some 37 years, wrote about his experience in a newspaper article. He said the encampment was led by pro-Hamas advocates "who are seeking to justify Islamist terrorism by normalizing antisemitism." He said most of the agitators weren't even students at all and that, for the most part, university faculty went along with their encampment.

"With my kippah proudly on my head, I tried to enter the encampment to speak with those inside. For my efforts, I was not only barred from entering but I was also cursed, sworn at, abused, and told I should go back to where I came from. This all happened in plain sight of the campus police, who merely stood back and refused to get involved when I asked for their assistance."[9]

In his article Green said some of his Jewish students refused to attend classes for fear of facing a threatening mob every day. He said all this has a source in an ideology that has gripped the minds of the vast majority of university professors—"a neo-Marxist ideology that despises the values of liberal democratic society."

Said Green: "We should not blind ourselves. A target has been painted on the faces of all Western people, first on the Jews, but then ultimately on all defenders of western liberal democracies. Israel is merely the low-hanging fruit, attacked through the soft target of the universities."

Well, I decided to go and see that pro-Palestinian encampment at the University of Toronto for myself and, for the record, I am a graduate of that same institution. There was a fence around the whole thing and the only way in was with consent of the protestors. There were signs all over the place. Like this one: "UofT divest from South African apartheid—1990. Israel apartheid—May 2024."

Now it may be chic for students to equate Israel with apartheid South Africa, but the comparison illustrates a profound ignorance of history. South Africa imported its anti-black racist laws directly from the playbook of Nazi Germany, while the modern state of Israel is a democracy with free elections. No matter your stand on the war in Gaza, it's a fact that more than 20 percent of Israel's population is Arab and the Knesset—Israel's parliament—has elected members who are Arabs.

Other signs at the encampment cried out *This is the Intifada, Revolution Until Victory, Our tuition will not be spent on GENOCIDE,* not to mention ALL COPS ARE BASTARDS. There were also signs that raised ignorance to new levels.

"Queers for Palestine and Queer and Palestinian Liberation is intertwined."

Try appearing in drag in the streets of Gaza, never mind anywhere else in the Middle East, and see where it gets you. Correction. Anywhere in the Middle East—except Israel. But the most injurious sign at that encampment said "From the river to the sea" which is the stated mandate of Hamas and it means no Jews between the river Jordan and the Mediterranean. No Jews and no state of Israel.

Ayaan Hirsi Ali said the new woke mainstream makes antisemitism *okay* and it certainly seemed okay with UofT administration for more than two months until a court order forced the encampment to disband. Of course, the UofT was but one of many universities in Canada and the US with such encampments. I will take leave of Ali with another comment she made in that ILTV Israel interview when speaking about those who live in the West, and keep in mind this is a black woman who had been raised as a Muslim.

"Our guilt has been weaponized. The West's success has been weaponized against itself. Westerners have been told that you're white and you're privileged and I think we should never have accepted that but we can climb out of that. We have to put a stop to feeling this guilt. We have to put a stop to all these stupid questions of unconscious bias training. We have to acknowledge that the privilege we have is the outcome of centuries of hard work."[10]

But there are people who don't want to hear this. One of them gave an online seminar I happened to attend with the title *Systemic Racism in Canada.* The organization behind it was a group called Moms Against Racism, which calls itself a federally-registered non-profit. The founder described herself as a 'biracial, cis-gender woman of African, English, Swedish and Irish who identifies as black.' Now let's stop right there. My family has Jewish roots going back to Poland, Belarus and Romania but I don't call myself a straight Polish-Belarussian-Romanian male who identifies as Jewish. I just call myself Canadian, and when you see me if white male is what comes to mind, then good on you. For the record, never in my life had I enrolled for a seminar that asked in advance what my ethnicity happens to be.

But this one did.

According to the literature, the convenor and her family 'live as guests on the unceded traditional territories of the Lək̓ʷəŋən people, colonially referred to as Victoria, BC.' It actually said *colonially referred to as Victoria, BC*. So even though this program was called Moms *Against* Racism, it was obvious to any discerning individual that race—and making judgments—before the thing even begins are front and centre.

Go on the organization's website and you see that the MAR (Moms Against Racism) Shift learning series is funded in part by the Government of Canada. Its mission? To 'educate adults in anti-racism, cultural competence, and decolonization so they have the tools and support to dismantle racism in themselves, their families, and their communities.'

So what was the content of that seminar? In a nutshell, it was a cherrypicked look at Canadian history through an anti-white bent in order to show that this country, its history, and all that it stands for, is inherently racist. Over and over again, we heard about white supremacy and white-dominated society and the ills of colonialism. There was nothing positive revealed about this country nor its history. Nothing.

But here is an interesting point.

A list of 13 *historical racist events* was presented including that infamous day of July 1, 1867—what we now call Canada Day—when "colonizers worked together to establish one country." Another event was creation of the Northwest Mounted Police which was described as a "colonial para-military force." The Indian Act was mentioned, along with the head tax slapped on Chinese immigrants to Canada, mission schools in the 17th and 18th centuries, residential schools in the 19th and 20th centuries, the internment of Japanese-Canadians during World War II, the destruction of the black community Africville in Halifax in 1964, not to mention Islamophobia. There was even the Underground Railroad. I always thought the Underground Railroad was an intricate network that smuggled enslaved blacks from the United States and brought them to freedom here. No, not with this interpretation of history.

"Self-liberated slaves came to Canada via the Underground Railroad but found more slavery when they arrived."

Also on the list was the Komagata Maru incident of 1914 when a ship with would-be South Asian refugees—many of them Sikhs from India—was denied entry at the port of Vancouver. Fair enough. But I figured if she includes that she'll have to mention what happened 25 years later in 1939 when a ship with Jews arrived in Canadian waters. The ship was the German ocean liner the MS St. Louis and it had 908 Jews on board who were fleeing the Nazis. The ship was denied entry in Cuba, the United States and Canada. Just like those Sikhs from India who weren't allowed in at the outbreak of the Great War—World War I—these Jews were not allowed in either, a few short months before the beginning of World War II. That ship wound up going back to Europe and hundreds of those people died in concentration camps.

Nope. Not on the list. Didn't make it. Nor was there any mention in that seminar about rising antisemitism taking place across Canada while the war in Gaza raged. Not a word of antisemitism in a seminar called *Systemic Racism in Canada*? And so, with that glaring omission, the whole thing we call Canada was summed up in three little words.

"Our shameful history."

What's more, the attendees were even encouraged to take "a few deep breaths" in order to handle all the stress they were going through from this most disturbing history lesson! In addition to giving seminars, the organization in question offered programs called Group Unlearning and Diverse Book Baskets, the latter an effort to promote books. Of course, there is sometimes a flipside to book promotion and that is book banning. Not long ago, the Peel District School Board in Ontario came under fire for removing books from its libraries. One of the books removed was *The Diary of a Young Girl* by Anne Frank. There was even a move to remove all books published before 2008!

As mentioned, Moms Against Racism and its learning series is funded in part by the Government of Canada. Government funds going to programs like this is not unusual and in recent years has been given a boost. Dave Snow knows all about that. He is an associate professor of Political Science at the University of Guelph and a senior fellow of the Macdonald-Laurier Institute, a national public-policy think tank based in Ottawa. Snow did a report for the Macdonald-Laurier Institute called 'Promoting Excellence or Activism? Equity, Diversity, and Inclusion at Canada's Federal Granting Agencies.'

What did he find?

That federal granting agencies, the main source of Canada's research funding, with a total combined budget of nearly $4 billion, are heavily into DEI. Wrote Snow in his report:

> DEI has now become fully infused into all three of Canada's granting agencies—the National Sciences and Engineering Research Council (NSERC), the Canadian Institutes of Health Research (CIHR), and the Social Sciences and Humanities Research Council (SSHRC). Their DEI initiative range from specialized race, gender, and diversity grants to revised definitions of 'research excellence' to mandatory 'bias training' for most peer reviewers. As a result, a growing proportion of grants are rewarded to projects with explicitly activist subject matter. All this adds to the idea that Canada's research funding process has become politicized, further undermining the public's faith in universities.

Snow says one of those granting agencies, CIHR, even embeds activist DEI into how it evaluates success by updating its 'research excellence framework' with language like this: "Research is excellent when it is inclusive, equitable, diverse, anti-racist, anti-ableist, and anti-colonial in approach and impact."

Says Snow: "Canada's granting agencies claim that equity merely means the removal of systemic barriers, but in practice, SSHRC-administered Canada Research Chair positions often exclude applicants who are white and male."

In his report Snow assessed more than 2,600 individual SSHRC awards between 2022 and 2024. He said "activist DEI language" was present is as many as 63 per cent of project titles for what he called identity-focused, Future Challenge grants.

"These grants are supposed to promote research excellence," he says. "Instead, they are funding projects with titles such as Just Kids: Children and White Supremacy."

He recommends removing all references to DEI from agency guidelines, eliminating DEI-themed grants, and ending the practice of equity targets and what are known as preferential awards. But Snow also says *not* to ban DEI-driven research from award consideration—which is now government policy in the United States—but instead to let activist DEI scholars make the case that their research deserves funding by the taxpayer.

Snow told me he's inundated with EDI emails from his university every week and sometimes must "roll my eyes" because much of what he sees is activism dressed up as academic research. "The mandate is to support research excellence, but if you already know the answer what do you need research funding for? The reliance on evidence is almost not there at all. It's often poor scholarship."

In the Conclusions to his report for the Macdonald-Laurier Institute, Snow acknowledges that there has been pushback in academia to all this. In May, 2024, 40 scholars submitted a brief to the House of Commons Standing Committee on Science and Research. They recommended the abolition of DEI from the three federal granting agencies, and cited the significant costs of EDI, the administrative burden on smaller institutions, and weak evidence for its benefits. Snow also says that, according to one study, many faculty are "scared even to question" policies relating to equity, diversity and inclusion.

Mike Ramsay is a school trustee and past Chair of the Waterloo Region District School Board in Ontario. He's been a school trustee since 1989 and is also a former soldier and police officer. What's more, he's an outspoken critic of DEI ideology. He got upset when the Toronto District School Board (TDSB)—the largest school board in Canada—issued a teaching guide that said the Canadian education system is "colonialist" and designed to uphold the dominant white culture. In fact, one document called Facilitating Critical Conversations issued through TDSB's Equity, Anti-Racism & Anti-Oppression Department said that "education is a colonial structure that centres whiteness and Eurocentricity and therefore it must be actively decolonized."

In an article entitled 'Divisive DEI ideology is harming our students. It's time to ditch it,' Ramsay said this:

> I often wondered what good could come from paying DEI consultants upwards of $500 an hour to teach kids that if they are white the successes they experience are not due to personal effort. Meanwhile, racialized students are being taught that despite personal effort, their chances of success are diminished because society is racist and therefore biased against them."[11]

Mike Ramsay, obviously no fan of EDI, is a black man.

Finally, we come to a conference that was held at Memorial University in St. John's, Newfoundland in the spring of 2024—the inaugural International Equity, Diversity, Inclusion and Anti-Racism (EDI-AR) Conference. One of the scheduled presentations caught my eye—'Navigating Whiteness in EDI-AR Leadership: Reflections and Actions.' The person delivering it was the Special Advisor for Equity, Diversity, and Inclusion from a Canadian university. The paper and slide presentation she gave had this title—The Unbearable Whiteness of Being. Needless to say, I didn't make the conference but she was kind enough to send along her presentation.

In this presentation she talked about "the bastion of whiteness" in universities and academia.

She talked about how "whiteness exists in a spectrum—where we are on the spectrum determines how we wield our whiteness."

She talked about how to "identify and disrupt patterns protecting white supremacy."

When I asked her for the key takeaways from her paper she was only too happy to comply.

She told me how EDI and AR work is dominated by white folks and that, in universities, decision-making and authority are typically white which means the work is defined and directed "in a way that may not be meaningful, substantive, or sustainable."

She told me about people practicing white habits and protecting white/status/culture and who create "cultures of harm instead of healing."

She told me that the habits and patterns of whiteness/white supremacy protect white folks from hard work and do harm unto equity-deserving folk or EDI practitioners who are trying to advance robust change.

And this gem:

> It is necessary to create white learning environments (white affinity groups) led by experienced and knowledgeable white facilitators (not just people who have a 'passion' or an 'interest') to unpack whiteness and rewire power/privilege/white habits into productive ones so we can act in solidarity with equity-deserving groups.

Incidentally, that facilitator was Indigenous—not white—which raises a phrase they like to use and begs the question: Is this not cultural appropriation? Nope. Not the way they see it.

We've been Aunt Jemima-ed.

CHAPTER 4

How we got here

IN 1997 THE Dominion Institute was established as a national charity to promote history and civics education in Canadian high schools. It was founded by journalist Rudyard Griffiths. Since that time Griffiths has been busy doing all kinds of things such as organizing the Munk Debates, which brings world-class speakers to Canada where they debate issues of the day before a live audience, not to mention publishing *The Hub* which has become a distinctive new media voice in the country. Note—I have written many pieces for *The Hub* myself and have also attended a number of those Munk Debates; I heartily recommend them for anyone who wishes to learn about key topics of the day and become better informed.

Something the Dominion Institute did was produce national surveys that addressed public knowledge, or lack thereof, about politics, civics and wars of the past. In 2009 the Dominion Institute merged with the Historica Foundation. The Historica Foundation had been co-founded and endowed by Charles Bronfman in 2000 with "a mandate to engage young Canadians in the history of their country." This new merged entity was called Historica Canada and if you go on the website it says: 'Historica Canada is a charitable organization that offers programs in both official languages that you can use to explore, learn, reflect on our history, and consider what it means to be Canadian.'

That is all fine and good. The organization has been involved in such programs as Heritage Minutes, those popular 60-second vignettes presented on TV that re-enact important events from our history.

From 1998 to 2003 a consortium with a mandate that looked at Canadian history, led by Historica Canada, sponsored a Biennial National History Teaching Conference. From 2001 to 2003 it also sponsored the Summer Institute for Teaching Excellence in Canadian History. What happened with those things? Let's ask Paul W. Bennett. He is an education consultant and Adjunct Professor of Education at Saint Mary's University in Halifax, Nova Scotia. He leads an organization called Schoolhouse Institute, which according to its website, 'provides independent, relevant, and sound commentary and research on critical issues in education.'

Says Bennett: "All this activity managed to energize Canadian history enthusiasts, but it ran foursquare into provincial school systems where the subject discipline continued to occupy a diminishing place with limited course offerings."[12]

Bennett is the author of ten books about education. One of them is 'The State of the System: A Reality Check on Canada's Schools.' In this book he says:

> Curriculum trends such as the rise of Canadian Studies with its sociological emphasis, the dissolution of national history, inquiry-centred approaches, and 'skills-mania' all contributed to the subject's gradual disappearance. While the teaching of Canadian history then experienced a revival, fuelled from 1997 to 2010 by the Dominion Institute and Historica Canada, it proved short-lived.[13]

But why was the Dominion Institute formed in 1997 in the first place? And why did the Historica Foundation come about three years after that? Because enlightened individuals—dare I add the word 'courageous'—recognized that our schools were doing a lousy job teaching young people about our history.

A year after The Dominion Institute was formed, historian J. L. Granatstein came out with his landmark best-seller 'Who Killed Canadian History?,' published by HarperCollins. Of course, dismissing Granatstein as a historian and leaving it at that does the man little justice. Yes, he was indeed a long-time professor of history at York University and even became Distinguished Research Professor of History Emeritus, but he is also an expert on the Canadian military—he graduated from the Royal Military College of Canada, and for a time was CEO of the Canadian War Museum. As well, he holds a Masters degree from the University of Toronto and a PhD from Duke University in North Carolina. And on top of that he is a member of the Order of Canada and a prolific writer who has authored more than 60 books! But for my money 'Who Killed Canadian History?' is the key one.

I have referred to this book many times in presentations and lectures about history, and why it's so important to preserve it. Books in Canada reviewed 'Who Killed Canadian History?' and the review started like this: 'After thirty years as a professional historian, Jack Granatstein is well placed to comment on the way Canadian history is taught. This book warns that a frightening future awaits Canada if we continue down a path towards historical amnesia.'

In the book Granatstein decried the lack, and in many cases total absence, of any viable history program in the schools. He said educators "use history to search for villainy" but that was way back in 1998 when he said this. More than a quarter-century has come and gone since then and what has happened? Things have only gotten worse and you need look no further than the same York University where Granatstein carved out his illustrious career as one of the country's leading historians. Here is what it says in the 2023 calendar for York's History department: "Our courses focus on the thematic areas of Indigeneity, culture, gender, social, political, environmental and sexuality."

That sounds more like a social commentary with an activist edge to it than the curriculum for a history program. And it is. One might even call it a form of *brainwashing*. Indeed, an epidemic of social revisionism—never mind historical revisionism—has taken hold of our schools and that includes our public schools from kindergarten up, our junior high and secondary schools, and most definitely our colleges and universities.

Is it any wonder that in those same colleges and universities you see students carrying signs promoting Hamas? And supporting the ideology of Osama bin Laden on social media? And giving capitalism, and everything that a modern liberal democracy stands for, the finger? In short, it seems to me that a group I will call for lack of a better term 'left-wing-nuts'—armed with a strong ideological edge and agenda—basically controls the state of public education in Canada today.

I got my first taste of this as a minority member of that Parents Advisory Council at my kids' high school, but that was a long time ago. A generation. What does J. L. Granatstein say about young people and their knowledge of history?

"Most young people cannot place important global historical figures such as Winston Churchill or Franklin Roosevelt. Hitler is all but unknown, and Stalin and Mao Zedong are names they may have heard once or twice. Few are able to give the dates of the First or Second World War, or the combatants, or even which side we were on. And beyond this century, their ignorance is complete. In effect, most students are culturally illiterate about everything beyond their generation's immediate experience."

But how could a young man or woman who is twenty years old in this country not know who Winston Churchill was? Or

Franklin Roosevelt? How could someone of university age not know which side Canada fought on in World War II?

Well, what Granatstein said is true and I found this out for myself. I discovered it when I was teaching at four different community colleges in Ontario and later when I produced my video in which university students in Canada's biggest city were interviewed and asked questions about the war. The fact is what they don't know is scary.

What's more, this phenomenon isn't only scary but dangerous. But who is to blame? It's easy to say the schools are guilty. But who runs the schools? In each province and territory there is a Ministry of Education that establishes curriculum, and so, we can point our collective finger at the Minister of Education in each one of those jurisdictions, not to mention the Premier of every province and territory. And yet, I don't hear any discourse at the provincial level decrying the abysmal state of historical knowledge among young people today.

A personal aside. Some years back there was a provincial election in Ontario and my local Member of Provincial Parliament just happened to be the province's Minister of Education in a government led by then Premier Kathleen Wynne. The minister was Mitzie Hunter. During the election campaign I contacted her office and requested a meeting. After all, I was her constituent and she was my local MPP. At the meeting I planned to bring along my laptop and show her that nine-minute video I produced that went viral around the world—with Ontario university students who don't know much about World War II.

I phoned and emailed her office, and left messages. But I never heard from them. It was just like the time I wanted to meet with my son's high school English teacher to discuss his marks, but the teacher wouldn't see me. Such is democracy in action provided you never ask them to account for themselves.

The Dominion Institute came out with its first national study of Canadian high school curriculum for the school year 2008–2009. It provided an analysis of the official curriculum in each province and territory, but according to the aforementioned Paul Bennett from Saint Mary's University, not much resulted from that development. Says Bennett: "In spite of all the advocacy, curriculum remained ossified and it was difficult to determine whether it penetrated the system and reached classroom teachers."

Bennett went on:

> The first Canadian History Report Card revealed that history was still imperiled and losing ground, even in the more holistic social studies curriculum. Quebec ranked first with a B+, scoring 42 out of 50 points (85 percent), largely on the strength of requiring two full years of Quebec-Canada historical study before Grade 11 graduation. Only four provinces required students to take a Canadian history course before graduating—Quebec, Ontario, Manitoba and Nova Scotia—and they were not only singled out but fared better than others. Benchmarked against the Ontario model of self-standing history courses, most provinces were found wanting in terms of providing all students with exposure to at least one Canadian history course before graduation.

I live in Ontario and if my experience with students in this province is any indication, that summary does not bode well for the country.

Historica also conducted Canadian History Report Cards in 2016 and 2021, but according to Bennett they focused more on diversity in the history curriculum, resulting in an ever-shrinking footprint. Bennett's conclusion?

"Granatstein's worst fears have been realized."

Rory Gilfillan teaches history at Lakefield College, a private educational facility in Peterborough, Ontario. He, too, laments at what passes as history curriculum in the school system and says nowadays we hold historical figures to standards that either weren't available at the time or were part of a worldview that is no longer valid, and then we judge them to be lacking. What's more, he says the problems in education go back a long time. Decades.

"The ideals we have instilled over the last forty years have bred complacency and indifference," he says. "Where our grandparents responded to evil with action, we deny its existence, wear rubber bracelets, post on Twitter, mouth platitudes from a great distance, and then wait for others to take our place on the sharp end. Consequently, we have the country we deserve."

Back in 2016 I came across an article posted on the site of an organization called The National Association of Scholars, a non-profit that seeks to reform higher education. It is American and based in New York City. But the article was about Canada and had this headline—'It's Something, But It's Not History: Canadian History in Ontario Schools.'

At the time I had started doing my history presentations and showing that video. By and large, most people were shocked when they saw it. But there were also people who were not shocked, and time and again they would turn out to be former schoolteachers who had taught in Ontario's public school system.

In the article mentioned the author begins with a reference to Granatstein's book *Who Killed Canadian History?* and then admits to being a teacher before citing an Ontario Ministry of Education document from 2013.

> The Ontario Curriculum (2013) replaced historical narrative with abstract thematic units designed to stupefy students—Social, Political, and Economic Context; Communities, Conflict, and Cooperation; Identify, Citizenship, and Heritage. Moreover, the Curriculum's sample questions skew towards explorations of multiculturalism, gender inequality, and racism. There is nothing wrong with this in

principle—these topics are part of Canadian history, and they should be part of what we teach. But they aren't all of Canadian history, and certainly not all of Canadian history worth studying. The disproportionate emphasis on these topics amounts to a slanderous retelling of Canadian history as a chronicle of villainies.[14]

The author then provides an example.

One of the Curriculum's suggested questions for the study of the settlement of the Loyalists in Niagara after the Revolutionary War asks how the First Nations would have felt about being "forced off their land" to make room for the Loyalists. Not only does the question contain an unwarranted assumption, it invites a misreading of the actual history. The Crown purchased the land from the Mississaugas, one of the many First Nations tribes with whom the Crown had a good relationship. Whether or not the price for the land was a fair one is worthy of debate. But as it stands, the investigation of this question will leave students believing that, inarguably, there was nothing but exploitation devoid of even a shred of fair dealing in Loyalist settlement in particular and in European imperialism in general.

The author went on to say how the Curriculum highlights the experiences of slaves in New France and British North America, but never says that John Graves Simcoe, Lieutenant-Governor of Upper Canada, enacted a law that would effectively put a stranglehold on slavery in the colony and make Upper Canada the first jurisdiction in the entire British Empire to do so. The article ends with this observation: "The Ministry of Education endorses the Curriculum's narrative of victimhood."

What is most telling about this article is that the author, an Ontario high school teacher, had to resort to using a pseudonym in the byline because fessing up would have been damaging to their career.

Now I write novels that contain a large dose of history. Call it historical fiction if you want. One of those books mentioned earlier, *The Last Witness*, is about the last living survivor of the Holocaust in a near-future world that doesn't know history. When the novel was finished I went to New York City and attended a writers' conference called Thrillerfest. My aim was to land a literary agent for the book and I did.

At that conference I had the pleasure of meeting the late Nelson De Mille, an author of action and suspense novels who passed away in 2024. Many times he was on *The New York Times* bestseller list with sales in the millions. I told him about my just-completed novel and he asked me to send him the manuscript. A week or two went by and then in the mail I received a letter from Nelson De Mille. Yes, a letter! In fact, De Mille was a writer, and a very successful one, who didn't even use a computer. He wrote all his novels in long-hand and then had the manuscript typed. Well, whatever works, and as I say his sales are in the millions. This is what De Mille said in that letter.

> As a history major in college I can't believe how little history young people know. The curriculum in schools has been corrupted and politicized so I blame public and private schools for this ignorance of history, civics, and even simple geography. Students can't learn what they're not taught, and what they are taught is often politically skewed.

He said the premise of my novel is a good one and wished me luck. It has now been ten years since I met Nelson De Mille and his observation still holds true; it's even more true today than it was then, especially because of the *politicizing* that he referred to. And Canada is a good example.

In 2019 the Government of Canada, through Parks Canada, issued a news release about the new Framework for History and Commemoration; National Historic Sites System Plan 2019. The date of the announcement was June 19 and was made by The Hon. Catherine McKenna, Minister of Environment and Climate Change and Minister responsible for Parks Canada. Here is the first paragraph of that news release: "Parks Canada places reflect the diverse heritage of the nation and provide an opportunity to learn more about our rich and sacred history, including the history, cultures, and contributions of Indigenous peoples."

The agency said it was investing $23.9 million to "recognize and integrate Indigenous peoples' histories, voices and perspectives at heritage places administered by Parks Canada" and was embarking on a new approach to "review existing national historic designations and their associated plaque texts. In cases where there is *controversy* (my italics) or new research findings, the review could result in the addition of new plaque text, changing the reasons for designation, or adjustments to the name of a designation."

Remember my analogy with American sprinter Jesse Owens who shattered the world record for the men's 100-metres at the 1936 Olympic Games in Berlin? He did it in a time of 10.3 seconds. I then compared that to the still current world-record time of Jamaican sprinter Usain Bolt who ran it in 9.58 seconds in 2009. Put the two men together and run them in an AI-generated race and it's no contest. But the world—even the world of sprinting—was a lot different in 2009 than it was back in 1936. In short, only a fool would *judge* what Owens did against what Bolt did and then proceed to label Owens a lousy runner.

Jesse Owens was not a lousy runner. He was a great runner and an incredible athlete, and also a very courageous one who did his thing right in the heart of Nazi Germany and in front of Adolf Hitler himself. It's the same when we compare, measure—and judge—earlier periods of history, when everything was different, against the time we find ourselves in today.

The upshot of all this is that history has been rewritten, and continues to be rewritten, in order to fit a narrative that embodies politics and ideology, and panders to elements in society with an agenda. For evidence all we have to do is examine what has happened to the legacy of our first prime minister.

Sir John A. Macdonald.

If he were alive today he might well file charges of defamation and slander against those who have sullied his name. And he would have a case, as would others whose names have been unfairly besmirched. In Ontario we can include the likes of Egerton Ryerson and Henry Dundas. In Atlantic Canada a prominent name from history who has received similar treatment is Edward Cornwallis, the founder of Halifax. And in British Columbia, longtime judge Matthew Begbie has had everything associated with him kicked into the trash can as well.

How about we see for ourselves and look at the historical record of each of those men? We'll start with Macdonald for he has suffered the biggest fall from grace. Based on what we hear about him now—the man died in 1891—it would seem that he has a contentious track record. But does he? And how did Canadians feel about him when he was alive? What's more, how did they feel and what did they think about him after his death? Most important of all, what exactly was his legacy?

Let's find out.

PART II

The Lynching of the Innocent

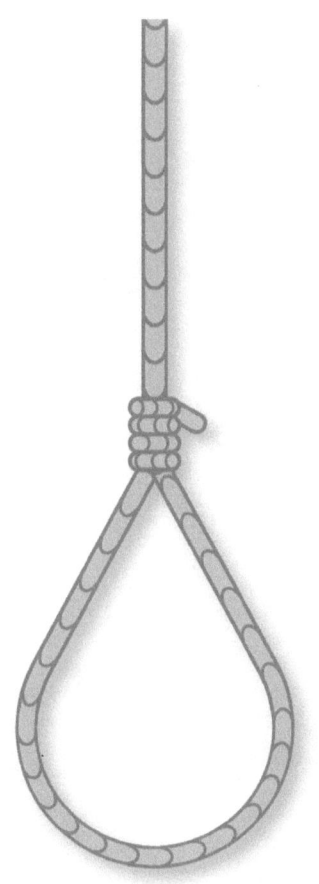

CHAPTER 5

The trashing of John A. Macdonald

THE DATE WAS FEBRUARY 17, 1891, and the place the Academy of Music in Toronto. The first building in the city to be fully electric, it sat on King Street where University Avenue now crosses the south side of King in the middle of the financial district. Built as a concert hall two years earlier, the Academy of Music would present not only concerts but operas, operettas and recitals. It had seating for more than 1,500 people, including box seats for private viewing. The floor was on an incline so there were no bad sight lines and in a few years a little girl named Gladys Mary Smith would make her stage debut here. She would go on to become Mary Pickford, the first big star of the silent film era, and known around the world as America's Sweetheart even though she was from Toronto. But on this day people were coming to hear a speech.

It was unseasonably warm for February and Canada in the middle of a federal election, the main issue being trade relations with the United States. The Liberals had Wilfrid Laurier running his first campaign as party leader and he supported reciprocity or free trade with the US. The Conservatives, still led by Prime Minister John A. Macdonald—he'd been at the helm of the party since 1867—pushed the National Policy, a three-pronged strategy for building the economy of this still fledgling country that lay immediately north of an upstart America. The policy involved high tariffs on imported manufactured items to protect Canada's manufacturing industry, growing the infrastructure—especially roads and railroads—and immigration into western Canada. Building the Canadian Pacific Railway would be a big part of that.

Canada had been a country for only 24 years and it was from the get-go a very divided country. In 1891 it was but 26 years since the end of the American Civil War and Abraham Lincoln's assassination. It would be another 27 years before women would win the right to vote, even though Macdonald had pressed for that in the previous decade; Canada's parliament was the first legislature in the world to debate the issue. Macdonald had also supported extending the franchise to Canada's Native people. In 1885 he persuaded parliament to give the vote to Indigenous inhabitants in central and eastern Canada, on the same terms as white inhabitants, but this was rescinded by the Liberals in 1898. And as far as the former attempt was concerned—giving women the vote—even Macdonald's own wife Lady Agnes thought it a bad idea!

Such were the times.

He was 76 and in just over two weeks would win his sixth federal election. To this day no politician has won more, although Macdonald would later share the distinction with Mackenzie King as leaders with the most election wins in Canadian history. However, on that day he was ailing and in poor health, but the masses came out for him.

At six o'clock, there were a few thousand of them and then 15,000. A sizeable police presence had been established outside the Academy of Music, but only 4,000 people could get into the building and they did with a tremendous surge. According to reports, women fainted and seats were ripped out to make room. Some got in by breaking a basement window or climbing a ladder that had been brought by an enterprising boy who charged for the privilege. First a nickel, then a dime, then a quarter. Finally, Macdonald appeared. He arrived by carriage just past 7.30 p.m.

Alice Freeman was a reporter for the *Toronto Empire*. The first female columnist in Canada, she wrote a column called 'Women's Empire' which tackled women's issues of the day. She was also a schoolteacher and to protect that job had to hide the fact about being a journalist, a profession considered demeaning, and wrote under the pseudonym Faith Fenton. She was a member of the Women's Christian Temperance movement, which considered alcohol the prime cause of many of society's ills and which pushed for total prohibition of all alcoholic beverages.

When everyone was inside the building and Macdonald was spotted, a roar burst through the crowd. Wrote Freeman: "[It] broke in great waves over the house, falling and rising again and again, spontaneous, irrepressible, magnetic."[15]

Charles Tupper, former premier of Nova Scotia who five years later—and for a mere three months—would become Canada's sixth prime minister, took the stage.

"I always knew our great leader was a very popular man," he said. "But I never appreciated it fully until I attempted to gain entrance to this hall tonight."

Then Macdonald started to speak and it would be the last great speech of his long career. Alice Freeman a.k.a. Faith Fenton wrote what she saw and heard that night.

"The old man stood up, and as, in the fullness of his years, he leaned slightly forward there was a sudden outburst from the audience that fairly shook the building from its vaulted roof to its foundations. The entire gathering arose and yelled. Handkerchiefs, hats, umbrellas, walking sticks, programmes, and in fact everything within reach, were waved by the audience. The enthusiastic uproar was deafening. This was one of the rewards that fall to the lot of a man who has spent his whole life labouring for the benefit of his race. It was a proud minute for Sir John."[16]

We must remember this was 1891. Indeed, any journalist in Canada today who crafted such words as *for the benefit of his race*—especially in reference to whites—would be tarred, feathered and quartered. At least, in a figurative sense. That actually was a popular method of execution in Britain and other European countries during the Middle Ages, a statutory penalty for men convicted of high treason. It was always men. If the guilty party was a woman, she would be burned at the stake. Nevertheless, in such a public spectacle the guilty party got hanged within a whisker of death, then disembowelled, beheaded and quartered. Their remains would go on display at the Tower of London or wherever. But the practice lasted beyond the Middle Ages.

The last official execution like this occurred in 1782 and, according to reports, a crowd of 20,000 people attended and when it was over they fought over pieces of the corpse which they wanted as trophies. How big a crowd is that? Think of a hockey arena—the Scotiabank Arena in Toronto or Bell Centre in Montreal—at full capacity. But even after that, in 1803, seven convicted men were placed on sledges attached to horses and pulled around the *gaol* yard before being hanged and beheaded. Some 20,000 people watched that one, too. It happened in Dublin, Ireland.

When we talk 1803 we find ourselves in *the same century* as when John A. Macdonald made his final speech at the Academy of Music. The difference between the two dates—88 years—may be construed as a single lifetime today. So, here we have Macdonald's speech in 1891 and one lifetime earlier tens of thousands would gather for a public execution, and not in Saudi Arabia but Dublin, which was part of the United Kingdom of Great Britain and Ireland. For the record, public execution by hanging, drawing and quartering wasn't legally abolished in Great Britain until 1870—three years *after* Canada became a nation.

My point is when we talk about history we have to recognize the time period being discussed. Customs and values were different in 1891 than they were in 1803. In the last decade of the 19th century no public execution with 20,000 witnesses taking part in the festivities would occur anywhere in the British

Commonwealth. Why? Society had *changed* in the span of one lifetime. By the same token, many beliefs and thoughts that were widespread and acceptable in 1891 would not pass the litmus test today. People evolve and society evolves with them, hopefully, for the better.

Thus, customs and values were *different* in the Canada of 1891 than they are now. The people were different. Work was different. Life was different. As were prejudices. But the fact remains John A. Macdonald was an immensely popular leader among the people of this country, even in the twilight of his political career, and that makes him unique for a prime minster of Canada.

In 2015, when Stephen Harper was in his last year as prime minister, one would be hard-pressed to find a more disliked figure in the country. It was the same for Brian Mulroney in 1993, Pierre Trudeau in 1984, and the younger Trudeau when he announced in 2024 that he would be resigning. Twenty years before that Jean Chretien's own party forced him to step down. But such was not the case with Macdonald. He was loved, and not only that, he was a man ahead of his time. Still, today he is trashed unmercifully from coast to coast by those who don't know better. They certainly don't know much about him nor the times he lived in, and are in a complete vacuum when it comes to Canadian history. So let's try to remedy that.

Who exactly was John A. Macdonald?

He was born in Glasgow, Scotland in 1815 and there is some discrepancy about the date. Official records say January 10 but according to his father's notes it was the next day. Contemporary Canadians might find such inconsistency amusing, but discrepancies in the date of one's birth may be for a reason and I can point to my wife's family.

My mother-in-law was born on January 2, 1932, in a small village in northern Greece, but this presented a problem; local authorities refused to register a female as the first official birth of the year. Instead, they waited until a boy was born the following day and registered him, and only then would they register her birth the day after that, which was two days after her actual birth. To this day all official documents for my mother-in-law—birth certificate, citizenship papers which made her Canadian, passport, etc.—have her birth recorded as January 4 even though that was not the day she was born.

Such was the place. Such were the times.

Macdonald's family came from Sutherlandshire in the Scottish highlands. His father, a shopkeeper, was 33 when John was born and his mother 37. The senior Macdonald had two shops and they both failed. In 1820, when John was five, the family packed up and left. They took a steamship across the Atlantic to Quebec City and went on to Montreal and then along the St. Lawrence River to Kingston in what was then Upper Canada. Many of the residents there were Scots like them.

The journey from Montreal to Kingston came courtesy of a Durham boat, a flat-bottomed craft made of wood. It was slow and crude and there were places along the route where passengers had to disembark and portage to make it through the rapids. That trip alone took three weeks.

It wasn't long before tragedy struck the family. When John was seven he witnessed with his own eyes the death of his little brother James. As the story goes, one day both their parents were out and a family worker who was known to be a drinker struck the boy who had been crying. He fell and hit his head on an andiron—a bracket support that holds logs over a fireplace—and he died. On May 3, 1822, the *Kingston Chronicle* ran the obituary. "On Monday the 22 ult., James, second son of Mr. Hugh Macdonald, Merchant of this town, aged five years and six months."

No charges were laid and it left John the only son. He has written that he never had a boyhood because at the age of 15 he left school and went to work, not that this was unusual back then. He was a good student who studied Latin, French, English and Math, and one of his contemporaries, Oliver Mowat, would later become Premier of Ontario. The young Macdonald wanted to apprentice at a law firm. Doing that required an in-person exam before a panel of judges at the Law Society of Upper Canada in Toronto. He did the exam and passed, and still not 16 years of age, went to work as a law clerk before finding employment in the office of an eminent Kingston lawyer who called him the most diligent student he ever had.

John worked during the day and spent his evenings poring over textbooks. At 21 he was called to the Bar of Upper Canada and became a barrister, and two years after that was going up against some of the top lawyers around. At 29 he was asked to run for public office and in accepting the invitation this is what he said:

> In presenting myself to the electors of Kingston as a candidate for their suffrages, I have no object of personal ambition to gratify, except a desire to advance the interests of the town in which I have lived so long, and with whose fortunes my own prosperity is identified, as well as to maintain those principles of public policy which you justly style "sound and liberal," and which have always actuated our loyal old town. In a young country like Canada, I am of opinion that it is of more consequence to endeavor to develop its resources and improve its physical advantages, than to waste the time of the Legislature and the money of the people in fruitless discussions on abstract and theoretical questions of government.[17]

The message was not politicking on his part because Macdonald believed what he was saying. He wasn't interested in furthering his own personal riches. Indeed, if he had forgone politics to remain a lawyer full-time, he would have earned much more money in his life. But he wanted to serve his constituents and build a country, and he would remain true to these principles throughout his career. However, at that time he felt he had to continue to run his still growing law practice.

He once defended a Mohawk who had been charged with killing another Mohawk. Another time he defended a black man, a slave who had escaped from the United States where slavery was the letter of the law; the man had been arrested in Upper Canada for stealing a horse south of the border. Macdonald said the magistrate who initiated the proceeding should be discharged from his duties.

For him both careers—law and politics—were on the upswing. By the time he was 35 he was one of Kingston's top lawyers. He was made a Queen's Counsel and soon became Receiver General for Canada and head of the Crown Lands Office. He organized those departments and people regarded him as an excellent administrator.

In 1843 he married Isabella Clark. Richard Gwyn's award-winning, two-volume biography of Macdonald—*John A: The Man Who Made Us* (published in 2008) and *Nation Maker: Sir John A. Macdonald: His Life, Our Times* (published in 2012) says of that union:

> The first two years of his marriage to Isabella would be the single span of time in John A. Macdonald's entire adult life in which he experienced a normal marriage and family life. In place of the small daily epiphanies of any couple, whether they are in love or merely companionable, Macdonald's entire life would be politics. This was one reason—the tragic one—why he became so good at it.[18]

They were married for 14 years until her death in 1857, but for their last 12 years together she remained a bedridden invalid constantly prescribed opium by her doctors. Macdonald, in his despair, would turn to drink. That despair was compounded by the death of their infant son, also named John, yet another calamity in a long line of personal tragedies that would befall him throughout his life. Then there was his mother who suffered 12 strokes, not to mention his two unmarried sisters. Macdonald, embroiled in the two careers of law and politics, was responsible for the entire lot of them.

He and Isabella would have another son, Hugh, who later became estranged from his father and went on to forge his own career in politics as Premier of Manitoba. After Isabella's death, Macdonald thrust himself even more into public service and was named Attorney General for Upper Canada, and with that role came responsibility for laws, penitentiaries and appointing judges. The same year Isabella died a royal commission was formed to recommend "the best mode of so managing Indian property as to secure its full benefit to the Indians without impeding the settlement of the country."[19]

This would be a fine line to navigate.

South of the border in the United States some 45,000 Indians—estimates run as high as 60,000—were slaughtered in one Indian war after another and that was to be avoided here. The royal commission recommended ways to protect them "from contamination by the white settlers," while at the same time, enable them to "assimilate the habits" of white men. It culminated in the Gradual Civilization Bill of 1857 which aimed to assimilate Indigenous people by giving them citizenship and the right to vote, but in the process they would lose their Indian status.

What was the world like in those days?

The Grand Trunk Railway connecting Sarnia and Montreal was finally finished, but in debt to the tune of $7 million, no small sum back then. The British North American Exploring Expedition surveyed—for the very first time—the prairies and the West. On the last day of the year Queen Victoria named Ottawa capital of the Province of Canada.

Meanwhile, in the United States, the Supreme Court ruled that blacks were not citizens and slaves could not sue to win their freedom, which would help lay the groundwork for the coming

Civil War. What else happened? The first elevator was installed in New York City and the era of skyscrapers began. A band of Sioux massacred 40 settlers in Iowa and took four women hostage. The first national financial crisis stemming from widespread speculation in land and railroads led to bank closures.

The next year—1858—gold would be discovered in the Fraser River area and lead to creation of the Colony of British Columbia. The gold rush attracted scores of people. In one incident American miners raped a young Native girl. Her tribe found and killed the perpetrators, decapitating them in the process, and tensions between whites and many Native tribes would remain high. Also that year the Province of Canada released its first decimal coinage and the government levied tariffs on goods manufactured in the US in order to pay for some of those railroad debts.

Canada wasn't a country yet and south of the border a young nation was flexing its muscles and marching inexorably to what would be a long, cataclysmic war. Also, one year later—1859— an English naturalist named Charles Darwin would publish his book *On the Origin of Species* which forever changed how people looked at God and religion.

This was the world in which John A. Macdonald and the people of Canada found themselves. Since the mid 1850s he had effectively been running things in the country that wasn't quite a country, but in 1857 the Gradual Civilization Bill became law. It passed in the Legislature by a vote of 72 to 1, the only naysayer being William Lyon Mackenzie—who in 1834 had been the first mayor of Toronto—and he posed this question of the Indians: "Why should we wish to civilize them?"

Said Richard Gwyn in Volume 1 of his biography:

> Macdonald's own views about Indians were the same as those of most Canadians at this time: they should be protected from whites but assimilated into white society. In two

respects he differed from the general opinion. The letter of the law itself and the treaties negotiated with the Indians were of cardinal concern to him. Macdonald consistently rejected requests by individuals, including Conservative, for permission to buy reserve lands that they had persuaded bands to sell them.[20]

Notwithstanding what was said earlier about tarring, feathering and quartering, the fact is when Macdonald was in his final term as Prime Minister—this would be 1891—executions were still taking place in Canada and would continue for many decades afterward, only not with 20,000 people watching and not by decapitation. It would be a hanging inside penitentiary walls. Macdonald himself ended the practice of public executions in 1871, two years after Canada's last public hanging. And yes, according to reports, thousands of people turned out to watch that event but had to go away disappointed when things were moved up an hour and they missed it.

Such were the times.

Taking the values and customs from the 21st century and applying them to a hundred or 200 or 1,000 years earlier, and then making judgments about the character of people from that time—in essence, trying to gain insight into their minds but only through the lens of today—is, in a word, absurd.

It makes as much sense as calling Jesse Owens a lousy sprinter.

Macdonald, first and foremost, was a nation builder and that nation is Canada. He has been described as a master of herding cats. Indeed, along with the English and French, the Catholics and Protestants, not to mention Anglicans, Methodists, Americans, Brits, Scots, Native peoples, and every group and party along the political spectrum—he more than any other individual managed to weave all those disparate elements together and create a country. And not only that, he made this country separate but not totally apart from Great Britain, and at the same time, distinct from the United States.

Politically, the man was a magician.

Three conferences were held to discuss confederation, the last of them in December, 1866 in London, England. Many fathers of confederation attended that gathering and the first thing they did was elect Macdonald chairman. Macdonald biographer Richard Gwyn points out that Sir Federic Rogers, the most senior person there from the British Colonial Office, described him as "the ruling genius" and Rogers was not alone in expressing such sentiment. British Colonial Secretary Lord Carnarvon called Macdonald "the ablest politician in Upper Canada." Sir Hector-Louis Langevin, who represented the interests of Quebec at that conference and who had attended two earlier conferences in Charlottetown and Quebec, wrote: "Macdonald is a sharp fox. He is a very well informed man, clever and very popular. He is *the man of the conference*."[21]

How did Macdonald sign the guest book at the Charlottetown conference of 1864? He wrote his name and added two words—cabinet maker. And so, we come to confederation.

Now I'm a history junkie with an office full of old maps and newspapers. One of those newspapers is *The Globe* which in 1936 merged with the *Mail and Empire* to form the *Globe and Mail*. But on July 1, 1867—a Monday—the paper was still *The Globe* and I have a replica of that day's edition.

You can tell a lot about the time period from old newspapers. This one was a broadsheet running nine columns across with type so small most people today would need a magnifying glass to read it. There was no white space, no graphics and no photos. The lead story began at the top left corner with the headline CONFEDERATION DAY and this was how that story started:

> With the first dawn of this gladsome midsummer morn, we hail the birthday of a new nationality. A united British America, with its four millions of people, takes its place this day among the nations of the world. Stamped with a familiar name which in the past has borne a record sufficiently honourable to entitle it to be perpetrated with a more comprehensive import, the Dominion of Canada, on this first day of July, eighteen hundred and sixty-seven, enters on a new career of national existence.

I began my career as a newspaper reporter and can assure you that any editor would have a field day with copy like this now. But not back then. And just as you can tell a lot about the time period from the news and how it was written, you can also discern things from ads. One in particular stands out. It was an ad taken by a man who had just divorced his wife, and in it he urged people not to conduct any business with her! The name of the woman was printed in full for all to see.

If a newspaper or any publication, online or whatever, published such a thing like that today it would be sued and good luck in court. But in 1867 women didn't have the vote and wouldn't have it until 1918—more than half a century later! What's more, anyone of Asian extraction wouldn't get the vote until 1948 and if you happened to be a First Nations man or woman you had to wait until 1960. Such were the times, and when you think about this it makes Macdonald all the more remarkable for some of the things he tried to do.

Canada's first census took place in 1871. At the time the young country consisted of Ontario, Quebec, New Brunswick and Nova Scotia. More than 80 percent of its people lived on farms and the biggest city was Montreal with some 115,000 inhabitants. Quebec

City and Toronto each had 60,000. For the most part, Canada was agrarian and rural, and in Quebec almost half the population over the age of 20 couldn't even read or write.[22]

Drinking was widespread and certainly not confined to Macdonald. As for religion, 43 percent of the citizens were Catholic, most of them of French or Irish descent, but the great majority of the population was definitely Christian. One question concerning religion on the 1871 census allowed for 'no religion' and only 0.15 percent of respondents selected that option—a paltry one-seventh of one percent! Compare this with the 2021 census, which included the category of 'non-religious.' How many ticked off that box? *Just under 35 percent of all respondents, which is more than one in three!* What does it mean?

The times, not to mention the views of the public, changed a lot.

What were the prospects of this new nation making a go of it in 1867? Well, neither the Brits nor the Yanks were particularly optimistic. *The Times of London* didn't think it would survive because it lacked "the body, the vital organs, the circulation and the muscular force that are to give adequate power to these widespread limbs." Said *The New York Times*: "When the experiment of the 'Dominion' shall have failed, as fail it must, a process of peaceful absorption will give Canada her proper place in the great North American republic."[23]

But those newspapers didn't take into account John A. Macdonald.

If ever there was a person who *invented* Canadian politics it was he. He popularized the concept of going on tour, speaking to the public, and not from a prepared text. He was well read, learned, and possessed a keen sense of humour. Once, when speaking to a group of farmers, he stood on top of farming machinery only to be told it was a manure spreader. How did Macdonald, leader of the Conservative party, respond?

"This is the first time I've stood on the Liberal platform."

The man who called his profession 'cabinet maker' was just that. He formed a Cabinet by taking representation from each of Canada's provinces, and his list of accomplishments is more than considerable. Thanks to him we have the Bank Act of 1871, which has resulted in fewer bank failures than in just about any other country. He was also chief architect of the Northwest Mounted Police (NWMP) which became the Royal Canadian Mounted Police, and Macdonald biographer Gwyn is effusive in his praise about that. Says Gwyn:

> The NWMP was never perfect, but it was extraordinary. Because of it, law and order prevailed in Canada's West, while below the border the gun ruled, wielded either by the army or by vigilante squads. Above the border, most of those hauled into the courts by the policemen were whites accused of crimes against Indians; below it, few whites were ever tried, because the all-white juries refused to find them guilty. The Mounted Police did all this with a few hundred men in an area half the size of Europe.[24]

Contrast that with you saw in Chapter 3 of this book when an organization called Moms Against Racism—funded in part by the federal government—dismissed the NWMP as a "colonial, para-military force" in a seminar called Systemic Racism in Canada. What does that tell you?

It pays to do research before making unsubstantiated claims.

Indeed, if that organization had looked a little deeper it may have learned about Chief Asapo-Muxika of the Siksika Indian band in Alberta. Better known as Crowfoot, he was a supporter of Treaty 7 which established the police force. What did he have to say?

> If the [NWMP] police had not come to this country, where would we all be now? Bad men and whiskey were killing us

so fast that few of us would have been alive today. The Police have protected us as the feathers of the bird protect it from the frosts of winter.[25]

Biographer Gwyn recognizes that the plight of Canada's Indigenous community was an ongoing challenge for Macdonald. Macdonald's policy was essentially the same as British policy, namely, protecting Aboriginal people from destructive contact with settlers and "to place [Indians] on a footing of equality with their white brethren."[26]

But such a sentiment did not endear him to other politicians and lawmakers of his day. When he proposed giving them the vote, there was pushback. When he argued for women having the vote, more of the same. Thus, if one happens to be a politician in a democracy, as Macdonald was, that person is not a dictator. They must lead and learn the art of compromise, which is where Macdonald stood without peer.

In 1879 he and his second wife Agnes had a daughter, Mary, who was born with hydrocephalus, a condition that kept her in a wheelchair her entire life and in constant need of care. This is a man who saw his little brother of five murdered, killed, what have you. After two years of marriage his first wife turned into an invalid. His first son, on whom he doted, died as an infant. He had to look after a sickly wife, sickly mother, two unmarried sisters, and later a daughter confined to a wheelchair. Despite it all, what mark did he leave? Let's again turn to Gwyn, who devoted some seven years of his life to researching the man.

"Any reasonable ranking of nineteenth-century democratic leaders would be Abraham Lincoln, Benjamin Disraeli, William Gladstone and John A. Macdonald."

That is heady company to be in. According to Gwyn, when looking at the history of Canada and all its leaders right up to the first decade of the 21st century, "no one else came close to

Macdonald." He concludes: "Had there been no Macdonald, there almost certainly would be today no Canada. In a great many ways, what Canadians have become began with him. He, a nation-maker, made us."[27]

Gwyn's two-volume biography wasn't published until well over a century after Macdonald's death which fell on June 6, 1891. But another book—*Anecdotal Life of Sir John Macdonald* by Emerson Bristol Biggar—came out the same year he died. And this is how Biggar described Macdonald's passing.

> Never was a man so widely lamented, and never did a death strike a whole nation with such a feeling of personal loss. In hundreds of churches on that day memorial services were held, and for a week or more there were few courts that sat, from the Supreme courts down to county courts, few city councils or municipal councils, and few public bodies that assembled, without making some allusion to Sir John, expressing sorrow at his death or praise of his many great qualities. Of these qualities surely not the least was his affectionate loyalty to the Empire, of which he was from the Canadian point of vision so colossal a figure.[28]

This does not sound at all like the man we see portrayed today. From coast to coast no historical figure from this country's past has been besmirched to such a degree as Sir John A. Macdonald. His statue outside the Ontario Legislature in Toronto was boarded up after protests in 2020 and remained that way for five years. Another statue in Montreal was toppled by a mob that cheered when the head came off. Other statues were taken down in Hamilton, Victoria and elsewhere. In Kingston his statue was removed and in Ottawa the Sir John A. Macdonald Parkway was renamed *Kichi Zibi Mikan*, which means 'Great River Road' in the Algonquin language. Across the land schools bearing his name are considering making a switch. In short, he is being trashed from one end of the country to the other.

After including Sir John A. Macdonald Day—his birthday—in its university calendar, McMaster University in Hamilton felt it had to make a public apology for the oversight. It resulted in this email:

> We inadvertently included the mention of Sir John A. Macdonald day, which is a day that commemorates a person who was responsible for the genocide and oppression of Indigenous peoples in Canada. We are committed to creating a culture of diversity, inclusion, and respect in our department, and we recognize that our calendars should reflect the values and identities of our members and the communities we serve.

Macdonald did *not* create residential schools which was pointed out in a letter published in *The Globe and Mail* on June 26, 2023. The renaming of the street bearing his name in Ottawa was too much for Mary Lazier Corbett of Picton, Ontario. Here is her letter in full.

> Re 'NCC (National Capital Commission) renaming of Sir John A. Macdonald Parkway to Kichi Zibi Mikan' (June 22). I realize that these days people are working to be sensitive to past wrongs done to Indigenous peoples, but the residential schools were established around 1831, when Macdonald was about 16 years old. They were not his creation.
>
> As a trained historian, I strongly believe that the past has to be understood in terms of the realities of the times. The American Indian Wars were designed to "remove" Indigenous peoples so U. S. whites could settle on their land. Modern historians view it as a form of genocide. That horror

was a key factor behind Macdonald's drive to create a land from sea to sea, by building a national railway, and creating a border between the two countries. He did not want that misery spreading north.

Given Macdonald's support for various Indigenous communities in his private work as well, I am saddened by the sloppy historical work that is behind the destruction of his name. If lies continue to replace legitimate history, then his legacy is at serious risk.

While Catholic nuns and priests did run earlier versions of residential schools as early as the late 1600s, the first officially sanctioned one was in Brantford, Ontario in 1831. Federal funding didn't begin until 1883. I will tackle this subject in more detail later, but am compelled to address the charge of *genocide* alleged by McMaster, not to mention numerous others who are just as misinformed. The term 'genocide' was first used in the 1940s to describe what Nazi Germany was doing to European Jews—the systematic murder of millions of people. Nothing like that has ever occurred in Canada. In fact, the closest thing to a genocide in Canadian history does concern Indigenous people, namely, the Huron-Wendat. In 1649 they were pretty much wiped out—tens of thousands of them massacred with no mercy—but this happened not at the hands of the white man, but *another* Indigenous group, the Iroquois, who were attacking their neighbours in Huronia.

When it comes to residential schools, those who levy the charge of genocide should research actual history and that means research without an ideological bent. Anyone who climbs down this rabbit hole and screams 'genocide'—and lays it all at the hands of John A. Macdonald—is a victim of historical revisionism and subject to mob rule. History has shown time and again where that leads. Put another way, this is succumbing to *brainwashing*. The Merriam dictionary defines that as 'persuasion by propaganda and salesmanship,' which accurately describes how the Government of Canada, through Parks Canada, handled the reopening of Bellevue House in 2024 after a six-year hiatus.

Bellevue House is the one-time Kingston home of Macdonald. It had been under wraps since 2018 because of restorations and then Covid. Administered by Parks Canada, it offers tours and I opted for one called 'Unpacking Macdonald.' But after taking it I found myself thinking of the Hitler Youth.

Adolf Hitler established the Hitler Youth to introduce children and youths of the Fatherland to Nazi ideology. It was a way to educate and indoctrinate them, and create bona fide Nazis. There were rallies, training academies, propaganda—and historical revisionism—to foster the myth of Aryan supremacy.

Now a personal aside. I was once a guest of the Canadian Armed Forces who invited me to speak at our military bases in the former West Germany. They even provided a car and chauffeur to tour my wife and me around the Black Forest region. In one town we were at a stop sign and saw a group of long-haired young people on the sidewalk. Our German driver, a man in his 50s, took one look and said: "Hitler did a lot of bad things but he wouldn't put up with that."

This was 42 years after the end of World War II. I figured our driver must have been in the Hitler Youth and, well, old habits die hard. What now passes as history on Sir John A. Macdonald at Bellevue House in Kingston is a different form of education and indoctrination, but it's clear no effort has been spared to shove ideology down your throat. For lack of a better term, let's call it *woke history* and it starts when you go on the website.

> Hello. Shé:kon. Aaniin. At Bellevue House National Historic Site, many voices present the complex legacy of Canada's first prime minister, Sir John A. Macdonald.

If this is history, it's through a filtered lens. Bellevue House has little connection to Macdonald. He rented the house for barely a year long before becoming prime minister, living there with his sickly wife Isabella and first son John, who died in infancy. While the restored house is beautiful, the impression left with you is that Macdonald was of the upper class and did everything he could to show it. Nothing could be further from the truth. During his brief time in Bellevue House he was struggling to make a living as a lawyer, never mind caring for his wife and being responsible for his unmarried sisters and mother. But Bellevue House implies that he was a man of wealth. This is pure fallacy.

While the house is furnished according to the time period, there is only one artifact from Macdonald. His son's crib. However, a great deal is *suggested*. For example:

> As you move through the house, you will discover that a wealthy Victorian home can offer clues through architecture, furniture, and contents that express the occupants' power and privilege. You'll encounter difficult stories about the past and be invited into discussions and moments of personal reflection about how Canada's future can be more inclusive.

There is signage at Bellevue House about the internment of Japanese-Canadians during World War II. What does that have to do with Macdonald? There are references to slavery, as if what was going on in Upper Canada mirrored what transpired south of the border. In fact, Lieutenant Governor John Graves Simcoe abhorred slavery and in 1793 an Act was passed to prevent the introduction of slaves to Upper Canada, making that jurisdiction the first in the British Commonwealth to do anything like that. The not-so-subtle implication at Bellevue House points to the sorry treatment of anyone in these parts who wasn't white; that means everything from the head tax on Chinese migrants who worked on the railway to the plight of Indigenous people.

If you believe what is presented at Bellevue House, then the head tax on Chinese migrants was due to Macdonald the racist. But again, a little research helps. In fact, Macdonald was pressured by British Columbia to discourage Chinese workers from coming there. He argued that they were building the Canadian Pacific Railway and agreed to appoint a commission to study the matter. The commission recommended a head tax of $10, but British Columbia wanted $100. The government eventually settled on $50. Later, when Wilfried Laurier was prime minister, his government doubled the head tax to $100 before raising it to $500.

As for the Indigenous community, it apparently had more than passing influence on the treatment of Macdonald at Bellevue House. Parks Canada admits that prior to the reopening it had formed working groups with Indigenous partners, culturally diverse members of Kingston, and other 'collaborators' to share stories and develop 'new exhibit content.' Said Parks Canada in its news release of May 18, 2024:

> Visitors are encouraged to engage with stories that reflect the diverse lives lived in the 1800s, including those of Indigenous, racialized, working-class, and upper-class individuals. Themes of wealth and power, incredible achievements and feats of engineering, and personal loss and tragedy, are interwoven with issues such as colonial expansion, racism, misogyny, and exploitation.

Outside the house you can tour the gardens and there is signage along the way. One of the first signs has unattributed statements allegedly made about Macdonald. *He was a monster. He was a product of his time. He's done some good things and some bad things.* That one brought to mind the earlier quote about Hitler.

Macdonald biographer Richard Gwyn died in 2020 and I have mentioned a few things he said about his subject. But if Gwyn, who as I said devoted seven years of his life to our first prime minister, was alive something tells me he wouldn't have been consulted by Parks Canada for the reopening of Bellevue House. No, he would have been *persona non grata*.

Was there anything at Bellevue House about young lawyer Macdonald defending Native Canadians or blacks who had escaped from the United States? Was there anything about him pushing for women's voting rights? Or writing 50 of the 72 resolutions in the British North America Act which gave Canada nationhood? Or being the only member of a British commission in Washington, DC that was discussing trade with the Americans who stood up to fight for Canada? In fact, the US president of the time, Ulysses S. Grant, wanted to annex Canada, and if not for Macdonald, he might have.

British journalist Douglas Murray calls Macdonald "the nearest thing the country has to a founding father" in his best-selling book *The War on the West*. After referring to the statues coming down in the wake of the Black Lives Matter movement, Murray said:

> During this strange stampede in Canada, as in so many other cases, the whole history of the country and the wider West became strangely perverted. Both truths and lies were exaggerated and then spun along through a cycle of outrage. Assumptions of obvious guilt were made, followed by a scouring search for culprits to blame.[29]

The train wreck that is Bellevue House—I don't know what else to call it—comes courtesy of Parks Canada, an agency of the federal government. That same government and agency issued a news release in 2019 announcing a new Framework for History and Commemoration: National Historic Sites. In a nutshell, it stressed the diverse heritage of the nation and the contributions of Indigenous people. What you see today at Bellevue House is a direct result of that policy and it gets worse.

The place offers education programs for schools. If the 'Unpacking Macdonald' tour is any indication, we can assume that our first prime minister is not only unpacked, but sealed up in a crate as he is presented to students. This is brainwashing or, better still, *indoctrination* and that is defined as 'the process of teaching a person or group to accept a set of beliefs uncritically.' But this is exactly what has been happening in our schools—at all levels—not to mention the government itself.

Should Canadians be concerned about this? No. They should be *horrified*.

In 2015, on the 200th anniversary of Macdonald's birth, three experts were gathered together by *Maclean's Magazine* to discuss his legacy. They were his biographer Richard Gwyn, Patrice Dutil, a professor at what was then called Ryerson University and co-editor of a collection of essays about Macdonald that wound up in a book, and Jane Hilderman who belonged to a group called Toronto's Friends of Sir John A. Macdonald. They met with Maclean's reporter Aaron Wherry in the very building in Kingston which housed Macdonald's law office from 1849 to 1860. When asked what should be celebrated on this 200th anniversary, Gwynn said:

> I think you could compress it into a sentence. No Macdonald and none of us would be Canadians. There would be no Canada. Everyone took it for granted that Canada wouldn't last. It made no sense as a nation. We were divided between the French and English, between Catholic and Protestant, between Aboriginal and European, etc. Macdonald got us

through that period when we were very, very vulnerable and could have just been lost like that. And that's a big deal.[30]

The discussion that followed got into Macdonald establishing the prime minister's office as a strong, centralizing force. Creating a national park—Banff—some 30 years before the National Park Service was established in the US. Not to mention the railway, the man's work ethic, his intelligence, and advocating for women's right to vote long before anyone else would dare suggest such a thing. The three experts also despaired of what they felt was the cartoonish display of Macdonald as nothing but a drunk.

In the years since that gathering the writ on Macdonald has only gotten worse. He has been accused of being a racist and bigot when it comes to minorities and especially to the Indigenous community. Nevertheless, Patrice Dutil had something to say about this at that 2015 meeting.

> What's interesting about him is that his ideas evolve in his life. His ideas toward women evolve. His ideas toward Catholics evolve. His ideas toward Aboriginal Canadians evolve. There's an evolution to this man, a march toward rethinking his own prejudice that I think makes him a modern man and a man worth emulating.[31]

I once sent a friend an article I had written about the travesty at Bellevue House. He then sent me something in return—*Sir John A. Macdonald Fact Sheet*. It had come from his daughter and was what she had been reading about our first prime minister when attending university. Under the headline 'Racism and Oppression Committed by Sir John A. Macdonald' was a series of bullets outlining all the crimes he had committed and the first one was this:

"Cleared the prairies through the deliberate starvation and detention of the Indigenous peoples in order to make way for European settlement and the construction of the railroad."

Here are the facts.

North America's buffalo herds collapsed in the late 1870s and buffalo had been the prime food source for Indigenous Peoples out west. In 1882 there was an exchange in Parliament between Macdonald, a Conservative, and an opposition Liberal member named David Mills. The discussion was about government programs for famine relief. The Liberals wanted to spend *less* on this. Said Macdonald: "When they fall into a state of destitution, we cannot allow them to die for want of food."

It's all there in Hansard if you want to read it.

The famine peaked in 1884 and by that time the Canadian government's budget for famine relief *exceeded* that for National Defence. However, eastern Canada was in the middle of a severe economic recession and money set aside for rations was being reduced. The Liberals pushed to reduce it even more. Macdonald the Conservative fought them on this. But when you look at history, lead with your conclusion and don't bother to check the facts, it's easy to say John A. Macdonald was prime minister and monies going to famine relief were being cut.

Ergo, the man was starving our Indigenous Peoples.

This is the sort of reasoning that runs rampant in the ideology of Woke-minded history. But real history doesn't work that way.

I once attended a function put on by the Town of York Historical Society at St. Lawrence Hall in Toronto. St. Lawrence Hall is a striking building that went up in 1851, and for the last half of the 19th century and into the next one it served as the cultural centre of the city. The front façade has three grand archways and incredible stone carvings. In front of the building is a replica of an old gas lamp that still works. Inside, on the third floor, is the Grand Hall with an ornamented plaster ceiling rising more than ten meters above the wooden floor. The room is huge and there is an enormous crystal chandelier hanging from the ceiling.

In Canada's centennial year, 1967, St. Lawrence Hall was restored to its original, stately grandeur, which is a good thing because it means you can experience the place just as it was back in the day. John A. Macdonald spoke in the Grand Hall many times. I found myself thinking about that during this event and if only our first prime minister—the man who created our country—could be granted the respect, dignity and restoration he rightly deserves. Just like that beautiful old building. Then perhaps he would be seen as he was and not as the sorry, despicable figure portrayed by those with an axe to grind.

CHAPTER 6

A paragon of education and an institution of lower learning

ON JUNE 6, 2021 A STATUE that had stood for 134 years came crashing down on the grounds of a Toronto university. The statue was of Egerton Ryerson and the university had been named after him. Back in the middle of the 19th century Ryerson almost single-handedly set up the foundation for public education—in essence, schools—for Ontario. This was before Confederation and what he did in no small way led to what became our system of education in Canada. Two weeks before the statue came down there had been an announcement about the graves of 215 Indigenous children being discovered on the site of a former residential school in Kamloops, BC and emotions were running high. That day—June 6—the Bring Our Children Home March with 1,000 people taking part, many in traditional Native clothes and clad in elaborate headdresses, began marching at Queens Park, seat of the Ontario government. They wound their way eastward through the downtown streets of the city before congregating on the main campus of Ryerson University. Shoes—215 pairs—had been placed around the base of Ryerson's statue representing the lives of all those lost and perhaps murdered kids up in Kamloops.

The statue, erected in 1887, had been splattered with red paint one week earlier and Black Lives Matter Toronto had taken credit—three people were charged—but that was only a defacing.

This time the crowd meant business. A rope went around the statue and there were loud cheers when the brass figure of Egerton Ryerson tumbled over and fell to the ground. Then a man wielding a sledgehammer started bashing away at the head—Ryerson's head—and soon someone else was taking a grinder to his neck, grinding away, and when the head was finally severed more cheers erupted. Marchers, demonstrators, what have you, stepped on the severed stone head of the man. Kicking it. Stomping on it. Over and over and over.

It was a mob scene much like that which had descended on the statue of Saddam Hussein in Baghdad three weeks after the United States launched its invasion of Iraq in the first Gulf War. That happened in 2003. The US Army had just made mincemeat of the Iraqi military and Iraqi civilians, furious with the now fallen dictator who had cost so many lives, tried to bring his statue down. But they couldn't. That prompted US marines to get into the act and they lent a hand, not to mention rope, and it wasn't long before the statue came down with cheers erupting everywhere. Soon the sledgehammers were doing their thing and then Saddam's head, the neck included, was separated from the body. The decapitation complete—this was more than symbolic—a chain was placed around the head which was then paraded through the streets. The feverish, enraged Iraqis proceeded to kick it and stomp on it.

These people in Toronto on June 6, 2021 were just as angry with Egerton Ryerson as those Iraqis had been with Saddam almost two decades earlier.

Sam Howden was there that day. She was one of the organizers and told Global TV News how it felt when the statue toppled:

> I was blown away. It was very moving. It was the community that took it upon themselves to deal with the problem and you can't stop people's anger. You can't stop people's sadness . . . they would look like they were supporting white

supremacy and colonialism if they were to put that statue back up.³²

The reporter doing the interview took it all in, looked straight into the camera, and explained to her viewers how Ryerson had been "influential in shaping Canada's residential school system." In another interview Sam Howden gave, this one with CBC News, she mentioned "the stolen and murdered children that were found in Kamloops."

Virtually all the TV networks at the site had their news reporters refer to Ryerson as the "architect" of residential schools. The word *architect* was used time and again in their on-the-spot coverage. The story even went international. The next day a report by BBC News led with this tagline: "Protestors toppled the statue of a man who helped create schools in Canada that forced Indigenous children to assimilate." That was followed by: "People gathered to remember 215 Indigenous children who were found in a mass grave at a former residential school." And finally: "Statue toppled of 'shameful' school founder."³³

In the afternoon of June 6, about an hour after the mob departed, a truck arrived to take away the base of the statue. The number 215 had been painted on it with 'DIG THEM UP' in big letters. On the side of a university building adjacent to where the statue had stood, and written in paint, were the words 'GO BACK WHERE U CAME FROM. ME AND MY GIRLS HATE COLONIZERS.' Scribbled on a window of the same building was a stark message—'FUCK YOU RYERSON.' The next day his severed head, still splattered in red paint, was found on top of a spike at a 'reclamation camp' set up by Six Nations of the Grand River in Caledonia, Ontario.

The president of the university announced that the statue would not be restored or replaced, and one person involved in the proceedings said how the toppling of the statue "marks the beginning of healing for an entire nation." Hundreds of members of the university faculty signed a petition calling for a name change with the school and many of them had already started calling it something else—X. Three student groups at the university—the Indigenous Students Association, the Continuing Education Student Association of Ryerson, and the Ryerson Students Unions—came out with their list of demands:

1. Remove the statue.
2. Create an Indigenous-only space.
3. Mandatory Indigenous content in all programs.
4. Change the name of Ryerson University.

It was clear to all and sundry that this Ryerson guy had been one bad dude. As bad as they come. Not only was the mob of demonstrators saying it, so was the media. It was a good thing only a statue had received the brunt of everyone's fury that day; if by some miracle the man himself could have transcended time and space and been there in the flesh, there is no telling what might have happened. Chances are good he wouldn't have come out alive, such was the hostility of the demonstrators who wanted blood but only got a statue. And it was all because of what he had done. And what exactly had he done? And why had his name been bestowed on the university in the first place?

Egerton Ryerson was born in 1803 in Charlottesville Township near the north shore of Lake Erie. His father had been an officer for United Empire Loyalists in the American Revolutionary War and when it was over he left the United States and came to Canada. In the War of 1812 he again took up arms against the Americans. The family made no apologies for being staunchly pro-British and that's how the young Egerton grew up. He got married in 1828 and his wife died four years later after the birth of their second child. A son, John, died of dysentery at the age of six and a daughter, Lucilla, would die of consumption at 17, but Egerton had remarried by then and would have two more children with his second wife. None of these circumstances, although tragic, were particularly unusual for the time.

There were a few constants in the young Ryerson's life that were important to him—his faith, most notably Methodism which would evolve to the United Church of Canada, and education. He became a Methodist minister at a young age and would go on to be an influential person in Upper Canada, especially in that area of education. Indeed, it is no stretch to call him the father of public schooling in this country.

In 1829 he became the first editor of *The Christian Guardian* and his reputation as a learned man and intellectual grew. Over the course of the next two decades he recognized the chaos of what then masqueraded as a system of education. In fact, there was no system. Most boys had some schooling and then went to work on the family farm. For girls there was even less education, if any.

He was appointed Superintendent of Education for Canada West in 1844 and took the job seriously. He went away for a year to study educational programs in Great Britain and Europe, and the United States, New York state in particular. At the time what constituted education here was not remotely close to what had been going on in those jurisdictions.

In 1846 Ryerson proposed major reforms and their reach would eventually go far beyond the borders of what was then called Canada West. The Common School Act called for creation of a General School Board to govern education and recommended curriculum for 20 school districts. There would be regulations for improved teacher-student ratios, rules for school management, not to mention text books written for and by Canadians. As Superintendent of Education, Ryerson would chair the General School Board himself.

Only about half of school-aged children in the province were even attending classes back then. Ryerson wanted to make education a universal right, which meant schooling for everyone. In 1850 the Common School Act was revised and with its inception schools would be funded by local governments, but this didn't become the case for all districts until after Confederation when Ontario passed the Comprehensive School Act of 1871. That made education mandatory for any child up to age 12.

Ryerson also had a deep interest in post-secondary schooling. He helped found the Methodist Upper Canada Academy in Cobourg, Ontario which would become Victoria College, and years later that would be part of the University of Toronto. As well, he was involved with the Normal School in Toronto which was dedicated to teacher training.

As for Indigenous people, he had a deep and abiding interest with them. He was the first Methodist missionary to live among the Credit Mississaugas, and as with his role in education, he also took this seriously. He learned their language—Ojibwe—and would also learn French and German when studying educational systems abroad, and even become capable in Hebrew. It was at the tender age of 23 when Ryerson first worked with and lived among the Mississaugas. He wrote this in the *American Methodist Magazine* in 1827:

> I was at that time a perfect stranger to Indians, and but little acquainted with their customs. But the affectionate manner in which they received me, and the joy they appeared to feel on the occasion, removed all the strangeness of national feeling, and enabled me to embrace them as brethren, and love them as mine own people.[34]

This relationship with Indigenous people would last him the rest of his life. He got involved in their attempt to secure a title deed to their lands at the mouth of the Credit River in what is now the City of Mississauga, 12 miles west of Toronto. The way he saw things it was about protecting their land that still remained and keeping it from the ever-encroaching British Canadian settlers. At the time Indigenous people constituted less than 1 percent of the population of Canada West. Ryerson's wish was that they would become farmers and be able to sustain themselves.

At a council fire in December, 1826 the Credit Mississauga formally 'adopted' him and gave him the Ojibwe name *Cheechok* which means 'Bird on the Wing.' He became the lifelong friend of a man named *Kahkewaquonaby* or Sacred Feathers, later known as Peter Jones, and he would become chief of the Mississaugas.

In 1846—two years after Ryerson was named Superintendent of Education—government officials met with 30 chiefs at The Narrows of Lake Simcoe and Lake Couchiching in Orillia, Ontario. This is the same Orillia that many years later would give Canada its famous songwriter Gordon Lightfoot. At that meeting it was decided that schools would be a good idea and the chiefs agreed. Some of them even said they would use part of their treaty payments to help support these new schools.

On March 18, 1847, the Civil Secretary in the Indian Department—George Vardon—asked for Ryerson's advice in "establishing the Manual Labour Schools for education of the Indian youth in this Province." Ryerson had already returned from his studies and travels in Britain and Europe. Added Vardon in his request: "You are aware that there are numerous persons in the colony, though actuated by different motives, who will alike rejoice in the failure of a plan which tends to place the Indian on a footing of perfect equality with their White Brethren."[35]

In response, Ryerson, an acknowledged expert in education and widely regarded as a progressive, submitted a 3,000-word letter recommending Indigenous training schools. The focus would be on agriculture. He had a model in mind for these schools. In 1845 he had visited a boarding school for the rural poor in Berne, Switzerland. The idea was that admission would be voluntary and the goal for Indigenous people to learn about using tools and equipment for the purposes of farming. What's more, Ryerson's approach was that graduates would eventually run these schools themselves.

This led to two schools being set up. They would be supervised by the government and run by the Methodists, as were most of the schools already in existence on reserves. Teaching was courtesy of those who had been trained as teachers in the regular school system. Not by clergy. Children were free to speak their own language, it was all voluntary, and religion was but one subject in the curriculum.

However, these initial schools failed, largely because the government refused to give them proper funding. Some of the students were living far from their homes and while they had been promised farmland upon graduation, that never happened. So how does all this connect with the toppling of Ryerson's statue and his *complex* legacy?

On August 18, 2021, the Standing Strong Task Force of Ryerson University—it was still called that at the time—released its report and recommendations. This was during COVID and everything had to be done remotely. The two co-chairs of the task force were Joanne Dallaire and Catherine Ellis. Dallaire was Senior Advisor, Indigenous Relations and Reconciliation for Ryerson University, and Ellis a Professor in the Department of History at Ryerson University. Both were members of the school's Board of Governors. Their report said upfront that The Task Force "approached its mandate through an Indigenous lens" and what was the mandate?

1. Conduct thorough, open, transparent consultations with Ryerson students, faculty, staff, alumni and others.
2. Examine and more fully understand Egerton Ryerson's relationship with Indigenous Peoples, his links to the education system in Ontario, and his role in the

education system in Ontario, and his role in the development of residential schools in Canada, as well as interpret those findings in both their historical and modern context.
3. Examine how other universities had dealt with the issues of statuary, memorials, and requests to rename and identify best practices.
4. Develop principles to guide the recommended actions that Ryerson could take to respond to Egerton Ryerson's legacy and the findings of the consultations.
5. Provide a final report to the President with recommendations and principles by end of summer 2021.

Now here is an admission. I reached out to both co-chairs of that Task Force report with the prospects of doing an interview with them when researching this book. One of them—Catherine Ellis—responded, only to refer me to the media relations department of the university. The other—Joanne Dallaire—never got back to me at all.

The report said that nearly 9,000 students, faculty, staff, alumni and others had been consulted about Ryerson's legacy. It went on to mention the "devastating news" about the remains of 215 Indigenous children in unmarked graves near Kamloops and how the statue of Ryerson became the site of a memorial "to the children whose remains had been discovered." It also described what had transpired with the statue of Ryerson on June 6, 2021 as "a peaceful demonstration."

What's more, the report said that over 11,000 individuals had been engaged in total for this exercise. In addition, it said that some 22,860 responses were collected, more than 195 participants were involved in YouTube videos, more than 18 community conversations had taken place with more than 250 participants, and over 250 'direct communications' had occurred with the Ryerson University community. Here are some observations as stated in the Task Force report:

- The school structure Ryerson recommended reflected his belief in racial hierarchy through his presumption about the capacities of Indigenous people and his resulting assessment that their educational needs differed from students in common (or public) schools.
- Ryerson's goal was to produce "industrious" Indigenous farmers through very long hours of manual labour, extensive religious teaching and limited academic instruction.
- The 1850 Act opened the door to separate schools for "coloured people," which were frequently underfunded and provided lower-quality education. Ryerson also subsequently recommended the creation of separate schools for lower-class students and deaf and blind students, and he opposed girls' attendance at grammar schools.
- The legacy of Ryerson's ideas—that is, the mark that he has left upon numerous communities within Canada—is evident in colonial policy and through enduring perspectives on religious conversion, education, the assimilation of Indigenous People and separate schools for Black students.

Finally, on the very last page of the report, we see where the word 'architect' came into play.

"Seven years after Ryerson's death in 1882, Senator John Macdonald first referred to him as the "architect" of a system of education. What the architect is to the building that was Egerton Ryerson to our school System."

(Note: The man in question was not Sir John A. Macdonald, but another politician with the same name.)

Patrice Dutil is a Professor in the Department of Politics and Public Administration at the university and has been a member of the faculty since 2006. He has written articles about Canadian historical figures whom he feels have been unfairly judged, not to mention books. His most recent is *Sir John A. Macdonald and the Apocalyptic Year 1885*, published by Sutherland House Books in 2024. What did he have to say about the Standing Strong report?

"The whole thing was railroaded."

According to Dutil, the Standing Strong report, in Appendix B, claimed that a long list of organizations had provided information to it. The list cited includes the Canadian Civil Liberties Association, LEAF (The Women's Legal, Education Action Fund), Urban Race Relations, and various Indigenous groups.

"But the university refused to provide the briefs," he says. "We tried to access information and were refused."

He calls Appendix B a "fake appendix."

Dutil co-authored a lengthy article about this published in *The Dorchester Review* on August 12, 2021. This was one week before the Standing Strong report got released. The article was called 'The Imbecile Attack on Egerton Ryerson—An Assault on Decency.' His co-author, Ron Stagg, was a professor of history at the university which was still called Ryerson at the time.

Wrote Dutil and Stagg in that article:

> The movement against Ryerson belongs to a wider trend to indulge in rage against "white men" who dominated Canada's history. But this case is special because Egerton Ryerson is patently innocent of the charges. The Progressive Conservative government of Ontario agreed in the late 1940s with the notion of dedicating a new post-secondary

institution in his honour because Ryerson represented everything that was good in educational policy.[36]

Dutil, who was mentioned in the previous chapter about Sir John A. Macdonald, calls Ryerson "a beacon of educational reform, a fighter against injustice of all sorts, and a kind and generous man." He said his good name was first challenged when the Truth and Reconciliation Commission "began casting its highly political and sometimes unhistorical shadow in 2008."

Said Dutil:

> The TRC soon made the news for suggesting that Dr. Egerton Ryerson was involved in creating the Indian residential schools that existed after the 1870s. Was it true? No. But no matter. It sounded plausible that an obscure 19th-century figure would have a dark side, and anyway would be highly damaging if you are a cultural warrior out to deface any glint of nobility in our forebears.

Back in 2010 Ryerson University's Aboriginal Education Council issued a paper about Ryerson the man having played a defining role in establishing residential schools. According to Dutil, that document contained misspelled names and statements not backed up by references, was based on limited research, not subject to peer review, and did not circulate outside a small circle of administrators. He also points out that the Sinclair Commission itself recognized that Ryerson was not party to creating post-Confederation residential schools.

Murray Sinclair, who passed away in the fall of 2024, was one of the first Indigenous people in Canada to become a judge. In 2009 he was named Chief Commissioner of the Truth and Reconciliation Commission and in December of 2015 that commission came out with its report. Nothing in that report says Ryerson created, or was responsible for, residential schools. This is something that people like Dutil and former Member of Parliament Lynn McDonald hammer at time after time.

McDonald is professor emerita at the University of Guelph and a Fellow of the Royal Historical Society. She has done presentations and written articles making the case for the unjust treatment of Ryerson. She refers to a long record of scholarly publications about him by "serious researchers" from the years 1937 to 2021, and says that in this entire body of material there is no evidence to implicate him. Nothing. Included in the list are the two-volume Life and Letters by C. B. Sissons, published in 1937 and 1947, respectively. The biography of Ryerson by Clara Thomas published in 1969. A biography of Ryerson's closest Ojibwe friend by history professor Donald B. Smith published in 1988. Another book by Smith about Ryerson's connections with the Mississaugas published in 2013. There is also a history of residential schools by Jim Miller published in 1996, as well as academic materials prepared by Hope MacLean which involved her Master's thesis from 1978 and two papers based on that thesis which were released in 2002 and 2005. According to McDonald, that thesis and the two papers "reported on the voluntary, bilingual schools that Ryerson did report, which involved no forcible taking of children from their parents."

In an article published by *The National Post* on September 9, 2021, McDonald wrote the following:

> In a university, academic standards and respect for primary sources should be paramount. But they have been missing from action throughout these discussions at Ryerson. The residential school system instituted by the Canadian government in 1883 bears no resemblance to the schools Egerton Ryerson supported in the 1840s and 1850s. Nor could he have fought its introduction: he died in 1882. Moreover, its

worst aspects came much later: making attendance mandatory, in 1920, and giving over guardianship of the children to the principals of the schools from their parents.[37]

After the Standing Strong Task Force produced its report, McDonald said she used the Access to Information Act to try and get briefs claimed to have been sent to the Task Force, but got "stonewalled."

Says McDonald: "As a Member of Parliament I've given briefs to royal commissions and at some point those briefs become public but that wasn't the case here."

However, in the greater scheme of things and despite the efforts of people like her, the historical record of Egerton Ryerson as perceived today has been dimmed to such a degree that he is widely considered a demon; if he did not create residential schools, he certainly had a prominent role in them. In 2018 Ryerson University—the name had not been changed yet—unveiled a plaque next to the statue of Ryerson that was still standing. This is what it said:

> Egerton Ryerson is widely known for his contributions to Ontario's public educational system. As Chief Superintendent of Education, Ryerson's recommendations were instrumental in the design and implementation of the Indian Residential School System. In 2015, the Truth and Reconciliation Commission reported that children in the schools were subject to unthinkable abuse and neglect, to media experimentation, punishment for the practice of cultures or languages and death. The aim of the Residential School system was cultural genocide.

Lynn McDonald is involved with an organization called The Friends of Egerton Ryerson which is trying to set the record straight about his legacy. The group has 300 members, including retired university professors, historians, and journalists. They organized to try and prevent the university from changing its name. Ryerson University officially changed its name to Toronto Metropolitan University in 2022. As for the plaque that went up in 2018, she calls it "dishonest."

Patrice Dutil says the university placing that plaque there made a mockery of the monument it stood next to. And of the Standing Strong Task Force, he said: "The committee's composition does not accurately reflect the university community and is obvious for all to see. Given that there is no basis for the claims to begin with, this entire review of Egerton Ryerson should collapse like a house of cards."

Only it doesn't. The man and his legacy remain tarnished—no, ruined—in the public domain. Never mind the litany of misinformation out there on social media, we can look at how the Canadian Encyclopedia, which was founded in 1985 and went digital in 2013, speaks of Ryerson. What does its entry say about him?

It talks about his role in education and his leaving a mark on cultural institutions. After all, he founded the Methodist Book Room which later became Ryerson Press before being sold to US publisher McGraw-Hill in 1970. It mentions his trips to Europe in the 1850s which led to early collections of items that eventually evolved to museums and galleries, among them the Royal Ontario Museum. Today that is the largest museum in Canada. It says how Ryerson's imprint can be felt on the Ontario Agricultural College at the University of Guelph, and the Ontario College of Art and Design University in Toronto. But it also says that since 2010 there has been controversy about his influence on the development of residential schools.

However, according to people like Dutil and McDonald, there was no controversy about Ryerson until the Truth and Reconciliation Commission came along.

Ron Stagg, who co-authored that article about Ryerson with Dutil, retired in 2024 after 50 years of teaching history at Ryerson cum Toronto Metropolitan University. For ten of those years he was Chair of the school's history department. On the website for Toronto Metropolitan University there is a writeup that calls him "a specialist on late 18th- and 19th-century Ontario" and it says for many years he was considered "the university's unofficial historian." When Stagg was asked why *he* was not part of the Standing Strong Task Force, he just laughed.

"It was a put-up job," he says. "The people behind the whole thing wanted to decolonize the university and the way to do that was to change history. They started with a conclusion and then went looking for the evidence. They did some very limited research looking for proof but had to distort the historical information to get there."

Stagg then provides examples. He points to the Task Force claim that Ryerson considered Indigenous people uncivilized. Says the Standing Strong report: "Ryerson maintained that religious training was the prerequisite for all other forms of education in the mission to "civilize" Indigenous Peoples."

Stagg—keep in mind he is a historian and an expert on Ontario in the 1800s and 1900s—says that word had an entirely different meaning in the middle of the 19th century than it does today.

"It didn't mean the same thing. This is what it meant. There were three stages of development. The first was nomadic. The second was hunter-gatherer. And the third was civilized which means what the Europeans had reached. The meaning of the word has changed over time."

The Standing Strong Task Force also maintained that Ryerson advocated separate schools for blacks. But this is not true, says Stagg. He says Ryerson was approached by white settlers who didn't want their schools to accommodate blacks, many of whom had come here through the Underground Railroad to escape slavery in the United States.

"He (Ryerson) was horrified by that so a compromise was reached where it would be left to the individual district to decide. In fact, most of Upper Canada did not have separate schools. That Task Force report was a distortion of history designed to prove that Egerton Ryerson did not deserve to have his name on the university."

Stagg, who says he was "horrified" when the statue of Ryerson came down, also contends that all the business about early schools being centres of assimilation, mandatory attendance, and forced conversion to Christianity is nonsense. But he adds that most students at the university today, not to mention the faculty, do not know their history. And then he added this gem that occurred not long before he retired after a half-century of teaching.

"In one of my classes I was talking to my students about Egerton Ryerson and they didn't know who he was."

Which is another way of saying ignorance abounds. In Chapter 2 of this book—*They don't know what they don't know*—I referred to my video in which I interviewed university students and asked them questions about World War II. The video went viral. Indeed, when Canadian university students don't have the faintest idea who Winston Churchill was, what happened on the Beaches of Normandy on D-Day, or which countries fought on the side of the Allies, it's obvious we have a problem. In that video the university was never identified, but I'm revealing it now. It was Ryerson University. The students interviewed were first-year students, most if not all, graduates of Ontario's public school system. Their lack of knowledge about history may have had far more to do with the sad state of curriculum in Ontario than it did for anything at Ryerson, as it was called then.

But maybe not.

Two weeks after the Israel-Gaza War broke out in October, 2023, 74 students attending the Lincoln Alexander School of Law, the law school at Toronto Metropolitan University, signed their names to a letter saying how they stood with Palestine, and not only that, but supported the terrorist group Hamas.

> Israel is not a country. It is the brand of a settler colony. So-called Israel has been illegally occupying and ethnically cleansing Palestine since 1948, when the British unlawfully conceded Palestine's territory. We, the undersigned, recognize that the apartheid state referred to as "Israel" is a product of settler colonialism. We stand in solidarity with Palestine and support all forms of Palestinian resistance and efforts toward liberation.

The letter went on to say that Israel was responsible for *all* loss of life in Palestine. "To say otherwise is to accept and endorse colonialism in all its forms: there would be no death if not for Israel's apartheid regime."

Right off the top this letter illustrates a profound lack of knowledge about Middle East history, but as with the case concerning the legacy of Egerton Ryerson, let's not muddle the argument with facts. Nevertheless, those students—aspiring lawyers every one of them—quickly learned that hitching their star to Hamas does not open doors to law firms. The administration of the law school issued a statement condemning "the sentiments of antisemitism and intolerance expressed in this message" while a number of prominent lawyers said they would never consider job applications from anyone who signed that letter.

What does all this demonstrate? The management and administration of the university—right up the office of the president—showed itself sadly lacking when it came to the hatchet job done on Egerton Ryerson. And that goes for accepting the shoddy work done by the Standing Strong Task Force, inaction when the statue came down, erecting a plaque with incorrect historical information, and allowing a culture of ignorance and, as far as Hamas is concerned, hate to be perpetuated on its campus.

Toronto Metropolitan University, once known as Ryerson, has been developing a reputation and that reputation continues. The university recently embarked on launching its very own medical school which, according to the literature, says the following:

> The school will use a multifaceted, holistic approach to identify students who possess the necessary academic capabilities, interpersonal skills and personal attributes required to excel in the medical profession. The TMU School of Medicine is founded on equity, diversity and inclusion, decolonization and reconciliation, and our admissions process will seek to identify applicants who have lived experience and/or are committed to advancing these principles.

Good luck with that.

In closing, I cannot leave the sorry tale of Egerton Ryerson without a note about Donald B. Smith. He is professor emeritus of History at the University of Calgary and was mentioned in the list of works cited earlier by Lynn McDonald. He specializes in Canadian Native studies and has written several books, one of them *Sacred Feathers: The Reverend Peter Jones (Kahkewaquonaby) and the Mississauga Indians*. It was published by University of Toronto Press in 2013 and is considered the first modern account of the Mississauga Indians. The 408-page book is based on the letters, diaries and sermons of Ryerson's long-time friend Peter Jones.

The Ontario Historical Society published an article Smith wrote largely based on that book. It's called 'Egerton Ryerson and the Mississauga, 1826 to 1856, an Appeal for Further Study.' In this article he says: "Any attempt to portray Egerton Ryerson as anti-Indigenous should sound an alarm. As should the frequently advanced opinion that casts him as one of the 'architects' of the oppressive, non-Indigenous controlled Indian residential schools of the late nineteenth century and beyond."[38]

Smith makes the point that much of the so-called controversy over Ryerson stems from the year 1898—sixteen years after his death—when the government's Indian Department under the direction of Clifford Sifton, Superintendent of Indian Affairs, printed a half-century-old letter (Statistics Reporting Indian Schools) with Ryerson's 1847 report attached.

Says Smith: "Read in 1898 without any historical context it gave the erroneous impression that Egerton Ryerson had designed the draconian repressive system, both ugly and real, that Clifford Sifton now administered. It would be hard to advance a view farther from the truth."[39]

Notwithstanding the reality of social media and how outright fabrications—lies—go viral, not to mention the culture embedded today across the landscape of Canadian colleges and universities, and the ease with which those who have a political agenda advance it, we can see how the good name of a person responsible for public education in Canada—and who advanced the cause for cultural institutions—has been vilified and destroyed. Alas, Egerton Ryerson does not deserve this fate and to this day he is really guilty of only one thing.

He was a white man.

CHAPTER 7

The slaver who wasn't

CITIES AROUND THE WORLD erect plaques and monuments to honour names from the past and to celebrate their history. Years ago I was involved in one of these things—an event to commemorate Babe Ruth's first professional home run—which I alluded to earlier. Indeed, the greatest name in baseball hit his first pro homer not in the United States, but at an old ballpark at Hanlan's Point on the Toronto Islands. It happened September 5, 1914. Ruth was a lanky, 19-year-old pitcher for the AAA Providence Grays—that's one level below the major leagues—and that day he pitched a one-hit shutout against the Toronto Maple Leafs baseball team and hit a three-run homer. It was the only minor-league home run he ever hit. Today there are places in the US that lay claim to his first home run—one of them in a pre-season game, another in an inter-squad game, what have you—but there is no disputing historical fact.

On September 5, 1914, George Herman 'Babe' Ruth hit his first pro home run in an official league game in Toronto. It is recorded history.

In 2006, on the anniversary of that home run, the New York Yankees were in Toronto to play the Blue Jays and both teams were involved in the ceremony with Paul Godfrey, then President of the Blue Jays, presiding. I had known Godfrey from my reporter days when I covered municipal council and he was a local politician. He was also president of *The Toronto Sun* when I was a columnist for that newspaper. Anyway, I was very much up on Babe Ruth, having done extensive research on him for my first novel.

There had been a small plaque on a rock at Hanlan's Point with information about the 1914 home run, but was hard to find. So, at this event two new plaques—more substantial than what had been there before—went up. One marked the 1914 home run and the other the city's long history of professional baseball which dates back to the 1860s. We worked with Heritage Toronto, an agency of the city that handled historical plaques and monuments, and the whole thing involved a submission-and-acceptance process that took time, as well as money.

Those two plaques are still there, but to see them you must take the ferry from the city's mainland. In 2013 the Toronto Island Ferry Docks got a new name—the Jack Layton Ferry Terminal—to honour a man who had been a city councillor and later federal Leader of the NDP. A bronze statue of Layton on a bicycle—he died of cancer in 2013—was also unveiled.

I met Layton once. Many times I had been a guest on the CHCH-TV talk show *Cherington* with host Tom Cherington. It was based out of Hamilton, Ontario. The topic? The criminal justice system. I had written a book about crime victims and was still doing my *Toronto Sun* column called *Justice For All*. Layton, then a Toronto city councillor as was his wife Olivia Chow, was no friend of the police and made no apologies about it. The fact is never in my life had I encountered a politician—at any level of government—so disdainful of the police as Layton, and I wrote a column about it. He was considered patron saint of an anti-police group called CIRPA (Citizens Independent Review of Police Activities) and not only that but he let them hold their meetings in his office at city hall, which meant taxpayer-funded.

On that day the two of us were Cherington's guests. Layton was anything but cordial to me, but that's beside the point. While it was the only time I ever met him, something else comes to mind when I hear his name. A story later circulated that he and his wife were living in subsidized public housing while both served on city council and drawing a combined, six-figure income—$120,000 to be exact—which wasn't chicken feed in those days. As it turned out, they were eventually cleared and said not to have done anything illegal.

Why get into all this?

In 2023 Olivia Chow became Mayor of Toronto and in that position has presided over Canada's largest city disparaging the name Henry Dundas. Nowadays anything in Toronto with the name Dundas, as far as city council is concerned—I'm talking streets, signs, public squares, subway stations, libraries—is strictly *verboten*. Dundas, you see, is deemed to have been a proponent of slavery, but there is this sticky point. The historical record says otherwise, and not only that, it turns out he was anything but pro-slavery; the man was a confirmed abolitionist.

It makes as much sense as calling Egerton Ryerson public enemy no. 1 of Indigenous People, but this is what happens when Far Left ideologues win the ear of elected officials, some of whom also occupy that side of the political spectrum. Put another way, it's what happens when loud voices rise far and above their actual number only to insert themselves into the public discourse and drive decisions that make no sense. And it's all driven by ideology.

Not history.

Andrew Lochhead, a PhD candidate at—you guessed it—Toronto Metropolitan University, was author of a petition to rename Dundas Street, a major east-west artery in Toronto. He was easy to find on the university website where his areas of expertise were listed: Public Memory, Commemoration, Landscape, Museum Studies, Community-engaged Arts & Research, Arts & Heritage Sector. Then it went on to say this:

> Andrew's research focuses on contemporary, artist-led interventions into mnemonic infrastructure - statues, plaques, street names, historic sites—that celebrate white supremacy

and ongoing colonial violence. Specifically, he is interested in how these curatorial approaches can inform public heritage sector practices aimed at creating spaces of repair, the making of reparation, and toward answering the Truth & Reconciliation Commission of Canada's Calls to Action. His project is in part driven by his experiences as the author of the Let's Rename Dundas Street petition, which played an important role in the creation of a process to rename Toronto's longest East-West thoroughfare and the development of a new commemorative framework for Canada's largest city.

Never mind that three former mayors of Toronto all said this was wrong and bone-headed. Or that legitimate historians both in Canada and the United Kingdom contend that Dundas was no slaver. It didn't matter. In 2021 Toronto city council, led by then mayor John Tory, voted to rename Dundas Street. After Olivia Chow became mayor she endorsed that decision. Also up for grabs was removing the name Dundas from two subway stations, a public library, parks, some 730 street signs, and the big one—Yonge-Dundas Square—merely *the* public square in Canada's largest city.

Today that place is called *Sankofa Square*. It sits in the middle of the city's downtown and on every side are huge neon signs overlooking the central space. The two main signs introduce visitors to the city. The first one tells you about Indigenous Land Acknowledgement:

> As we gather in the heart of Tkaranto, we acknowledge this land is the traditional territory of many nations including the Mississaugas of the Credit, the Anishnabeg, the Chippewa, the Haudenosaunee and the Wendat peoples and is now home to many diverse First Nations, Inuit and Métis peoples. We also acknowledge that Toronto is covered by Treaty 13 with the Mississaugas of the Credit. We invite you

to join us in honouring and celebrating their rich past, present and future.

I was born and raised in Toronto. I went to public school, junior high and secondary school there, and graduated from the University of Toronto. I also studied history and had never heard of *Tkaranto*. And so, I checked it out. The first thing that turns up when you google the name is an article with the title 'This is why more people are now referring to Toronto as Tkaranto.' Below the headline is a photo of a banner displaying 'TKARANTO' in big letters and right under that the words 'ABOLISH THE POLICE.' The article went on to say that "Using Tkaronto in place of Toronto is merely one small step toward abolishing the systemic oppression of Indigenous people."[40]

As for the Haudenosaunee reference on the sign at Sankofa Square, that would be the Six Nations of the Iroquois, and I knew about them. But other groups like the Anishnabeg were news to me, as was Treaty 13. According to the historical record, a sale was completed in a 1787 treaty but the land boundaries weren't clear. Fast forward to 1998 when the Mississaugas of the Credit filed a claim against the Government of Canada, and 12 years later those same feds settled things and forked over compensation of $145 million which at the time was the largest claims settlement in Canadian history.

But I digress.

If I were American or a tourist from Europe or anywhere else standing in the middle of that big public square in downtown Toronto and visiting for the first time, I might think these First Nations people were everywhere. They must be. And what about the second sign that welcomes you at Sankofa Square? The title of that one is African Ancestral Acknowledgement.

> As we gather on Sankofa Square, we acknowledge all Treaty peoples, including those who came here as settlers, migrants

either in this generation or in generations past—and those of African descent who came here involuntarily through the Trans-Atlantic Slave Trade and Slavery. Please join us in paying tribute to these ancestors and their spirit of resilience, honouring the past to build a better future, together.

We have some serious problems here.

First, as far as the City of Toronto is concerned, these signs reflect public policy. As related earlier, my grandparents were Jews who left the persecution they found in such countries as Belarus, Poland and Romania, and came to Canada where they built a better life for themselves. There is no mention of them on these signs. As also related earlier, my wife is Macedonian and came to Canada with her family from Greece when she was three. They came for the same reason. No mention of them either. But then maybe there is. We are all lumped together as an afterthought—along with the French, English and Dutch who first came to these shores, never mind everyone else who is not Indigenous or African—only to be dismissed as 'settlers' and 'migrants.'

And there is more to be alarmed about. Much more. In fact, anyone who regards history as a key building block of a nation should be very alarmed about this because what passes as history on that sign is wrong and deceitful. No one of African descent came here "involuntarily through the Trans-Atlantic Slave Trade" because slave ships didn't come to these parts. They journeyed from Africa to South America. And to islands throughout the Caribbean. And to the Thirteen Colonies which became the United States. The American ports that received slave ships were in Boston, Massachusetts. And Newport, Rhode Island. And Charleston, South Carolina. It's all in the historical record. But slave ships never came here.

Blacks who found themselves in Upper or Lower Canada, or Canada West and Canada East as they would be known, arrived through the Underground Railroad to escape slavery in the US where it was not only legal but a staple of the economy, especially in the south. That was not the case here. After the American War of Independence got going in 1776, blacks including those who had been enslaved south of the border came by ship to Nova Scotia with United Empire Loyalists loyal to the Crown. These people were promised their freedom. However, it's true that some slaves—estimates range from 500 to 700—were living in the province after their slaveowners brought them.

But it's not true that slave ships came here from Africa.

Thus, we have Sankofa Square—a huge open space of misinformation, deceit, and lies about our history in the central public square of Canada's biggest city, a place no longer affiliated with the besmirched name of Dundas.

This would be like renaming Times Square in New York City. Indeed, in 1626 the Indians sold the island of Manhattan to the Dutch for $24 worth of beads and trinkets. In fact, there is a document in the Dutch National Archives, a letter written by Dutch merchant Pieter Schaghen on November 5, 1626, to directors of the West India Company. The English translation is as follows: "They have purchased the Island of Manhattes from the savages for the value of 60 guilders."[41]

That worked out to twenty-four bucks US.

Let's imagine for a moment that what transpires for history and heritage in the biggest city in Canada happened south of the border in the biggest city in America. Times Square wouldn't be called Times Square anymore. There would have been a movement to recognize the alleged theft that took place early in the 17th century and then a few activists with an axe to grind would have circulated a petition. This would have got going after the murder of George Floyd. These people would have obtained thousands of names from their network of like-minded friends and friends of friends. Never mind that most of them didn't even live in Manhattan. They would have made a formal presentation to New York City Council and referenced the Dutchman Pieter Schaghen who had the temerity to refer to the natives as *savages*, thereby demonstrating to all that he was a rabid racist.

Having won the ear of the mayor of New York City, this small group would lobby left-leaning members of city council, not to mention staff, none of whom possessed a post-secondary degree in US history and who get what they know about the past from Wikipedia. Pretty soon a motion to rename Times Square honouring those Native Americans who had been victimized by evil white men passes. They prepare a short list of new names to consider and promise to hold public consultations since they are big on democracy and inclusion—they are *very* big on inclusion—but as things turn out they don't do that. They consult only with their own DEI (diversity, equity, inclusion) cohorts, and with selected members of the black and Indigenous communities. Eventually they settle on Kənär´sē Square—or the English equivalent—*Canarsee Square*. And what the hell is that? Why, that's the name of the tribe said to have done the deal in the first place and who were taken advantage of by those nasty Dutch traders.

Never mind that Times Square was called that because in 1904 *The New York Times* moved its headquarters to a brand new building, Times Tower, and this is where the name came from. That might be true but this is white, settler colonial history and may be dismissed.

Thus, Canarsee Square it is. So, going forward, whenever we bring in the New Year with parties and friends and everyone's eyes are glued to the tube we can now count down the seconds and watch that big ball drop on Canarsee Square and then we top it off with a rendition of *Auld Lang Syne*.

However, if anyone in the United States ever started a movement to rename New York City's Times Square—and bestow upon it a moniker as ridiculous as *Canarsee Square*—all hell would break loose. Say what you want about Americans, but they don't like it when you screw with their history. Not so in this country. But then that isn't totally true. Some people were pissed off about this.

Like Jennifer Dundas.

She is a descendant of Jacobites and Highlanders from Scotland who were driven off their land in the mid 1700s and made their way to Ireland. They became part of the Scottish enclave there. While she is not a direct descendant of Henry Dundas himself, she says her Scottish forebears were related to him and adds that Dundas represents one of the oldest clans in Scotland. She can, however, trace her family name and history in Canada as far back as the year 1815.

Jennifer Dundas is a former political affairs reporter and TV news anchor for the CBC in Winnipeg. She spent 18 years with the CBC. When the public broadcaster made some massive cuts she took a severance package and decided to go to law school at the University of Manitoba. She was a crown attorney for many years before retiring in 2022, but by that time we were in the post-George Floyd era and a certain commodity had already hit the fan as far as Mr. Dundas was concerned. Jennifer and a cousin of hers, Linda Dundas, were well aware of the long history of their namesake back in Scotland—as I say, the man was a lawyer, politician and leading abolitionist—and they formed a group called the Henry Dundas Committee of Ontario. The mission? To set the record straight.

What I just hypothetically recounted about the renaming of Times Square to *Canarsee Square* in New York City is what happened in Toronto, a municipality that made a fool of itself by kowtowing to special-interest groups who had their facts wrong. These groups are pencil-thin on content, especially in terms of history, but very thick on ideology. And the whole mess began at city council.

When it became apparent that changing the name of Dundas Street would have required changing 730 street signs, Toronto City

Council decided there might be better ways to spend $8.6-million—the numbers were as high as $12.7 million—and so, council decided to abandon that part of it. But not two subway stations that contain the insidious name. And not the local branch of the Toronto Public Library that has it. And not Yonge-Dundas Square.

So what is Sankofa anyway and why did the City of Toronto choose it? Good question. If you go online this is what you find.

> On December 14, 2023, the City of Toronto announced that Toronto City Council adopted a motion to change the name of Yonge-Dundas Square to Sankofa Square. The name Sankofa is the result of two years of careful work by the City of Toronto convened Recognition Review Community Advisory Committee (CAC), whose conversations were informed by consultations with the public. The 20-member CAC was made up of Black and Indigenous leaders, along with other diverse residents and business owners living and working along Dundas Street.[42]

But what exactly is it?

> Sankofa (SAHN-koh-fah) is a Twi word from the Akan Tribe of Ghana that loosely translates to "go back and get it." Its literal translation comes from the Akan proverb, "Së wo were fi na wosan kofa a yenkyiri" meaning "It is not taboo to go back for what you forgot (or left behind)." Sankofa is a phrase that encourages learning from the past to inform the future. While Sankofa originates from the Ghanaian Akan language, it broadly resonates across African and Black communities globally as an expression of cultural and political affirmation.

What any of this has to do with Toronto, not to mention Canada, is another good question. But it seems no one on the Recognition

Review Community Advisory Committee (CAC) bothered to ask such a thing. And for the record, the country of Ghana, previously known as the Gold Coast on the west coast of Africa, was a major departure point for the slave trade, a place where slaves were sold to European slave traders. Slavery wasn't abolished in Ghana until 1874. Compare that to England which abolished the slave trade in 1807 and Scotland which forbid the owning of slaves in 1778. But there is an interesting footnote about the Scottish experience.

Giving slavery the boot in that country was largely due to the efforts of a lawyer who helped defend an escaped enslaved man. This black man had been purchased as a slave in Jamaica and then taken to Scotland. The lawyer successfully pleaded the case on appeal and won over a majority of the Scottish lords, some of them slaveowners themselves. It wasn't unanimous, but a majority and that was enough. The upshot of all this was that the slave got freed and it was ruled there could be no slavery in Scotland which meant all other slaves in the country were also freed.

The lawyer's name was Henry Dundas.

Dundas later became a prominent politician in Scotland and in that capacity appointed John Graves Simcoe as the first Lieutenant-Governor of Upper Canada. We are now talking 1791. Like Dundas, Simcoe was a confirmed abolitionist. In 1793 he introduced the Act to Limit Slavery in Upper Canada, making it the first jurisdiction in the British Empire to limit slavery. This is all in the historical record and should be celebrated as part of our heritage. Because of that law more than 40,000 black men, women and children would flee the United States over the next seven decades. They would risk their lives to come to Upper Canada through the Underground Railroad.

And that isn't all Dundas did. He also ordered the governors of Nova Scotia and New Brunswick to honour Britain's promise of land grants to 4,000 former slaves who had fought for the British in the American Revolution. This was significant. It meant offering free passage with the help of the British Navy to those who wanted to return to Africa.

So why all the fuss about Dundas?

In 1792 he stood up and spoke in the British parliament about the complicity of *African* leaders in the slave trade. This was a touchy subject. These are his very words.

"If once a prince of an enlightened character should rise up in that hemisphere, his first act would be to make the means of carrying off all slaves from thence impracticable . . . what reason had they to suppose that the light of heaven would never descend upon that continent? From there moment there must be an end of African trade. The first system of improvement, the first idea of happiness that would arise in that continent, would bring with it the downfall of the African slave trade, and that in a more effectual . . . way than if done by regulations in this country."[43]

This does not sound like a man who advocates slavery. At the time a motion was put forward by another parliamentarian, William Wilberforce, to abolish slavery outright. But it was defeated. Don't forget that many of those voting men—it was only men back then and would be only men for a long time to come—owned slaves. Recognizing the political reality he was facing, Dundas then introduced an amendment to bring about the 'gradual' abolition of slavery and, lo and behold, it passed. This would be the first step to legally abolishing the slave trade, but it would take years. Nevertheless, critics of Dundas dwell on this word *gradual* and accuse him of unsavory tactics to preserve slavery.

Lynn McDonald—professor emerita at the University of Guelph, former Member of Parliament, fellow of the Royal Historical Society, and one of the people consulted in the previous chapter about Egerton Ryerson—has also been active trying to clear the name of Henry Dundas. She wrote an article for The Macdonald-Laurier Institute, a national public policy think tank based in Ottawa, that was published May 23, 2024. The headline was: Toronto's *"Sankofa Square"—The terrible folly and historical injustice of erasing the legacy of abolitionist Henry Dundas.*

In the article she said the name Sankofa Square sends the wrong message because of the history of slavery, and the brutal violence associated with it, in Ghana where such practices as beheadings were conducted; the slaves of a chieftain were beheaded to serve their master in the afterlife. McDonald also had some choice words for slavery as practiced by Indigenous communities on our side of the ocean.

> Neglected is the documented fact that Indigenous societies themselves were slave societies. The losers of wars between Indigenous societies could be killed, mutilated, and/or enslaved, and even sold as slaves. Those more fortunate were adopted by the conquering group, in other words, assimilated—another no-no in today's world.
>
> No Indigenous society is known to have actually abolished slavery. Indeed, Indigenous slaves were among those freed by the abolition laws of Britain and Upper Canada. Nor did any African state ever abolish slavery or the slave trade of its own accord. It took decades of pressure from Great Britain and sometimes bribes from it, to achieve its abolition. Again, Dundas had some understanding of the key role of African leaders in slavery and the slave trade. As he stated in 1792 in the House of Commons when defending his amendment to William Wilberforce's motion for abolition of the slave trade, to make it "gradual.[44]

The controversy over Dundas initially began in Scotland before the torch was picked up in Canada. The Melville Monument is a towering column in St. Andrew Square in Edinburgh, and at the very top of the column is a statue of Henry Dundas, whom history had always portrayed as an enlightened liberal. This memorial to him was erected in the 1820s. But in 2016 an anti-Dundas campaign got launched by the former president of the Edinburgh University Student Association. His name was Adam Ramsey and it was all about this *gradual* business. Soon a petition containing many signatories was presented to city council.

Have we seen this movie before?

The next year a committee was convened to draft the wording of a new plaque to reflect "controversial" aspects of the legacy of Dundas. Geoffrey Palmer, a noted chemist and native of Jamaica, and the first black professor in Scotland, was chosen as Chair of the committee. Another committee member was historian Michael Fry. He was the biographer of Henry Dundas and said there was nothing sinister about the 'delay' campaign and that it was political expediency in order to get the amendment passed.

For whatever the reason, not much happened. Not until the murder of George Floyd and the emergence of the Black Lives Matter movement. Then, in 2020, with Palmer still chairing the committee, the makeup of the group changed as Michael Fry was booted out and more anti-Dundas voices joined the fray. Wording for a new plaque was then passed with these words.

> Dundas was a contentious figure, provoking controversies that resonate to this day. While Home Secretary in 1792, and the First Secretary of War in 1796, he was instrumental in deferring the abolition of the Atlantic slave trade. Slave trading by British ships was not abolished until 1807. As a result of this delay, more than half a million enslaved Africans crossed the Atlantic.

Shades of the Egerton Ryerson plaque about his role with residential schools on the grounds of the university bearing his name! And so, in Edinburgh the plaque went up and was "dedicated to the memory of more than half a million Africans whose enslavement was a consequence of Henry Dundas's actions." Thus, in the eyes of the 'anti' camp, Dundas was now personally responsible for all those enslaved Africans.

After the murder of George Floyd and the coming of Black Lives Matter, the anti-Dundas movement took what it could get from those happenings in Edinburgh and established itself in Canada. An article denouncing Dundas was published on a website called Open Democracy. The main editor for that site was Adam Ramsey, former president of the Edinburgh University Student Association, and the one who had initiated things in Scotland. The title of this article was *Henry Dundas, empire and genocide*. The author was Melanie Newton, an associate professor of history who specializes in Caribbean Studies and Atlantic World History at the University of Toronto. Here is an excerpt from her article:

> To be Black or Indigenous in North America and Europe is to live in the built environment of white supremacy, the physical embodiment of the apocalypse of colonisation and slavery. Every day we move through streetscapes, pass under the shadow of monuments, learn in buildings and live in towns named for the architects of the structural forms of violence that continue to shape Black and Indigenous lives, limit our choices, destroy our health and kill our children. These men were celebrated not in spite of the fact that they were white supremacists and, in some cases, mass murderers... but because of it.[45]

That article became ground zero for the hang-Henry-Dundas movement in Toronto.

Now let's return to Jennifer Dundas. And remember we are talking about a long-time investigative journalist, political affairs reporter and former CBC-TV news anchor in Winnipeg, not to mention crown attorney and prosecutor, and a woman committed to clearing her family name. She went through Newton's article with a fine tooth-comb and published her observations on a website for the Henry Dundas Committee of Ontario. She also wrote a letter to Toronto Mayor Olivia Chow and members of council.

She contends that the City of Toronto, which means the mayor and members of council, were misled by staff who manipulated them into supporting a proposal to get rid of the name Dundas. She says city staff presented false historical facts to council, made unfounded allegations that Dundas subjugated Indigenous peoples, defied instructions from Council to conduct public consultations, and "chose an understaffed, inexperienced Ottawa agency with a radical political agenda to lead the community consultation process."

As for Melanie Newton's article, Dundas the one-time journalist and prosecutor said Newton's commentary should have been deemed inconsequential since it had no citations and was published on the opinion pages of a website "that promoted left-wing activism." She said, in her view, the author showed a disturbing disregard for historical accuracy.

Nevertheless, according to Dundas, Newton became the favoured historian of the City of Toronto. She said city staff posted a link to her article on the city website and cited her name at the top of the list of experts they were consulting. In July, 2021, Toronto City Council voted to rename Dundas Street and invited Newton to co-chair the community advisory committee (CAC) that would choose a shortlist of possible names.

Says Jennifer Dundas: "In my opinion, based on my review of her article and her statements in the media, she produced propaganda, not legitimate scholarship. By disregarding the anti-slavery record of both Simcoe and Dundas, she engaged in unjustified character assassination. She denounced Simcoe and Dundas as white supremacists and mass murderers on the basis of their office and their race, while ignoring that anti-slavery track record.

This constituted a serious departure from the historian's duty of rigour, impartiality and sound judgment free of ethnocentric bias."

I reached out to Melanie Newton with the hope of doing an interview and she never responded, which is more or less what happened when I wanted to speak to the two co-chairs of the Standing Strong Task Force that dealt with Egerton Ryerson. Catherine Ellis referred me to the media relations department at Toronto Metropolitan University and the other, Joanne Dallaire, I never heard from at all.

Melanie Newton is a University of Toronto history professor specializing in Caribbean Studies. The official record says she is a native of Barbados with degrees from McGill University and Oxford University. She was also one of the UofT professors who spoke in support of the pro-Palestinian/pro-Hamas encampment which for several weeks in the spring and summer of 2024 occupied the middle of the UofT campus before a court injunction ordered the encampment to break up. In August, 2024 she took a selfie of herself and posted it; she was holding a sign in the colours of the Palestinian flag with the words 'DIVEST/DIVEST/DIVEST.' That same month she signed her name to an anti-Israel Faculty for Palestine Canada petition called 'University of Toronto Faculty Pledge for the Academic Boycott of Israel.'

It would appear then that Melanie Newton is an activist for various causes; one of them was to get rid of the name Henry Dundas on anything in Toronto.

A few days after Remembrance Day in 2024 I attended a presentation by Professor Patrice Dutil of Toronto Metropolitan University. It was about the toppling of statues and the changing of names of public squares and streets. This was supposed to be a *debate* about Henry Dundas and his legacy with Dutil there to speak on behalf of Dundas. Organizers said they reached out to 20 people from the black and Indigenous communities to take the other side, but none were willing to come.

Dutil said he wasn't surprised and didn't pull any punches. He said these groups have five things in common. First, they decide. Second, they create "committees of know-nothings" to legitimize their decision. Third, they don't do their homework. Fourth, they don't consult and refuse to meet in public debates "and it's OK to vandalize statues." And fifth, they then proceed with what was decided.

He also had sharp words for the City of Toronto. A native of Montreal, Dutil compared the official commemoration policies for those two cities. Montreal's 'Cadre d'intervention en Reconnaissance' talks about reinforcing the city's identity, recognizing the history, heritage and memory of Montrealers, and such things as giving expression to various aspects of the culture, identity and value of the Montreal community, and recognizing past contributions of those who contributed to the identity of Montreal.

But Toronto's Guiding Principles for Commemoration are very different. They include the following:

- Be informed by historical research, traditional knowledge, and community insights. Proposals for commemorative street names, property names, or monuments must be grounded in sound historical and/or community-based research.
- Proposals can be based on oral histories and traditional knowledge.
- Honour Indigenous ways of knowing and being.
- Prioritize commemorations significant to Indigenous Peoples, Black communities, and equity-deserving groups.

In other words, the policy for commemoration in Toronto is awash in wokeism which was much in evidence at the city's official Remembrance Day ceremony on November 11, 2024. After

Mayor Olivia Chow gave a speech about the sacrifice of Canadian soldiers, she was joined by Aretha Phillip, Chief of Protocol for the City of Toronto. In her remarks Phillip said: "The City of Toronto acknowledges all treaty peoples, including those who came here as settlers, as migrants—either in this generation or in generations past—and those of us who came here involuntarily, particularly those brought to these lands as a result of the Trans-Atlantic Slave Trade and slavery."

That was almost word-for-word for what is taken as history at Sankofa Square. It was all too much for General Rick Hillier. He was Chief of Defence staff for Canada from 2005 to 2008, which means he was the country's top soldier during the height of Canada's involvement in the war in Afghanistan. Said Hillier in his tweet: "We are nothing but 'sheep' to put up with this condescending lecture at any time, but especially today. A day devoted to those who served and sacrificed to build a country that doesn't have that."

He also added one more word.

Shame.

CHAPTER 8

Cancel culture in Atlantic Canada

But before I quit this part of my narrative, it will not be foreign to my purpose to give an account of their manner of scalping, that for the reader may both have an idea of the savage, and barbarous tempers of their inhuman cannibals, and at the same time be invited to set a proper value upon a country that is now civilized and which before the Romans came into it was a proverb and bye-word, among the nations for such was their brutality, that they should like Lycaon, kill and serve up their lodgers at their voracious entertainments. These Indians chain the unfortunate prisoner to a large thick tree, and bind his hands and his feet, then beginning from the middle of the craneum, they cut quite round towards the neck; this being done, they then tear off the skin, leaving the skull bare; an inflammation quickly follows, the patient fevers, and dies in the most exquisite tortures. In this situation was poor Brown found, while his comrades were thought to have undergone the [familiar] hardships, they not having been heard of, till accidentally some butchers going up to Minas to buy cattle, got intelligence of the matter, and informed Governor Cornwallis. He immediately wrote to the Commanding Officer of a little fort, belonging to Great Britain, in the neighbourhood of Minas, and recommended to him to make reprisals, to the intent that the English prisoners might be redeemed.[46]

SO BEGINS THAT PART of John Wilson's eyewitness account about the scalping of British settlers and militia by Mi'kmaq warriors in what became known as the *Dartmouth Massacre* which took place May 13, 1751. His mention of *Lycaon* refers to the mythical

Greek character who killed and cooked his son before serving him to Zeus. The full title of Wilson's account was 'A Genuine Narrative of the Transactions in Nova Scotia since the settlement, June 1749, till August 5th, 1751, in which the Nature, Soil and Produce of the Country are related, with the particular attempts of the Indians to disturb the colony.' Wilson, the sole survivor of the attack, would go on to provide gruesome details of what happened in another episode two weeks later. These were but two of several attacks by Mi'kmaq against British settlers in the colonies of Nova Scotia. Wrote Wilson:

> Though this might serve to illustrate the horrid barbarity of the Indians and to shew what little confidence is to be put in our neighbouring colony, yet, I have something equally surprising to relate. On the 27th of May last, a party of these Indians surprised Dartmouth, a small town opposite to Halifax, a little before four in the morning. They all at once appeared, fired through the windows and doors, and killed fifteen persons, including women and children; wounded seven, three of whom died in the hospital. Men were carried away and never heard of since. The party quartered there, being alarmed by the noise in the morning, were instantly drawn up by Lieutenant Clark of Colonel Warburton's regiment, who commanded there. They marched in haste to the Indians who discharged some shot, killed a sergeant dead on the spot, and wounded the superior officer in the leg; the former being very brave, right before the others, where he was attacked, and got several wounds. His right hand was cut off and the thumb and forefinger of his left hand. He was miserably mangled by their hangers and knives. Three soldiers were wounded.[47]

Wilson's account is not the only record of such Mi'kmaq attacks on settlers. Thomas B. Akins was a lawyer, historian and archivist. In 1857 he was appointed Nova Scotia's first Commissioner of Public Records and held that position until his death in 1891. He was held in such high regard that the government of Canada designated him a 'Person of National Historic Significance.' His *History of the Settlement of Halifax* was published in book form in 1895, four years after he died. But it had been published as a pamphlet half a century earlier, in 1847, and eight years prior to that—on April 18, 1839—he did a formal reading from his notes at the Halifax Mechanic's Institute. These are his words about the attack on Dartmouth:

> In the spring of the following year the Indians surprised Dartmouth at night, scalped a number of settlers and carried off several prisoners. The inhabitants, fearing an attack, had cut down the spruce trees around their settlement, which, instead of a protection, as was intended, served as a cover for the enemy. Captain Clapham and his company of Rangers were stationed at Blockhouse hill, and it is said remained within his blockhouse firing from the loopholes, during the whole affair. The Indians were said to have destroyed several dwellings, sparing neither women nor children. The light of the torches and the discharge of musketry alarmed the inhabitants of Halifax, some of whom put off to their assistance, but did not arrive in any force till after the Indians had retired. The night was calm, and the cries of the settlers, and whoop of the Indians were distinctly heard on the western side of the harbour. On the following morning, several bodies were brought over—the Indians having carried off the scalps.[48]

Edward Cornwallis, the governor referred to by John Wilson, is the founder of Halifax. He arrived on the shores of Nova Scotia on June 21, 1749 with 13 transports—boats or frigates—along with, in the words of archivist Thomas B. Akins, a "sloop of war." The precise records of Akins include a list showing each and every boat, names of the respective captains, as well as the tonnage and number of passengers. The total was 2,576 people and, of that, some 1,546 were males "exclusive of children." Of those adult males, more than 500 were "man-of-war sailors." The Akins account also refers to a letter Governor Cornwallis wrote to the Lords of Trade in which he, in effect, summarized his human cargo:

> The number of settlers—men, women and children—is 1,400, but I beg leave to observe to your Lordships that amongst them the number of industrious, active men proper to undertake and carry on a new settlement, is very small. Of soldiers there are only 100, of tradesmen, sailors and others able and willing to work, not above 200.[49]

Cornwallis reported the rest of them as being idle and worthless, but who embraced the opportunity to get provisions for a year without labour, or failing that, they were sailors who only wanted passage to New England. He also said many of them were sick and unfit to be settlers, and without sufficient clothing. During that first winter in Nova Scotia more than one-third of those settlers died.

The figure of Edward Cornwallis wields a significant presence in the history of Atlantic Canada and the biggest city in that part of the country. He was born in 1713 to an aristocratic family with a strong military pedigree. In 1745 he put down the Jacobite rebellion in Scotland and four years later, in 1749, King George II named him Governor of Nova Scotia. He would hold this position for three years and his mission was clear—establish and protect the settlement of Halifax. But the place wasn't initially called that. The Mi'kmaq called it K'jipuktuk which meant Great Harbour. To the French that translated to *Chibouctou* and to the English *Chebucto*. Nevertheless, Cornwallis renamed the settlement Halifax in honour of George Montagu-Dunk, the 2nd Earl of Halifax who at the time was President of the Board of Trade and Plantations, and responsible for planning the new settlement.

According to their oral histories and archaeological evidence, the Mi'kmaq had been living in Nova Scotia for a long time. Some say thousands of years. But with the coming of the Europeans things changed. Disease became widespread and by 1749 their numbers had dwindled, according to reports, as low as 3,000. By that time the French Acadian population had grown to almost 11,000. Between 1688 and 1763 there would be seven wars in northeastern North America between the two European powers—the French and English—with major impact on both settlers and Indigenous people alike. But for the Mi'kmaq two wars in particular were consequential—Father Le Loutre's War from 1749 to 1755, and the French and Indian War from 1754 to 1763.

Le Loutre was a Catholic priest and missionary for the French Foreign Missions Society. He was an ardent French nationalist who became leader of the band of French resistance forces which consisted of Acadian fighters and Mi'kmaq warriors. Thus, the Mi'kmaq were allied with the French and remained so during all those years of warfare in Nova Scotia. They also had a presence on the borders of Acadie, which is present-day New Brunswick. The French were based at Fortress Louisbourg on Ile Royale, now Cape Breton Island. Louisbourg had been established three decades earlier in 1720. While Ile Royale was in the hands of the French, mainland Nova Scotia was designated as British territory according to the Treaty of Aix-la-Chapelle in 1748.

When Cornwallis arrived in the spring of 1749, one of the first things he did was meet with Indigenous chiefs, including Mi'kmaq. There was an agreement to reaffirm the Peace and Friendship Treaty that had been ratified with the Wabanaki

Confederacy in Annapolis Royal in 1726. But on August 19, 1749, a Mi'kmaq attack took place on the settlement at Canso and on September 6 another one occurred on the settlement at Chignecto. Cornwallis then learned of an impending attack said to be in the offing for the settlement at Halifax, and so, he ordered the construction of five blockhouses connected by a palisade to protect it.

Cornwallis was a military man. The settlers he was duty-bound to protect had been promised by the British government passage across the Atlantic, free land, provisions for one year, and security. He aimed to deliver that.

On September 30, 1749, a Mi'kmaq raid involving 40 warriors took place in Dartmouth. They attacked six unarmed men who had been out cutting wood. Two men were scalped, two decapitated, one captured, and one managed to escape. This would be the first of eight Mi'kmaq raids on Dartmouth that took place over a ten-year period from 1749 to 1759. The settlement at Dartmouth, and especially the one at Halifax, were of strategic importance to the British to counter the French stronghold at Louisbourg.

The fortress of Louisbourg is something to behold and if you visit now you see it just as it was.

Many years ago, before our children were born, my wife and I went there. We still have the photos and I remember thinking how new it looked. The reconstruction was in the 1960s and 1970s, which would explain that. There is one photo of me standing between two members of the French 'militia' who are dressed in period attire, the three of us right behind a cannon. Louisbourg is not only a fortress but a town; a National Historic Site, it is the largest, reconstructed, French-fortified town in North America dating from the 18th century and everything looks exactly as it did back in the day. Of course, when we visited there was no Internet and no website.

Today Fortress Louisbourg Association (FLA) is administered by Parks Canada. Go on the site and you see it has gone *woke* in the same way as Bellevue House, the one-time home of Sir John A. Macdonald in Kingston, also administered by Parks Canada. This is what greets you:

> This territory is covered by the "Treaties of Peace and Friendship" which Mi'kmaq, Wolastoqiyik and Passamaquoddy People first signed with the British Crown in 1725. The treaties did not deal with the surrender of lands and resources but, in fact, recognized the Indigenous title and established rules for what was to be an ongoing relationship between nations.
> We are all Treaty People.
> FLA also recognizes the 400+ year history of communities of African descent and the 50 Strong and Resourceful African NS communities that exist today. We acknowledge our commitment to the struggle against systems of oppression that have resulted in profound inequities and the denial of self determination rights.
> FLA is committed to work actively to deepen our learning and provide learning opportunities about anti-racism and decolonization to the sector, and to develop partnerships with organizations serving and led by underrepresented groups.[50]

The website has no mention of Mi'kmaq from Ile Royale attacking Dartmouth nor of the subsequent massacre. And there is nothing about any Mi'kmaq attacks on British settlements that followed.

In 1745 a colonial force from New England aided by a British fleet captured Fortress Louisbourg, but three years later the French got it back under the aforementioned Treaty of Aix-la-Chapelle. One year after that, in 1749—the year Cornwallis arrived—the settlement at Halifax was established. And now we come to the heart of the matter concerning this man and what has been done to his name.

French authorities at Louisbourg had been paying bounties to the Mi'kmaq for British prisoners and their scalps. And so, on October 2, 1749, Cornwallis issued a proclamation of his own, offering a similar bounty for Mi'kmaq warriors. This is the wording of the proclamation:

> Whereas, notwithstanding the gracious offer of friendship and protection in His Majesty's name by us to the Indians inhabiting this province, the Micmacs have of late in a most treacherous manner taken 20 of his Majesty's subjects prisoners at Canso, and carried off a sloop belonging to Boston, and a boat from this settlement, and at Chignecto basely and under pretence of friendship and commerce attempted to seize two English sloops and murder their crews, and on Saturday the 30th of September a body of these savages fell upon some men cutting wood and without arms near the sawmill, and barbarously killed four and carried away one.
>
> For these causes we, by and with the advice and consent of His Majesty's Council, do hereby authorize and command all officers civil and military, and all His Majesty's subjects or others to annoy, distress, take or destroy such as are aiding and assisting them, and we further by and with the consent and advice of His Majesty's council do promise a reward of Ten Guineas for every Indian, Mickmack, taken or killed to be paid upon producing such savage taken on his scalp (as is the custom of America) if killed, to the officers commanding at Halifax, Annapolis Royal or Minas.[51]

Note that the proclamation says his scalp. Thus, the bounty was for the scalps of Mi'kmaq warriors for the reasons cited above. Women and children were not included, but were to be taken prisoner following the norms of British policy in such conflicts.

Murray Sinclair was chairman of the Indian Residential Schools Truth and Reconciliation Commission from 2009 to 2015. A lawyer, judge and member of the Canadian Senate, he was of Ojibway heritage. Sinclair passed away in the fall of 2024, but his words live on, especially these: "Reconciliation is about co-existence after all, and a relationship of mutual respect."[52]

Those are good words and we should take a long look at them when considering the treatment of Cornwallis who has been the target of a campaign that began more than 30 years ago. What transpired between the settlers he brought to Nova Scotia and the Mi'kmaq who were there already is dismissed in some circles as a case of 'good' versus 'evil.' Indeed, in what passes for history in today's woke world, anything Indigenous is deemed in a positive light while anything white, European or *colonial* is pure evil. Nevertheless, documented records from the time exist, such as from the likes of John Wilson and Thomas B. Akins. But despite that there are voices who boil things down to a black-and-white affair.

Rarely is history so cut-and-dried as that.

My wife was born in Greece but is of Macedonian ethnicity. After we were married I got a crash course in this sort of thing. There had been long-held friction between Greeks and Macedonians that goes back to Philip II of Macedon, who was obviously Macedonian. He was also the father of Alexander III, better known as Alexander the Great, and there is no dispute about that. Alexander the Great is merely the no. 1 superstar of Greek history and today a magnificent statue of him astride a horse overlooks the harbour of Thessaloniki, the second largest city in Greece after Athens. But try calling Alexander a Macedonian in the presence of a Greek national. The turmoil continues to this day. It's part of the reason why the country of Macedonia, which emerged from the former Yugoslavia after the fall of the Soviet Union in 1991, was renamed the Republic of North Macedonia in 2019. Fearful of territorial claims in its northern region, Greece had objected to the name 'Macedonia' ever since the USSR bit the dust. At every turn it had vetoed that fledgling country's bid to join NATO and the European Union. The new name settled things, but then, if you ask any Macedonian about it now you will likely be greeted with a smirk and a shrug.

Not long after my marriage I asked my father-in-law about this and he got into the history.

"When did all this happen?" I asked him.

"About 2,500 years ago," he replied.

"So who gives a damn?" I said.

As it turned out, a lot of people did. On both sides. What's more, they still do.

We all know Greece has a long and proud history, and the people of that country take great pride in it, as well they should. On the other hand, the history of Canada—the nation we know as Canada—embodies much shorter duration. But how much do we cherish our history, what little of it we have? To answer that question, let's return to Alexander the Great.

The statue of him on his horse was unveiled with pomp and ceremony in 1974 and to this day it commands the harbour of Thessaloniki. At an imposing height of more than six meters, or about twenty feet, it is the tallest equestrian statue in the country. As for Edward Cornwallis, the founder of Halifax, an equally impressive statue of him was unveiled in the downtown of that city in 1931. As with Alexander's statue, the city of Halifax held a dedication ceremony in Cornwallis Park. The original sculpture had been commissioned at a cost of $20,000 which was paid by Canadian National Railways, the province of Nova Scotia, and the City of Halifax. After all, this was part of the heritage and history of the city, the province, and the country.

But that statue is no longer there.

Cornwallis has been cancelled in the same way John A. Macdonald, Egerton Ryerson, Henry Dundas, and other notable figures from Canada's past have been cancelled by those who have an axe to grind. And they don't do it with history, but with their own *twisted* take on history which is deep in ideology and involves something other than the truth. To rub salt into the wound, the cost of removing the Cornwallis statue in 2018 from Cornwallis Park—that, too, has been renamed, it's now called Peace and Friendship Park—amounted to $25,000 of public money. Notwithstanding inflation, if we look only at the face value of currency, that number is *larger* than the payment made for the original sculpture back in 1931!

Scalping is front and centre in this 'controversy' which wasn't a controversy for the better part of two and a half centuries, not until a book by Mi'kmaq elder Daniel Paul was published in 1993. The book was *We Were Not the Savages: a Micmac perspective on the collision of European and aboriginal civilizations*. Paul, who passed away in 2023, was the 11th of 14 children in his family. He was born in 1938 in a log cabin on the Indian Brook Reserve in Nova Scotia.

In his book he laid the charge of *genocide* perpetrated against the Mi'kmaq squarely at the feet of Edward Cornwallis. He said the bounty proclamation was an "extermination" order and that Cornwallis had called for "the scalps of men, women and children." No sooner did he make this claim that other voices picked it up and built an anti-Cornwallis narrative in keeping with the story of the evil white man. In short, a number of people rallied with the cause and soon the Daniel Paul story became the official party line. The rest, as the old saying goes, is history.

But it's revisionist history.

This would be like the descendants of Darius III making a stink about Alexander the Great today. Darius was the last Achaemenid king of Persia whose army was defeated by Alexander at the siege of Tyre in 332 BC. That is deemed one of the great battles in history. But what if those descendants got together with other individuals who had their own fish to fry and defaced the statue of

Alexander in Thessaloniki? And what if they then demanded its immediate removal from that lofty perch overlooking the harbour? Why would they want to do that? Because when this epic battle was over Alexander had the temerity to sell all the remaining women and children from the losing side—those who had survived the siege—into slavery. We are talking the third century BC here and such things were not unusual for a victorious army. But how easy it is to look at this through the lens of current times and speak of Alexander's nerve!

For sure, life in 18th-century Nova Scotia was much different than anything from the third-century BC. But it was also different from 21st-century Nova Scotia. In fact, many historians have addressed that period of Nova Scotia history as a particularly violent time what with all the warring parties.

To make the analogy with Darius even more ludicrous, imagine that the current city council of Thessaloniki yields to the demands of those descendants of Darius. The councillors take a vote and agree to remove the statue of Alexander on his horse. Then they put it into storage. And never mind what the masses think.

But that is exactly what happened in Halifax.

After the death of Daniel Paul on June 27, 2023, this is what Global TV reported: "His research also helped persuade Nova Scotia politicians that statues, school names and even a coast guard ship should no longer bear the name of Edward Cornwallis, the province's first governor, who offered rewards for Indigenous scalps."

As far as that news report was concerned, this was the full extent of the Cornwallis legacy.

Back in 2020—on June 30—the CBC ran a story about the Mi'kmaq wanting to rename a coast guard icebreaker. The icebreaker had been called Edward Cornwallis. The CBC headline ran like this: "Founder of Halifax issued proclamation of bounty for killing Mi'kmag men, women and children." The story then ran a quote from Daniel Paul who said: "It's a good move toward reconciliation."

Look up the name Edward Cornwallis in the Canadian Encyclopedia and you get this:

> In October 1749, he issued an order that came to be known as the Scalping Proclamation. His government would pay a bounty to anyone who killed a Mi'kmaq adult or child in a bid to drive them off mainland Nova Scotia. It is not known how many people died, but several reports detail attacks on Mi'kmaq villages and mercenaries bringing in dozens of scalps to claim bounties.[53]

The person who made that contribution was Jon Tattrie who wrote a book called *Cornwallis: The Violent Birth of Halifax*, published in 2013. That, too, reiterated the already old trope about the scalping of Mi'kmaq men, *women and children*. Pretty soon anything with the name Cornwallis—a statue, park, street, icebreaker, what have you—was done for. And it all started with Daniel Paul.

Leo J. Deveau is an author, newspaper columnist, and authority on Nova Scotia history. This is what he says of Paul's claims:

> Paul's analysis ignored the wider context of the imperial wars of the period and the close alliance between the Mi'kmaq and the French in the struggle of empires. The history of that alliance records regular bounties paid for the delivery of scalps belonging to British soldiers and settlers obtained by Mi'kmaq warriors during numerous raids. Such bounties were paid by French officials at Louisbourg, and frequently also by the notorious Catholic missionary-cum-rabid nationalist, the Abbé Jean-Louis Le Loutre.

Deveau went on:

> Adopting the familiar 'good and evil' interpretation of history, Paul lays the charge of 'genocide' against Cornwallis, feeling that the term genocide 'aptly' described the barbaric behaviour of the British in colonial Nova Scotia. This in turn is meant to justify his wild exaggeration that the statue of Cornwallis represented 'white supremacist thinking.' For the author and his acolytes it seems everything comes down to genocide and white supremacy. This is grossly oversimplified history.

In June, 2011, the Halifax Regional School Board voted to rename one of its schools. The school was Cornwallis Junior High. According to a CBC report, the school had been named "after the city founder who ordered the mass killing of Mi'kmaq people." Daniel Paul was interviewed for the story and said he felt like "dancing in the street" after the decision was made. He said the next step would be to remove the statue of Cornwallis in Cornwallis Park, which happened a few years later. But not all media coverage at the time was sympathetic to Paul and his take on history.

Paul Bennett, who is the author of Canadian history textbooks, has enjoyed a long and distinguished career as an education consultant. At one time he was Adjunct Professor of Education at Saint Mary's University in Halifax. After the news report came out that the school was going to ditch the Cornwallis name, he wrote an article in *The Chronicle-Herald* with the title 'How solid is the case against Cornwallis?' In the piece he said this sets a dangerous precedent and took aim directly at Daniel Paul.

"While Paul is often described as an historian, his work is mostly popular storytelling since it's a fascinating mix of history, folklore, and personal testimony."[54]

Bennett went on to cite Paul's use of the word 'genocide' and his comparing the actions of Cornwallis against the Mi'kmaq to what Adolf Hitler did to Jews in World War II. Wrote Bennett: "Paul's analysis of Cornwallis is incredibly one-sided and enjoys little support among North American historians."[55]

I obtained a copy of the fourth edition of Daniel Paul's book, which was published in 2022. On the back cover it says he is a freelance lecturer and journalist, and "an ardent activist for human rights." Before the book even begins, this appears in the Dedication:

> To the memory of my ancestors, who managed to ensure the survival of the Mi'kmaw People by their awe-inspiring tenacity and valour in the face of virtually insurmountable odds! For more than four centuries these courageous, dignified and heroic people displayed a determination to survive the various hells on earth created for them by Europeans with a tenacity that equals any displayed in the history of mankind.

Not to minimize the very real plight of the Mi'kmaq, nor of any other Indigenous people after the coming of Europeans, but such words do not lend themselves as an authoritative work on recorded history. Indeed, how would that passage greet the ears of John Wilson who wrote in excruciating detail about the massacre at Dartmouth? It makes one think twice about something Paul Bennett said in 2011 when the only thing up for grabs, as far as Cornwallis was concerned, was changing the name of a school. Said Bennett in his article: "Basing public policy on Daniel Paul's writings can only lead to further historical injustices."

But that is what happened. For the record, this is how Daniel Paul describes the Bounty Proclamation of 1749 issued by Cornwallis.

In October 1749, he issued an order that came to be known as the Scalping Proclamation. His government would pay a bounty to anyone who killed a Mi'kmaw adult or child in a bid to drive them off mainland Nova Scotia/Mi'kma'ki. Several reports detail attacks on Mi'kmaw villages, with mercenaries bringing in dozens of scalps at a time to claim bounties.

Two points must be addressed here. First, there is no mention in Paul's book, or from what I can find in anything he has ever written, about the Dartmouth massacre. Second, while Cornwallis did indeed issue a bounty proclamation for Mi'kmaq warriors in retribution for Mi'kmaq attacks on various settlements, it was not for their women and children, who were to be taken as prisoners. Anyone can check the actual proclamation, but then that would dilute the story.

It brings to mind the classic Hollywood Western *The Man Who Shot Liberty Valance* and the wonderful line at the very end of it. Our hero James Stewart is a US senator whose political career got kick-started with his killing of a notorious outlaw when he was a young idealistic lawyer. Or so the story goes. In the film, the now much older senator relates what really happened back in the day to a newspaper reporter who is taking copious notes. When Stewart finishes telling the story, the reporter rips up his notes with dramatic flair.

"Well, you're not going to use the story, Mr. Scott?" James Stewart says.

"No sir. This is the West, sir. When the legend becomes fact, print the legend."

In May, 2014 a group of protesters gathered in Cornwallis Park and demanded that the park be renamed and the statue of Cornwallis removed. They spoke of his "very violent genocidal past." Just over a year later—in June, 2015—the Truth and Reconciliation Commission came out with its 'call to action.' By this time Halifax had already established its office of Diversity and Inclusion with major representation from the Aboriginal community. It was supposed to be based on truth, dignity and mutual respect.

Says Leo Deveau: "As it turned out, that meant little in the way of respect, dignity, or equal treatment for historical figures such as Cornwallis, but rather, a one-way cancellation campaign against the founder of Halifax."

Cornwallis has met the same fate as other nation-builders from Canada's past, including the nation-builder himself—Sir John A. Macdonald.

Early in 2016 the Halifax Mi'kmaw native Friendship Centre sent a letter to Halifax city council asking that Cornwallis Street be renamed. Then, in May that year, a member of city council introduced a motion to remove the name of Edward Cornwallis from all municipal commemorations. The mayor supported that but the motion was defeated 8–7. Shortly afterward the Cornwallis statue was ravaged by vandals with the now familiar dousing in red paint, meant to signify *genocide*. This is the same red paint and the same *genocide* that would soon mar the statues of other historical figures across Canada.

Later in 2016 a municipal election was held and both the mayor of Halifax and the councillor who had introduced the motion were re-elected. But now there were new councillors and they were swayed by a presentation delivered by the city's first Mi'kmaw poet laureate. In the presentation Cornwallis was depicted as a man "who prided himself on brutality" and who used Mi'kmaq scalps as "currency." Again, this was considered the extent of his legacy. Another vote about removing the Cornwallis name from all municipal properties was taken at city council and this time it passed 15–1.

Never mind that a CBC survey found that 58 per cent of the people of Halifax thought the Cornwallis name should remain on public parks, buildings and street signs. Don Mills, CEO of the company that did the survey, told the CBC: "Quite often the silent majority is not represented in these kinds of debate. In fact, it's almost two to one against removing the statue."[56] Another survey—a CTV Atlantic Web Poll—showed that 63 per cent wanted the statue to stay put.

It didn't matter.

In July, 2017 there were two organized protests against the Cornwallis statue with the result that a shroud was placed over it. Then the shroud was replaced by a tarp. Three months later Halifax Regional Municipality council voted 15–2 to launch a Special Advisory Committee with "equal representation from Indigenous and non-Indigenous backgrounds."

This sounds very similar to the task forces created at the university once known as Ryerson and the one set up at the City of Toronto to discuss Henry Dundas. Indeed, the Modus Operandi with historical revisionists tends to follow a playbook. Part of that playbook involves establishing an 'expert' panel with equal parts Indigenous and non-Indigenous, provided the latter are academics who have a 'progressive' bent.

One co-chair of the Halifax task force was Mi'kmaq Chief Roderick Googoo and the other was Monica MacDonald from Dalhousie University. The non-Indigenous MacDonald would later appear in a seminar about the subject of monuments. In November, 2020 she was on a panel for a presentation called 'Monumental Questions: Revisiting Controversial Monuments and Memorials.' The session can be found online. The other presenters were Melanie Newton of Henry Dundas fame and Lisa Phelps, then mayor of Victoria, BC. The political legacy of Phelps includes her presiding over the removal of a statue of John A. Macdonald in that city.

In the session Henry Dundas was introduced as "the active agent in the British parliament's delay of the abolition of the slave trade" while Edward Cornwallis was, as far as Halifax is concerned, "the city's first imperial administrator and a man with a questionable and violent legacy." Not five minutes in, a pot shot was also taken at John A. Macdonald.[57]

Thus, it would appear that 'Monumental Questions' was an anti-colonial, woke gathering of the first degree.

The upshot of the Halifax task force was that Mike Savage, the mayor of the city, met with Mi'kmaq chiefs who demanded the statue's immediate removal. And then it happened. On January 30, 2018, city council voted 12–4 to do just that and place it in storage where the statue remains to this day. The cost of the removal was $25,000 and the mayor was all fine and good with it, saying, "I feel strongly it's the right thing to do."

What is Leo Deveau's take on this?

> Cornwallis has unjustly become a lightning rod for all the grievances the Indigenous people have had since their first contact with European settlers. The mayor's rhetoric represented a denial of the historical fact that Halifax was established by Cornwallis and 2,500 dedicated settlers in 1749. Had Cornwallis not defended the British settlement in those critical years, there probably would not be a city called Halifax today, where peace, law and order, and eventually Canada's first representative government (1760), and later, elected responsible government (1849), would be born, where the fruits of the civilizing spirit of the Enlightenment would also take root and help shape the country that Canada has become.

As for the task force, Deveau says this: "The whole process was a done deal and rigged from the get-go and made to look like a public consultation."

When the statue was finally removed the verdict on Cornwallis was in. Reported Global TV: "It took one afternoon to take it down, but the calls to remove it have been coming for decades.

The statue of Halifax founder Edward Cornwallis represents white supremacy to many. He is infamous for among other things offering a bounty for Mi'kmaw scalps."

The CBC story about the removal of the statue led like this: 'Controversial Cornwallis statue removed from Halifax park' and then followed with: 'The decision comes after increasing controversy over Cornwallis's so-called scalping proclamation that offered a cash bounty to anyone who killed a Mi'kmaw person."

It even made international news. The headline in a story published by none other than *The Guardian* was "Canada confronts colonial past as Halifax removes statue of city's founder," followed by the sub-head: "In 1749 the city of Halifax's founder Edward Cornwallis offered rewards for ethnic cleansing—and now his bronze has been removed."

Cornwallis Park was renamed the Peace and Friendship Park.

Cornwallis Street was renamed Nora Bernard Street after a Mi'kmaw activist who had been murdered by her grandson back in 2007.

In short, Edward Cornwallis and anything associated with his name was as good as dead.

The man who started all this—Daniel Paul—passed away in 2023, and while no one likes to criticize the deceased, *alternate facts* accepted as history must be addressed. In the fourth edition of his book *We Were Not the Savages*, Paul dismisses Canada's first prime minister, Sir John A. Macdonald, with these words: "Macdonald himself left behind solid evidence that he was an unapologetic white supremacist."[58] Later he repeats this claim: "He was a white supremacist to the core."[59]

He compares the plight of the Mi'kmaq to European Jews in the Holocaust: "The hardship and discrimination they suffered in the midst of plenty, at the behest of English officialdom, does not greatly pale in comparison to that suffered by the Jewish people at the hands of Hitler in the 1930s and 40s."[60]

And what about Mi'kmaq attacks on settlers? This is what he said: "Most individual Mi'kmaw conducted themselves in a relatively humane and civilized manner during this trying period. The few that were involved in the bounty trade committed some atrocities, usually under the influence of alcohol supplied by Caucasians or in the employ of the French."[61]

As for the Mi'kmaq and their way of life, Paul says: "Civility and generosity were so engrained in Mi'kmaw society that to be rude or mean was unthinkable."[62]

Many times in his book and other writings he referred to the *genocide* carried out against his people, and to the Bounty Proclamation issued by Cornwallis in 1749, and how it involved bounties paid for the scalps of Mi'kmaq men, *women and children*. This is said over and over, and through the years it has been echoed and mined to the hills by members of the media who should have done their homework. It is also repeated by those who claim to be historians but are little more than purveyors of an ideology that is hostile to legitimate history. The point is this is not history and it is not scholarship. If we look at history it's easy to see what happens when public policy is based on commentary propagating things that are not true.

The Protocols of the Elders of Zion is a story that first appeared in a Russian newspaper in 1903. The claim being made was that Jews secretly conspired to rule the world by first taking over the economy, the banks, the media—what have you—and go on from there. After the Russian Revolution the story made its way to the West with an Arabic translation appearing in the 1920s. Today millions of people around the world, not to mention some governments, believe this to be true just as there are those who deny the Holocaust took place, that Arabs did not carry out the attacks on 9/11, and more recently that Jews themselves perpetrated what transpired on October 7, 2023 in Israeli communities near the border with Gaza.

On the other hand, there are also people who have doubts about humans landing on the moon or that Elvis is really dead.

John E. Grenier is an American historian. He is a Lieutenant-Colonel in the US Air Force with a Ph. D. in history from the University of Colorado, Boulder. In 2007 he won the Society for Military History's Distinguished Book Award for his book *The First Way of War: American War Making on the Frontier, 1607–1814*. But another book he wrote is *The Far Reaches of Empire: War in Nova Scotia, 1710–1760*. Published in 2008, it examines the wars in Nova Scotia during the 18th century from the perspective of a scholar who has no stake in the matter. One organization he thanked in his Acknowledgments is the National Archives of Canada.

Grenier readily admits that when it was all over the Mi'kmaq and their way of life would ultimately be no more. But he also said that the treaties the Mi'kmaq signed with the British in 1760 and 1761 were "far harsher" than previous ones, including the Articles of 1749 with Edward Cornwallis. Nowhere does Grenier say Cornwallis is an angel or saint. He calls him a British colonial official who used "brutal but effective measures" to "wrest control of Nova Scotia from French and Indian enemies who were no less ruthless."[63]

Grenier was one historical expert interviewed by *The National Post* for an article about the initial renaming of the Cornwallis high school. In the article he said: "It is complicated. But the PC [Political Correctness] crowd, if you will, prefers to remain ignorant of the historical record." He also added: "It is important to look at the context in which Cornwallis and the other Anglo-Americans made the decision to issue the scalp proclamation. The Mi'kmaqs certainly were not innocent, passive victims in that train of events."[64]

Another American observer of note is the late John Shy, a military historian who specialized in the American colonial and revolutionary periods, and who was professor emeritus at the

University of Michigan. He passed away in 2022. What Shy said about the wars in Nova Scotia is worth a look.

"We can exaggerate the frequency and intensity of colonial American military experience. Most American colonists, most of the time, lived in peace, and even in wartime daily life went on more or less untroubled by events on the frontier or at sea. Such, however, was not the case in Nova Scotia, which, after all, was the frontier. Nova Scotia, from an Anglo-American perspective, remained an unsettled marshland, infested with potentially hostile Acadians, Indians, and Frenchmen. There is no exaggeration in the contention that war, or the threat of war, often troubled the daily lives of the colony's inhabitants."[65]

John Wilson was one of those inhabitants.

No historian worth their salt examines any period or place through a one-way lens. That is to sacrifice both context and credibility. What's more, when a region, never mind a country, bases public policy on commentary that is rife with speculation, conjecture—and lies—a nation begins to lose itself and there is only one inevitable result.

Its history is vanquished.

CHAPTER 9

An honoured judge rewritten, renounced and removed

IF HE WAS AMERICAN they would have made a movie about him with Cary Cooper in the starring role. They would've done it long ago because Matthew Begbie was a character who had hero written all over him. He stood an imposing six-foot-five and when you put him on a horse with that handlebar moustache and van dyke he seemed bigger still. The man studied mathematics and the classics, played piano, and could sing with the best of them—even in Italian—and, of course, he shared a taste for fine wine. But he also studied law and became a judge and when he brought that to the Old West all hell broke loose.

With the upturned, white shirt collar around his neck, the stylish black tie, the black hat and black cloak of the judge that draped his formidable frame, Begbie cut a commanding figure. These were wild days and a lot of men carried firearms, but Begbie was no gunslinger. He was tougher and more feared than that. He was a circuit judge—the first one in these rough-and-tumble parts—who brought bandits and outlaws to justice as he travelled the highways, biways and rivers of the frontier. It was a time when there were no villages, roads or courthouses. No jails either. And so, he went on horse, on foot, or by canoe, carriage or steamship, and carried out the law through his own brand of circuit court that did its business in a courtroom but more often than not it was a log cabin, under an oak tree, or in the open wilderness.

He was an outsider who came from afar to mete out justice. For sure, he was respected, and in some circles, feared. But there was also another side to him with compassion for those whom he thought had been taken advantage of because they were Indians—this was the West and that's what they were called—or Chinese who had come to serve in whatever way they could after the gold was found.

He was a frontiersman who befriended the Native People and could communicate in Chinook jargon, their trade language in the Pacific Northwest. It came in handy and helped in legal matters with them and it didn't matter if they were the accused or the victim. He treated them all the same.

In 1860 Begbie told those in government that the Indians held aboriginal title to their land and this had to be recognized by the law. He would often commute their death sentences and not once did he ever do so for a white man who had been convicted of murder. He forced legislation to ensure Native women would share in the estates of their white partners, married or not, which was unheard of. One time he convicted a miner from California based solely on Native testimony; such a thing was not allowed in California courts.

Begbie went against the grain.

In 1865 he held court in every corner of his domain and in that one year alone it's estimated he rode 3,500 miles—or more than 5,000 kilometers—on horseback. He was known to walk hundreds of miles at a time just to become familiar with the rivers and valleys and exactly what he was dealing with in this land. He would put up his tent and spend the night after shooting game or catching fish for his dinner and sometimes he had to serve as counsel for both the defence *and* prosecution—and at the same time yet. His job was to uphold the law.

But Matthew Begbie wasn't American and didn't even ply his trade in the United States, although they knew about him down there. Everybody knew about him. He was an Englishman. The British had appointed him Chief Justice of the Crown Colony of British Columbia and he came to the interior of BC when it was still a colony of the British Empire. He was 39, a bachelor, and a bachelor he would remain for life. But in no small way he helped pave the way for BC to join confederation and in the process they named all kinds of things after him. There was Sir Matthew Begbie Elementary School in Vancouver and even mountains like Mount Begbie which is the biggest one to be seen from Revelstoke. There were also smaller peaks such as Begbie Summit, the highest point on the Cariboo Highway, and if that wasn't enough there were two lakes and a creek named for Judge Begbie.

In New Westminster they named a street after him. And a public square and a tavern. But the big thing was that magnificent statue in front of the city's courthouse and the likeness was a perfect match with the old photos. It was definitely him—Sir Matthew Baillie Begbie—and there was another statue in Vancouver outside the Law Society of British Columbia. It was fitting because the man pretty much wrote the law around here and for more than a hundred years everything was all fine and good.

Until they took it away.

In 1958 the National Film Board of Canada did a 30-minute docudrama about Begbie called *The Legendary Judge* and it started this way: "He was the form and substance of British justice sent out from England to challenge the wild west." The very first frame displayed the British Columbia coat of arms with the Latin SPLENDOR SINE OCCASU at the bottom; it translates to 'splendour without diminishment' and means the sun never sets over the British Empire.[66]

When he arrived exactly one century earlier, in 1858, he was the first and only judge in all of BC. His court was the Fraser canyon and everything beyond which meant Cariboo country. Gold had been discovered along the Fraser River and that spring 1,000 ounces was sent for processing to the San Francisco mint. Once word got out thousands of miners showed up and along with them came a certain commodity.

Trouble.

In January, 1947 the first edition of Volume II of *The British Columbia Historical Quarterly* was released. Published by the Archives of British Columbia in cooperation with the British Columbia Historical Association, it ran a series of essays and the lead essay was "*Dear Sir Matthew: A Glimpse of Judge Begbie.*" The author, historian Sydney G. Pettit, said the discovery of gold in the spring of 1858 led to 25,000 to 30,000 adventurers flocking to BC, "among them a lawless element of gamblers, claim-jumpers, and gunmen who were accustomed to scoff at the law and deride its officers."[67]

In his essay historian Pettit—he retired from the faculty of the University of Victoria 25 years later in 1972—described his subject: "Fearless and incorruptible, he made his name a terror to evil-doers who, rather than face his stern and impartial justice in the Queen's court, abstained from violence or fled the country, never to return."[68]

Directly below the title of that 1947 edition of *The British Columbia Historical Quarterly* were these words: "Any country worthy of a future should be interested in its past." We should keep this message in mind when examining Matthew Begbie's contributions to the building and formation of Canada's most western province. He played no small role in bringing BC into the fold of confederation and making sure it didn't become part of the United States which at the time was a distinct possibility.

The son of an army colonel, Begbie was born in 1819 on a British ship en route to the island of Mauritius. He lived there until returning to Great Britain at the age of seven. He graduated from the University of Cambridge, his area of study mathematics and the classics, and later became a successful lawyer in London.

When he eventually arrived in British Columbia he was the first judge—in *all* of BC—and would remain a judge for 36 years. What's more, for the first 12 years he would be the *only* judge in that vast territory.

It brings to mind the image of a solitary Clint Eastwood riding into an indiscriminate desert town in one of those spaghetti westerns except the man with no name was a cold-blooded killer who smoked long, narrow cigars while Begbie was a judge of more refined taste.

He preferred pipes.

He would hear his cases sitting on a log or high on the saddle, always with the judge's black robe and wig, the symbols of his office, and those symbols were important. Well known and respected in the toughest regions of the colony, he was knighted by Queen Victoria in 1875 before spending his later years in the courtroom which is now part of BC's Maritime Museum in Victoria. Long after his death they were still calling it *his* courtroom and for good reason.

Begbie is responsible for much of the early legislation in the fledgling province-to-be of British Columbia. The list is long and includes the Aliens Act of 1859, the Gold Fields Act of 1859, and the Pre-emption Act of 1860. Those statutes had to do with immigration, commerce and settlement. In 1866 he ruled that a law imposing high licence fees discriminated against Chinese because laundries at the time were the purview of this group of newcomers and he felt they were getting a raw deal.

But one case in particular—and a great many years after the fact—ultimately brought down the gavel on the very man who first wielded such an instrument of law in this part of the country. It meant once again that history is erased and the good name of our hero, be it Gary Cooper or Clint Eastwood take your pick, suffers a fall from grace and lands with a resounding thud in the land of purgatory. Or to use another word—disgrace—and it's all done in a way that only a self-flagellating country like Canada can conceive.

When gold was discovered in the Fraser Valley and tens of thousands of miners flocked to the interior of BC., life for those who dwelled there changed overnight. The Fraser River Basin was home to Indigenous communities. In the north were the Dakelh or Carrier People. To the west were the Wet'Suwet'en and to the south the Tsilhquot'n and Shuswap. To the far south of the basin were the St'at'im, the Nlaka'Pamux, and the Okanagan. On the coast, on the southwest, and taking it in what now constitutes Vancouver and all its environs and beyond were the Coast Salish.

In 1856 a member of the Shuswap, now known as the Secwepemc, discovered the gold but it was kept quiet until a sample was sent to San Francisco. Then word got out and in came the miners from California. Not all the miners were from there, but most were, with numbers said to be as high as 40,000 or even 50,000. No one really knows how many came.

Salmon fishing was vital to the Natives and they had fought their own inter-tribal wars over it. One of the worst massacres ever to occur in what is now Canada happened in 1745 in the Dakhel village of Chinlac and it was about salmon. The dispute was between the Dakhel and the neighbouring Tsilhquot'in, or as they came to be known, *Chilcotin*.

An account of the horrors and atrocities that took place was put in writing by Adrien Gabriel Morice, a priest who lived from 1859 to 1938. Morice came to British Columbia from France and learned the Carrier language of the Dakhel. He later produced a dictionary of the language and grew accustomed with their oral histories. In his book *The History of the Northern Interior of British Columbia (formerly New Caledonia), (1660 to 1880,)*, published in 1906, he described the Chinlac massacre in all its gory detail. The chief of the Dakhel village had been away only to return to the aftermath later. Wrote Morice:

The spectacle which met Khadintel's eyes on his return to his village was indeed heart-rending. On the ground, lying bathed in pools of blood, were the bodies of his own two wives and of nearly all his countrymen, while hanging on transversal poles resting on stout forked sticks planted in the ground, were the bodies of the children ripped open and spitted through the out-turned ribs in exactly the same way as salmon drying in the sun. Two such poles were loaded from end to end with that gruesome burden.[69]

Morice, who would later receive honorary degrees from two Canadian universities for his work with the Dakhel, said that any women who survived the day's events were taken off into slavery which was the custom. Three years later the Dakhel chief *Khadintel* avenged the massacre with his own attack on the Chilcotin and the carnage was no less. The Dakhel erected three poles of dead and mutilated children and the point was made. The old story of an eye for an eye often happened in inter-tribal warfare, especially between the Chilcotin and Dakhel. Many years later, in 1826 and 1827, there was yet more violence and brutality between the two in which "scalping and mutilation were practiced on both sides."[70]

But when the miners came with the gold rush once again there would be huge impact on the salmon fishery only this time it would be from the white man.

In 1846 the Oregon Treaty established the 49th parallel as the border between the United States and the western reaches of British North America, with all of Vancouver Island still remaining in British hands. The treaty meant that the states of Washington and Oregon officially became part of the US. Three years later, in 1849, the British set up Fort Victoria as a show of strength. The invasion of the miners—'invasion' pretty much sums it up—led to problems and one of them was about salmon. The miners occupied Native fishing sites and encroached on the salmon fishery. In their search for gold the miners would wash gravel through their mining sluices and this diverted the waters of rivers, creeks and lakes, which impacted the spawning grounds of the salmon. Whether that was the cause of the Chilcotin War or merely one aspect of it is up for discussion, but one thing is for sure. It would lead to the deadliest series of attacks by Indigenous People on immigrants in western Canada.

Ever.

In 1864 a businessman named Alfred Waddington wanted to build a road west of Williams Lake in the interior of BC and a road crew started working on it, but this was in Tsilhqot' territory and soon there was bloodshed even though some members of the Tsilhqot' were working on the road themselves. Over several days, a score of killings took place, nine of them in one fell swoop during the early morning of April 30 when the men were "shot or bludgeoned to death in their tents" as they slept.[71] The war party then moved to an advance camp where more murders and atrocities occurred. When it was over, 21 people—mostly workers but also some settlers—were dead with many of their bodies mutilated.

All the dead were white men.

Mel Rothenburger, a journalist and one-time mayor of Kamloops, BC, wrote about it in his book *The Chilcotin War*. He described how crew foreman Willy Brewster was found shot with his head smashed and his belly ripped up. According to Rothenburger, Brewster's killers carved out his heart and ate it, and cut off his penis and stuck it in his mouth.[72] He says Brewster was singled out because he had threatened to infect the Tsilhqot' with smallpox after bags of flour had been stolen from his crew, and for the Tsilhqot' this was no idle threat. It's estimated that 20,000 of British Columbia's 60,000 Indigenous People had been killed by smallpox over the previous two years with the Tsilhqot' losing half their population.

The colonial government set up a search party and eventually brought in the alleged perpetrators of the massacre, including their leader, a chief named Klatsassin. As the story goes, the gold commissioner of the province had threatened to kill all the Tsilhqot men, women and children unless these men gave themselves up, and so, they did. But some say they had been tricked.

Nevertheless, Begbie was the trial judge for the case and the court records are all there. He questioned Klatsassin in his jail cell. There were also eyewitnesses to what happened, including from the Indigenous community, and a trial by jury resulted in guilty verdicts for five of the eight men who had been charged with murder. Later, a sixth man was tried and also found guilty. In those days a guilty verdict of murder carried the death penalty—it was automatic—and all those found guilty were hanged.

Between 1859 and 1872 Begbie presided over 52 murder charges and 38 resulted in guilty verdicts. He offered clemency to 11 of the 38 and seven of those 11 were Native. But Begbie never once recommended clemency for a white man who had been convicted and sentenced to hang.[73]

Fast forward to 1993 and a report of the Cariboo-Chilcotin Justice Inquiry which examined the relationship between Indigenous Peoples of the Cariboo-Chilcotin and the justice system of BC. One recommendation in that report was a posthumous pardon for the six 'chiefs' although it is questionable if all of them were really chiefs, but that is beside the point. These men had been hanged in 1864. Said the report: "That episode of history has left a wound in the body of the Chilcotin society. It is time to heal the wound."[74]

More than two decades later British Columbia Premier Christy Clark and Prime Minister Justin Trudeau would both issue apologies for what transpired at the 1864 trial. In her statement Clark said the six chiefs were "fully exonerated of any crime or wrongdoing." Trudeau said much the same: "We now understand that the treatment of the Tsilhquot'in chiefs represented a betrayal of trust and injustice that has been carried by the Tsilhqot'in people for more than 150 years. And so these six native leaders, once convicted of murder, are fully exonerated of any crime or wrongdoing."

Thus, we then see a snowball effect. In 2014 Clark issued her apology and later that year a plaque was posted near the Fraser River in Quesnel, BC saying all those chiefs had been wrongfully hanged. In 2015 came the Truth and Reconciliation Commission report, and in 2018 the very public Trudeau apology. Add to that the 2020 murder of George Floyd and the Black Lives Matter movement and the rising Woke perspective on history where everything Indigenous is deemed good and everything white, colonial and settler is bad, and the future of Matthew Begbie's name was a done deal.

I went online to look for the actual wording of that plaque in Quesnel and had trouble finding it. But then it finally showed up under this headline: *Legacy of the crimes of British colonialists.*' The plaque said: "The Tsilhqot'in object to the chiefs being tried as criminals and continue to maintain that this was a territorial dispute between two warring nations." It went on to say: "This commemorative plaque honours those who lost their lives in defence of the territory and the traditional way of life of the Tsilhqot'in and to express the inconsolable grief that has been collectively experienced at the injustice the Tsilhqot'in perceive was done to their chiefs." [75]

Only after taking down those words did I notice what website I had chanced upon. It was none other than the site for the Marxist-Leninist Party of Canada!

As far as the good name of Matthew Begbie is concerned, the floodgates were now open for him to become the fall guy. But not everyone saw it that way. This is what Peter Shawn Taylor wrote in his chapter on Begbie in *The 1867 Project: Why Canada Should Be Cherished—Not Cancelled*. It was published by the Aristotle Foundation for Public Policy in 2023.

> What the law originally found to be a mass murder of 18 unsuspecting road workers and settlers is now officially recognized as a war between nations fully justified on the basis of a bio-terror threat, and which was lost only because of deception on the part of the white army. The final requirement for this new narrative affirming the natives as victims is the transformation of Begbie into a villain. His punishment is to have his reputation rubbished and his name scrubbed from the province's road maps and lobbies.[76]

And this is what happened.

Never mind that it was trial by jury which meant the members of the jury decided things and, as the presiding judge, Begbie's duty was to uphold the verdict and pronounce sentence. In 1864 the law was that if you were found guilty of murder, you hanged.

Never mind that two other members of the Tsilhqot helped find those who had been involved in the massacre and on the run, and that other non-Tsilhqot Indigenous People had tended to the survivors.

Or that one of the most descriptive testimonies of the attacks had come from a Clahoose Native who said the execution of the six was justified and that his own people had been "nearly annihilated" by Tsilhqot'in.

After the verdict was read it was up to the governor—not Judge Begbie—to grant clemency if he saw fit. And he did not. But in recent years the legacy of Begbie has paid the price. Leaders from the Tsilhqot'in community have had him in their crosshairs since the 1993 Cariboo-Chilcotin Justice Inquiry. Said Peter Shawn Taylor: "In the years that followed the case for exoneration was built on the unsubstantiated assumption that the killings were an honourable act of war, not murder."[77]

In 2001 the University of Victoria removed Begbie's name from the school's law building and after that a small statue of him in front of the building went missing. In 2008 a mural on the walls of the British Columbia Legislature was hidden from public view and to this day it remains hidden. The mural was said to portray Begbie. But according to historian John Lutz, a history professor at the University of Victoria who was on the panel that discussed the matter, it wasn't Begbie at all but a colonial military officer. It didn't matter. Even one who might *appear* to be him was now fair game.

Then, in 2017, the great statue of Begbie on his horse in the front lobby of the Law Society of British Columbia building in Vancouver was purged, as was a plaque that read: "His 36 years of fearless and impartial service made a lasting contribution to the administration of justice in the Pacific region of Canada."

No longer.

Those who had inspired all this—modern-day Tsilhqot'in leaders—then demanded even more. An entity calling itself the 'Tsilhquot'in National Government' of Williams Lake wanted Begbie's name removed from *all* public places "because he wrongfully convicted six Tsilhquot'in war chiefs of murder and sentenced them to death."[78]

As usual, the media played its sorry role in this sad misrepresentation of history. When Begbie's 'controversial' statue was removed from the BC Law Society, CTV News reported on June 3, 2017: "The Society previously featured the statue of Judge Matthew Begbie, who wrongfully convicted six Tsilhquotin War Chiefs of murder in 1864, sentencing them to death by hanging. The Law Society announced in April that it would remove the statue that is a negative symbol of the province's colonial past and replace it with a more inclusive image."

What's more, Chief Joe Alphonse got quoted in the story. He said: "The Tsilhquotin continue to honour the six War Chiefs who defended their territory and traditional way of life against a foreign aggressor."

Today the Tsilhqot'in Nation celebrates Klatsassin Memorial Day on the anniversary of the man's hanging back in 1864, Klatsassin being the one behind the massacre.

On July 7, 2019, Global News reported on "Begbie's role in the wrongful hanging of five Tsilhquot'in Nation chiefs in 1864."

On September 12, 2019, *The New Westminster Record* went one step further after a city councillor in the community moved that Begbie Square and Begbie Street ought to be renamed. "Thumbs up to New Westminster city Coun. Chuck Puchmary for his motion to have Begbie Square and Begbie Street renamed after Chief Ahan Square and Chief Ahan Street." This meant more plaudits for two of the Tsilhqot'in who had been involved in killing 21 people and mutilating their bodies.

Thus, the local newspaper was *endorsing* a motion to rename the square and street after perpetrators of the massacre. There would also be a move to change the name of a secondary school in New Westminster and name it after one of those who got hanged. And that wasn't the only school.

Late in 2022 Sir Matthew Begbie Elementary School in Vancouver was renamed and given an Indigenous moniker. According to a news report from Global News on December 9, 2022, the school would henceforth be called wəkʷanˀəs tə syaqʷəm which means "the sun rising over the horizon."

Sam Sullivan was the mayor of Vancouver from 2005 to 2008 after serving many years as a city councillor. He was twice elected as a Member of the Legislative Assembly of British Columbia and a member of the provincial Cabinet. He is also a member of the Order of Canada and founder of the Sam Sullivan Disability Foundation. Both his mother and his wife attended Sir Matthew

Begbie Elementary School when they were children and he, for one, is not happy with the name change. He's also not happy about what has happened to the legacy of British Columbia's first judge.

After the Law Society of British Columbia in Vancouver and New Westminster City Council both decided to remove their statues of Begbie, Sullivan was so incensed that he made a video. In the video he spoke about how the gold rush resulted in the formation of British Columbia. He spoke about the brutal, inter-tribal conflicts among the Indigenous People themselves. He spoke glowingly of Begbie and of his many contributions and how he supported the Native population and minorities like the Chinese.

"While just south of the border the US Army waged a dozen wars against Indigenous people, Judge Begbie risked his life in hostile environments for a more just society," said Sullivan in his video. "With a legal system that owes so much to him in a province whose very existence depended on the force of his personality, one must wonder if the justice he worked so hard for was done."[79]

Sullivan was in the room when then BC Premier Christy Clark made her apology in 2014 and said he was "shocked" hearing her words about the exoneration. He also said that the Law Society of British Columbia made its decision to remove the Begbie statue "in secret" and that there were no opportunities for legal historians to defend the man.

Sullivan is not the only one upset with the Law Society's actions.

Hamar Foster is Professor emeritus, Law, at the University of Victoria, and considered one of Canada's leading legal historians. He has written five books and more than 50 articles about the legal history of Indigenous and Non-Indigenous relations in western Canada. He contributed a lengthy essay for the book

'Voicing Identity: Cultural Appropriation and Indigenous Issues,' published by University of Toronto Press in 2022. The title of his essay was 'Sharp as a Knife: Judge Begbie and Reconciliation' and the subject was the decision by the Law Society of British Columbia to remove the statue of Begbie.

In this essay Foster makes several points:

1. In its report the Law Society of British Columbia said that Begbie "found (the Tsilhquot'in warriors) guilty" of murder and "ordered their execution," but this was not so since the jury found them guilty and at the time death was the mandatory sentence for murder.
2. The colonial governor, not Begbie, had the discretion to commute the death sentences and in Begbie's own report he wrote to the governor and said, "I do not envy you your task of coming to a decision" about whether to carry out the executions.
3. In Hamar Foster's own words: "After the decision to remove the statue was announced I spoke to a number of people, and almost everyone, lawyers included, whose only source of information about the events of 1864 was the media, believed that the decision to convict and sentence the men to hang was Begbie's, and his alone. Which is not true. Some also did not know what the hanged men were alleged to have done."

The report by the Law Society of British Columbia concluded that Begbie "epitomizes the cruelty of colonization" and his relationship with Indigenous people was "negative." Not so, said Foster. He said he's been researching and writing about British Columbia's legal history for over 40 years and had only come across one example of an Indigenous person saying anything negative about Begbie. That was in 1879 when a man who had just killed a constable called the judge a "grey-headed son of a bitch."

What does Hamar Foster—Professor emeritus, Law, at the University of Victoria, and perhaps the no. 1 expert in British Columbia on that province's legal history—conclude with regards to the Begbie saga?

"His record is much better than that of his contemporaries in Australia, the US, and the rest of Canada. And when his career is subjected to close examination, he stands out as both insightful and sympathetic when compared to most British Columbians of his day."

When I spoke with Foster he said the Chilcotin had very legitimate grievances about what happened in 1864 and rattled off their not being consulted about the road, the threat of smallpox, and sexual assaults against their women. As for the 21 white men who were killed and mutilated, he said the Chilcotin, in their own minds, thought of this as warfare and what transpired back then was "fairly standard fare."

But Hamar Foster has a major beef with how the Law Society of British Columbia made its decision about the Begbie statue. He said the full membership was not consulted and the benchers who rendered the decision did so based on an "incredibly one-sided report" prepared by the advisory committee. Foster also mentioned something else. He said he used to write a column about legal history for *Bar Talk*, the online publication of the BC Branch of the Canadian Bar Association, but quit doing that after they refused to publish a column he wrote about Begbie.

In other words, if you don't have something nasty to say about someone who's been cancelled, you are not free to express your view—even for one who is Professor emeritus, Law, at the University of Victoria.

The first biography about Begbie was by David R. Williams, a lawyer who wrote ten books, including novels. Williams had an abiding interest in history, especially in his home province of BC. In his 1977 book 'The Man for a New Country' Williams writes: "No other judge in Canada combines an historical reputation of national proportions—Canada might, without Begbie and a few others, have had its western boundary at the Rocky Mountains—with a distinguished contribution to the framing and shaping of this country's jurisprudence."[80]

Williams began the book describing two statues that once flanked the main entrance to the Parliament Buildings in Victoria.

> Set in niches, each larger-than-lifesize figure gazes with unblinking eyes over the Inner Harbour to the distant hills of Lower Vancouver Island. On the left, as one ascends the broad stone staircase to the arched entrance, stands Sir James Douglas, the first Governor of British Columbia, and on the right, robed and bewigged, stands Sir Matthew Baillie Begbie, its first Chief Justice. The statues of other notable personages in British Columbia history are ranged about the walls of the Parliament Buildings which were completed in 1898, but Begbie and Douglas have been given pride of place. The people of this province in this fashion acknowledged the obligation owed these men; without them, Columbia might not have remained British Columbia.[81]

So, according to those in the know, what is the bottom line here? Just this. If not for Matthew Begbie, there might not be a British Columbia today, at least, not as part of the country that sits immediately north of the United States. He was that instrumental, significant and important to the creation of the province and what it has become. And for this he is now deemed a villain.

Indeed, if Begbie had been American they would have made a movie about him with Gary Cooper in the starring role. You can see him riding into the big screen sitting tall and erect in the saddle, the judge's hat atop his head, the black cloak billowing in the wind behind him, and with his firm hand and complete and uncompromising devotion to the law, this incorruptible public servant brings justice to a harsh country. He lives on the land and becomes one with the people who have long been there. Firm but fair, he dispenses the law and is admired everywhere he goes. As for the history, it's all there—fully documented and laid out—with the cases, testimonies, verdicts, and the legislation he wrought himself. When he dies there is a huge funeral and a sense of public grief and then they build statues of him and name mountains after him and his legacy is steeped in honour and respect forever after. After all, this man is an American hero.

But in Canada we do things differently.

PART III

The Hijacking of Our History

CHAPTER 10

Was Winston Churchillian

I ENVY WINSTON CHURCHILL. He died in 1965 at the age of 90 and I remember watching his funeral on TV, but my envy has nothing to do with his distinguished leadership during World War II. It's that he could trace his family through so many generations. His father, Lord Randolph Churchill, was son of the 7th Duke of Marlborough and that line goes way back, while his mother Jennie Spencer-Churchill was an American socialite. When they attach the word 'socialite' to your name it means you come from money, but his father's side is what interests me.

Winston was a direct descendant of John Churchill who was the Duke of Marlborough, not to mention 1st Prince of Mindelheim, 1st Count of Nellenburg, and Prince of the Holy Roman Empire, and while I don't admit to being up on all those titles, they sound important. The Duke lived from 1650 to 1722, but the family lineage goes back even further because he was the son of another man also named Winston Churchill who was born in 1620 and, like his namesake, a politician. You can trace the family bloodlines all the way to the 12th century and what keeps turning up is one prominent person after another.

I can't do that. The little to be found is made even more difficult because the spelling of my family name isn't consistent with any documents I dig up. There is Amernic, Amernick, Emenek, Omenik and more variations still, and this is only back to my great-grandparents—poor Jews in eastern Europe—which is as far as we can go. I confess that my father removed the 'k' from the name so at least we know that one generation back it was Amernick.

Alas, no Dukes, Barons or Lords in this family tree, which isn't surprising for two reasons. First, there isn't a drop of blood from the United Kingdom anywhere down the line. Second, there is no wealth to speak of either. Now at one time, before the digital age came upon us, I was researching the family surname on my father's side and, lo and behold, discovered Amernick's Meat Market in the Manhattan telephone directory. For those of more recent vintage who may not know, that is what we used to call the white pages—a listing of registered, residential, telephone numbers. You could find the phone number for virtually anyone as long as their number was listed. From my vantage point this was very big news because I knew of no person outside my immediate family who had the name Amernic. With or without the 'k'.

Not one individual.

And so, I called them up, figuring we must be cousins. Unfortunately, that wasn't the case. They turned out to be two Italian families who had merged their surnames for the good of the business! Despite the letdown, I used this little anecdote as the lead for a magazine piece about tracing family roots.

The point I'm trying to make about Winston Churchill—full name Sir Winston Leonard Spencer-Churchill—is that perhaps the man may be forgiven for thinking he was hot stuff, and I'm talking long before he became Prime Minister of the United Kingdom. He was, of course, a master orator, consummate communicator, and an excellent writer who in 1953 was awarded the Nobel Prize in Literature for "his mastery of historical and biographical description as well as for brilliant oratory in defending exalted human values."[82]

Churchill wrote many books and one of the first was *My African Journey*, published in 1908. He was in his early thirties at the time, and the book was about his travels to Kenya and Uganda. If you check it out on Amazon you'll see that it offers "a rich blend of historical insight and personal experience." The International Churchill Society, established three years after his death in 1968, has a mandate "to preserving the historical legacy of Sir Winston Churchill." If you go on the website it says this about the book: "Those who impute racism to Churchill have never read the enlightened views expressed over East Africa in this entertaining travelogue."

Indeed.

I have always been a big fan of Churchill and often referred to him when I was conducting communications seminars because the man was truly a master of words. And then I read My African Journey. One passage in particular jumped out at me.

> It is unquestionably an advantage that the East African negro should develop a taste for civilized attire. In no more useful and innocent direction could his wants be multiplied and his desires excited, and it is by this process of assimilation that his life will gradually be made more complicated, more varied, less crudely animal, and himself raised to a higher level of economic utility.[83]

I couldn't believe what I was reading. This was *Winston Churchill* for God's sake! But there it was.

In 2002 the BBC undertook a poll throughout the United Kingdom to see who was the greatest Briton of all time and, according to the votes, he came in first. Other notables such as Charles Darwin (fourth) and William Shakespeare (fifth) each garnered about one-tenth as many votes as Churchill did, while Isaac Newton (sixth) got much less than that. It's been said that during the Battle of Britain when the German Luftwaffe was pummelling London every night Churchill picked up the English language and threw it into battle. The leadership he exhibited during the war is legendary. But it's also apparent that Churchill, at least the young Churchill, was of a certain family lineage and *breeding* that the above passage from My African Journey indicated what he thought of Africans at the time.

If that passage doesn't come off as racist, it sounds pretty close, but then I'm looking at these words from the purview of the third decade of the 21st century. I'm also looking at them *not* from one who is descended from a long line of Lords, Dukes and Barons, as was Churchill. In short, we must consider the *context* of what he was saying and, more importantly, *when* he said it.

In 1908, the year that book was published, people did not fly all over the word to places like Africa. In fact, 1908 was only five years after bicycle mechanics Wilbur and Orville Wright flew for the first time in human history at Kitty Hawk, North Carolina. That same year explorers Robert Peary and Ernest Shackleton set out to discover the North Pole and South Pole; Shackleton didn't quite make his destination but got farther south than anyone before him, while Peary claims to have reached the North Pole only to be challenged by another explorer who says he got there. Also in 1908 Henry Ford produced the first Model T automobile at his production plant in Detroit and this would very much impact how people moved around. Meanwhile, in Canada that year the Royal Canadian Mint opened its doors in Ottawa; this was only 41 years after Confederation.

Thus, the times were different and I would imagine that virtually all readers of My African Journey had never been to Africa or knew much about it. What's more, when looking at Churchill's comments from today, we must recognize that the meaning of such words as *civilized* has changed over the years.

In the earlier chapter about Egerton Ryerson, retired history professor Ron Stagg, an acknowledged expert on 18th- and 19th-century Ontario, said at one time *civilized* meant something much different than what it means now. It referred to what was considered the third stage of development—after *nomadic* and *hunter-gatherer*—which according to leading pundits of the time described the levels Europeans had attained. In other words, it was a term associated with culture and anthropology—the study of human behaviour, cultures, societies, etc. Today, however, if someone says people should "develop a taste for civilized attire" it comes across as a blatant insult steeped in racism. So, when presented this way, Winston Churchill could be depicted as a racist.

Another word that has undergone a lot of change is *gay*. One time when my granddaughter Emma was about seven she was sleeping over at the house. Before she went to bed I took out this children's book that's been in our family since I was a little boy. The book was about a small horse named Rowdy. I was sitting on the edge of the bed reading to her and we got to the part where we learn all about Rowdy who is described as a "gay little colt."

Emma stood up with a start.

"*Rowdy was gay?*" she said.

A seven-year-old!

My wife and I sometimes watch old movies such as those Fred Astaire-Ginger Rogers musicals. One of the earlier ones, made in 1934, was *The Gay Divorcee*. Try explaining to a younger person today—never mind seven-year-olds, I'm talking Gen Z and Millennials—that it's very innocent, a light romantic comedy. I'm sure they'll come at it with a completely different take.

But if some person, especially one with an axe to grind, wished to portray Winston Churchill as a racist and bigot—never mind his warnings about Adolf Hitler long before anyone else said such things, never mind the British PM's stellar leadership during World War II—they could pore through his speeches, his books, and all his writings which are considerable and find things to fit their agenda. They would snatch a snippet of something he is purported to have said, or take out of context a phrase from a speech or comment that he made, and make the case that this horrible man should not be honoured with statues, public squares, roads and highways and even cities that carry his name.

Alas, it is simple for anyone—informed or not—to go online and find allegations about Churchill advocating the use of poison gas in warfare, being a virulent anti-Semite, despising Mahatma Ghandi and all the people of India or—wait for this one—expressing admiration for Hitler! Put it altogether and hitch your wagon to others who take joy in cutting him down to size, and you have a movement.

Then it's like saying John A. Macdonald wanted to starve Canada's Indigenous population so we should write GENOCIDE in big red letters on his likeness wherever that likeness may appear.

Or we should knock down a statue of Egerton Ryerson because this awful man created residential schools.

Or change the name of Yonge-Dundas Square because Henry Dundas was a proponent of slavery.

Or damn anything associated with Edward Cornwallis because he was a warmonger who wanted the scalps of every Mi'kmaq man, woman and child out there.

Or Matthew Begbie should be renounced and eliminated because this despicable judge was responsible for hanging six innocent Chilcotin chiefs.

If it's on the Internet and if someone said it, then it must be true.

But Churchill was a monumental figure of the 20th century—maybe *the* monumental figure of the 20th century—and surely any young person today who graduates from a Canadian high school and is in university must know something about him and what he did. Well, sorry to disappoint. When I made my video interviewing first-year university students in Toronto and popped questions about World War II, I posited this one.

"Do you know who Churchill was?"

"Winston Churchill?" said the very first student I asked.

"Yes," I replied and then she looked off into space and laughed out loud.

She didn't know who he was, which prompted the young man next to her to issue something of an apology.

"Honestly it's embarrassing," he told me. "I know of the name and I know there's a statue of him near Nathan Phillips Square. There's probably one history class where they talked about him but I don't remember."

This was immediately after I had asked the two of them if they knew who the Allies were—they didn't—or if they knew who FDR was and they didn't know that either. With few exceptions, it was pretty much the same when I asked other students about the war. All of them first-year university students, almost all graduates from Ontario high schools. And yet, there are people today, many from the younger generation, who are quick to disclaim the name Winston Churchill.

A few years ago, shortly after the murder of George Floyd in the United States, a statue of Churchill was defaced during a Black Lives Matter demonstration in London. The words 'Churchill was a racist' were sprayed on the statue. Video footage showed the crowd chanting that over and over with protestors holding banners that said, 'British colonialism is to blame.' It got to the point where the statue had to be boarded up.

Closer to home, in June of 2024, a bronze, three-metre-tall statue of Churchill was unveiled in Calgary. It was the 80th anniversary of D-Day and Alberta Premier Danielle Smith presided over things with special guest Randolph Churchill III, the great grandson of the man himself, on hand. The statue was made possible with more than $300,000 raised by the Sir Winston Churchill Society of Calgary. Naturally, a group of protesters was present that day. Said one of them: "We don't think there should be a celebratory statue to this extremely controversial political figure.

This is 2024. Everything we put on these signs, these disgusting racist quotes, are things that are verifiable, incitable things that Winston Churchill said."[84]

Three years before then, when statues of John A. Macdonald were routinely being defaced and in some cases toppled across the country, a statue of Churchill in Edmonton got doused in red paint. This occurred in the wake of George Floyd and the rise of Black Lives Matter, not to mention the discovery of what were said to be "graves" at a residential school in Kamloops, BC. A young woman, poet laureate for the City of Edmonton no less, said this was all justified and then called for Churchill Square in the city to be renamed. In an interview with Global Television she said Churchill was known for not being opposed to "using poisoned gas against uncivilized tribes."[85]

Let's have a look at that.

In World War I, initially called The Great War, the Germans introduced the concept of poison gas as an instrument of war. When the war was over, a debate ensued about whether or not Britain should resort to using gas in a conflict against rebel tribesmen in northwest India and Mesopotamia, which is now Iraq. At the time Churchill was attached to the War Office and India was reluctant to use any type of gas against rebel tribesmen or anyone else. Churchill, however, was in favour of using *tear gas* and his words have since been misconstrued as an endorsement for the indiscriminate use of poison gas. This is what he said.

> I am strongly in favour of using poisoned gas against uncivilised tribes. The moral effect should be so good that the loss of life should be reduced to a minimum. *It is not necessary to use only the most deadly gasses*: gasses can be used which cause great inconvenience and would spread a lively terror and yet would leave *no serious permanent effects* on most of those affected.[86]

And then he added the following.

> If it is fair war for an Afghan to shoot down a British soldier behind a rock and cut him to pieces as he lies wounded on the ground, why is it not fair for a British artillery man to fire a shell which makes the said native sneeze?[87]

And so, this is what happens when you are wed to an ideology come hell or high water, and have no problem taking words and phrases out of context in order to achieve your ends. Or, to put things another way, how an enlightened man like Egerton Ryerson is deemed the creator of residential schools. Or a military man like Edward Cornwallis offered bounties for the scalps of Mi'kmaq women and children. Or a politician like John A. Macdonald starved untold thousands of Indigenous People in western Canada.

In actual fact, Ryerson did not create residential schools, Cornwallis never offered bounties for the scalps of Mi'kmaq women and children, and Macdonald never advocated policies with the intent of starving our Indigenous inhabitants. As far as the latter is concerned, Macdonald did just the opposite. He pushed for *more* government monies to go to famine relief after the disappearance of the buffalo herds, which is what triggered the food crisis out west in the first place. In the Canada of 1884 more money went to the cause of famine relief for Natives than to National Defence! It was the federal Liberal Party that wanted the government to spend less on the Indigenous file.

Not John A. Macdonald.

Unfortunately, what we often see today is that adherence to ideology overrides one's knowledge of history and exposure to the historical record—i.e., facts—prompting those who don't know better to take sides and wage battle. Another unfortunate thing is that there are people like this in public office, at all levels of government. This is why we get public policy based on error, innuendo, and to be perfectly blunt, lies about the past and it's no different with Winston Churchill.

One person who knew a thing or two about him was Sir Martin Gilbert.

Gilbert, who passed away in 2015, was a noted British historian, which is putting it mildly, and the official biographer of Churchill. He wrote the staggering total of 88 books. Among them are Churchill, A Life which is considered the definitive biography, along with other titles such as In Search of Churchill, Churchill—The Power of Words, Churchill and America, Winston Churchill's War Leadership, Churchill's Political Philosophy, and Churchill and the Jews.

In addition to all his work on Churchill, Gilbert was, arguably, the world's foremost chronicler of the Holocaust and it was in this capacity that I happened to meet him. At the time I was immersed in research for a novel I intended to write about the last living survivor of the Holocaust. The story would take place in the near future, in the year 2039, when knowledge about what had been dealt to European Jews during World War II is at record lows. I had just read Gilbert's epic book The Holocaust—A History of the Jews of Europe During the Second World War, which is almost 1,000 pages. For those who like to read history and are interested in World War II, it ranks right up there with The Rise and Fall of the Third Reich by William Shirer, a masterpiece which I admit having been through three times.

Luck would have it that Gilbert was doing a stint as a visiting professor at the University of Western Ontario in London, Ontario, a two-hour drive from my Toronto home. This was around the time when the institution was changing its name to Western University which is what it goes by today. While I graduated from the University of Toronto, I was familiar with the school having done one year there when enrolled in the journalism program.

I heard Gilbert speak and when he was finished I approached him and mentioned my novel which would be called *The Last Witness*. He seemed interested and with his wife accompanying him the three of us then met in a university cafeteria. Martin Gilbert was a true gentleman and could not have been nicer. Here was a man who had been knighted by HRH Prince Charles, a world-class historian of the first magnitude who had received 15 honourary degrees from universities in four different countries. He was Churchill's official biographer and the author of all those books. He didn't know me from Adam, but still took the time to chat. What's more, he agreed with my underlying premise that knowledge of the Holocaust was waning and waning rapidly, and even offered ideas for the plot of my novel.

Some time after that I saw him again at a book signing for his latest work on Churchill, *Will of the People—Winston Churchill and Parliamentary Democracy*. What I remember about that event was standing in line to receive an autographed copy from the author, and directly behind me in the line was a recognizable face.

Conrad Black.

Martin Gilbert's website is still active today and what he says there about the role of the historian is worth a look.

"What happened in the past is unalterable and definite. To uncover it—or as much of it as possible—the historian has several tools, among them chronology, documentation, memoirs, and the vast apparatus of scholarly work in which others have delved and laboured in the same vineyard."[88]

As far as the Holocaust is concerned, Gilbert's formidable book should be required reading for any course on World War II. It includes photographs and maps, each map specially prepared by Gilbert himself to locate every single place he mentions in the book. To call him meticulous would be an understatement and he took the same approach with everything he wrote. His website also says this.

"As a historian of the human condition, I have always tried to give a place and a name to those on whose shoulders fell the burden of the decisions of others—their rulers and their commanders—and those who did their duty without questioning, or seldom questioning, either the cause or the plan. Their stories deserve to be told in every generation, as an integral part of war, and as a testimony to human suffering and to the human spirit."[89]

I can only imagine how Martin Gilbert would have reacted to seeing a statue of Churchill defaced in England or, for that matter, statues of John A. Macdonald defaced and toppled in Canada. For sure, he would have been appalled. He would have been absolutely horrified. Gilbert, you see, had strong ties to Canada and always said he had a soft spot in his heart for this country.

He was born in London, England to parents who were Jewish refugees from Czarist Russia. World War II broke out when he was three years old and the family went to Cornwall to get away from the German bombing. The next year he was evacuated with thousands of other children to Canada where they would be safe. He lived with a foster family in Toronto for four years, returning to England in 1944 as a seven-year-old, and the family was reunited. They spent the last year of the war in Wales.

This is something else Martin Gilbert said: "One has to try to keep politics out of history, but history has implications for politics."[90]

Touché. When statues of such historical figures as Ryerson, Macdonald, Cornwallis and Begbie are town down or removed in Canada, it really has nothing to do with history because the people acting this out invariably don't know their history. They don't know the history at all. But this tearing down of our historical record has everything to do with politics. And ideology.

The same can be said for organizations that claim to be open and progressive, and are quick to accept government funding, when in fact they are steeped in racism from the get-go and ideology is the cloud that hangs over everything they say and do. This is why a group can call itself Moms Against Racism and put on seminars showing how hypocritical it actually is because of the inherent anti-white, anti-Canadian bias that permeates its core. This is why a conference that claims to foster such noble principles as equity, diversity, inclusion and anti-racism can deliver programs called 'The Unbearable Whiteness of Being' and remain oblivious to that same hypocrisy.

Martin Gilbert was not only an eminent historian par excellence, but he also lived through the war and his personal experience had great influence on his life's work. He visited many of those places where history was made. In 1952 he went to Vienna, Austria and then it was off to the Balkans and Turkey where he taught English. He travelled to Afghanistan and then India where he worked in an orphanage. In 1959 he visited Poland and while there went to see Treblinka. He travelled extensively and delivered lectures all over North America, not to mention such countries as Israel and the former Soviet Union, which is where he learned Russian. In 2004 he took a train all the way from Hong Kong to London, tracing the route of the Soviet gulag archipelago through Russia.

The man knew of what he wrote about and the person he was most familiar with from history is Winston Churchill. Gilbert once admitted that over a 20-year span—from 1968 to 1988—his research on all things Churchill involved reading "every page of an estimated fifteen *tons* weight of documentation." Gilbert said this revealed to him "every facet of policymaking, of success and failure, of friendship and opposition, of cause and effect, of mood and motive."[91]

When asked what aspects of Churchill's life needed more study, Gilbert mentioned the man's humanitarian and domestic policies, and pointed to the time Churchill served as Home Secretary. He said Churchill had pushed for clemency in capital murder cases, drastically reduced the practice of solitary confinement for prisoners, and, in fact, with his urging libraries made their first appearance in Britain's prisons. He also reduced the number of young men imprisoned each year from 12,000 to less than 4,000, and abolished automatic imprisonment for non-payment of fines; that in itself spared more than 60,000 people from having to serve short stretches in jail.[92]

According to Gilbert, one reason Churchill crossed the floor of the House of Commons to leave the Conservative Party and join the Liberals was Conservative enthusiasm for shooting 600 Tibetans who tried blocking a road during a British military advance into Tibet in 1904. Said Churchill at the time: "Surely it is wicked to do such things. Absolute contempt for the rights of others must be wrong. Are there any people in the world so mean-spirited as not to resist under the circumstances to which these poor Tibetans have been subjected?"[93]

Today Canada still honours and remembers Winston Churchill. There are statues of him in Edmonton, Halifax and Toronto. There is a bronze bust of him in Quebec City and another one in St. John's, Newfoundland. The largest underground powerhouse in the world is Churchill Falls in Labrador. There are high schools named after him in Toronto, Calgary and Lethbridge. There is Sir Winston Churchill Provincial Park in northern Alberta and Sir Winston Churchill Square in downtown Edmonton, the place which the poet laureate of that city said should be renamed because the man advocated the use of poison gas against human beings.

Alas, in the Canadian Rocky Mountains we have the Winston Churchill Range which sits in Jasper National Park, straddling the border between Alberta and British Columbia. It contains more than 30 peaks including Mount Columbia, the second tallest mountain in Canada's Rockies. The Athabasca Glacier, the most visited glacier in North America, is in the middle of the Winston

Churchill Range and for the past 125 years has been receding at an alarming rate.

No doubt, there are those who would like to change the name of that mountain range and there are some who might want to remove those statues in Edmonton, Halifax and Toronto. Not to mention the bronze busts in Quebec City and St. John's, and everything else that has the name Winston Churchill.

Churchill called Canada the "linchpin" between Britain and the United States. He once mused in a letter to his wife that if politics doesn't work out for him, he would consider retiring to the business world and do so in Canada.

Three times during World War II he met with US President Franklin D. Roosevelt on Canadian soil. In August of 1941, there was a secret meeting between the two aboard a US battleship off the coast of Newfoundland. Two years later, in August of 1943, Canadian Prime Minister Mackenzie King hosted a meeting with them in Quebec City and the leaders agreed on the invasion of Normandy, which would mark the turning point in the war the following year. Three months after D-Day, in September of 1944, another meeting between Churchill and FDR was held, again in Quebec.

But Churchill's most memorable visit to Canada was on December 30, 1941– three weeks after the Japanese attack on Pearl Harbor—when he addressed the House of Commons in Ottawa. The United States had just entered the war on the side of the Allies. Said Churchill:

> We have to win a world for our children. We have to win it by our sacrifices. We have not won it yet. The crisis is upon us. The power of the enemy is immense. If we were in any way to underrate the strength, the resources or the ruthless savagery of that enemy we should jeapordize not only our lives—for they will be offered freely—but the cause of

human freedom and progress to which we have vowed ourselves and all we have. We cannot for a moment, sir, afford to relax. In this strange, terrible world war there is a place for everyone, man and woman, old and young, hale and halt. Service in a thousand forms is open. There is no room now for the dilettante, for the weakling, for the shirker or the sluggard; the mine, the factory, the dockyard, the salt sea waves, the fields to till, the home, the hospital, the chair of the scientist, the pulpit of the preacher—from the highest to the humblest, the tasks are all of equal honour. All have their part to play. The enemies ranged against us, coalesced and combined against us, have asked for total war. Let us make sure they get it.[94]

The speech was, well, Churchillian and is considered one of the best of his career. Yes, it is easy to condemn when one knows only freedom and prosperity, and does not know the history, the times, the context, nor the man. How blissfully easy. But sad.

CHAPTER 11

Truth and reconciliation, falsehood and deception

A MAGNIFICENT STATUE of Joseph Brant stands in the old section of Brantford in southwestern Ontario. Three meters high and weighing 2,000 kilograms, the Joseph Brant Memorial Statue towers over the middle of Victoria Park Square as a commanding presence honouring the man the city is named after. While Brantford is also the birthplace of hockey star Wayne Gretzky and the long-time home of Alexander Graham Bell, inventor of the telephone, the place was named for Brant.

Nothing was spared with the monument. Bronze for the statue was melted down from cannons that had been used in the Battle of Waterloo and the Crimean War. A British sculptor was commissioned at a cost of $16,000 to make the statue that was unveiled in an elaborate ceremony in 1886, the Lieutenant-Governor of Ontario presiding. And it's not only Brant. On either side of him are three life-sized figures; to his right, three chiefs of the Mohawk, Tuscarora and Oneida Nations, and to his left, those of the Seneca, Onondaga and Cayuga. Altogether they constitute the Six Nations of the Iroquois, also known as the *Haudenosaunee*, which played no small part in the history of Canada.

Brant—his Mohawk name was *Thayendanegea*—lived from 1742 to 1807. During the American Revolution he was a steadfast British ally fighting for the Crown in North America. In 1780 the British commissioned him as a captain. He visited England to argue for

Mohawk interests when meeting King George III. He also met with George Washington and is widely revered as a great Mohawk leader and statesman. After the war he led Mohawk Loyalists and other Indigenous people to a tract of land on the Grand River in southwest Ontario. This was land granted to the Six Nations as compensation for their losses in the war.

The listing for Joseph Brant on Wikipedia—not a trustworthy source of information, but sometimes reflective of public sentiment—says he is "Perhaps the best known Native American of his generation."

There is another statue of Brant in Ottawa and on the plaque below that one it says, 'A Founding Father of Canada.' Also in the nation's capital is a distinguished portrait of him hanging in the National Gallery of Canada. What's more, schools are named after him, not to mention Joseph Brant Hospital and Joseph Brant Museum, both in Burlington, Ontario. To my knowledge, no one has ever defaced or toppled a statue of Joseph Brant.

Nevertheless, I have heard it said—and to my face—that education pioneer Egerton Ryerson was a slaveowner. Not true. And Scottish politician Henry Dundas, whose name became attached to many things in Toronto, was as well. This also is not true. I have been told that our first prime minister, John A. Macdonald, was a slaveowner and there are people who actually believe this. However, none of it is true.

But Joseph Brant *was* a slaveowner and the count is somewhere between 30 and 40 slaves.

While the names of those other figures are sullied and besmirched to the point where statues erected to honour them get defaced, decapitated, toppled, what have you—and streets and public squares named after them are expunged and given new names—there is no criticism of a real-life slaveowner who happened to be Mohawk and a prominent Native leader.

Indeed, while the Ottawa statue of Joseph Brant inscribes him, in bronze, as a *Founding Father of Canada*, the country's foremost founding father—John A. Macdonald—is decried as a racist at the Parks Canada-administered Bellevue House in Kingston. His statues are either boarded up for fear of vandalism or toppled and removed.

As for Egerton Ryerson, in his case insult is added to injury. Tyendinaga Mohawk Warriors were front and centre in vandalizing and tearing down his statue at the former Ryerson University in Toronto. A Mohawk flag was draped around the desecrated statue and the decapitated head of Ryerson wound up on top of a spike in a Mohawk compound. The campaign against him was waged to wrongfully vilify and convict him as the creator of residential schools when the historical record says otherwise.

How do we know Joseph Brant owned slaves? A book 'The Refugee: or the Narratives of Fugitive Slaves in Canada' was published in 1856. The author, Benjamin Drew, was an American educator and abolitionist who collected testimonies of more than 100 slaves who had escaped from the United States to what was then Canada West. One testimony was offered by Sophia Burthen Pooley, 90 years old at the time. She told Drew how she and her sister had been kidnapped from their home in Fishkill, New York and their kidnapper sold them to Mohawk Chief Joseph Brant who was then living in New York State. When the war was over and lost—as far as the British were concerned—Brant moved north, bringing his slaves with him. Pooley, who claimed in her testimony to have been abused by Brant's wife, lived with the family until she was 13 when Brant sold her for $100 to a white man named Samuel Hatt. She won her freedom in 1793 when John Graves Simcoe, the first Lieutenant-Governor of Upper Canada, passed a law to limit slavery. She then married a black man, Robert Pooley, who later abandoned her.

Many years on, the three-page testimony she gave to Benjamin Drew was expanded into a book by Andrew Hunter, a Hamilton writer and historian. *It Was Dark There All the Time: Sophia Burthen and the Legacy of Slavery in Canada* was published in 2022 by Goose Lane Editions. Hunter visited every location Pooley was known to have lived in or been to. His book hinted at sexual abuse in both the Brant and Hatt households, which was not uncommon with families owning slaves.

But we're talking about Joseph Brant here.

It doesn't matter. In the context of current historical revisionism as practiced in Canada, a slaveowner is glorified while progressive abolitionists are vilified. And it's all right as long as the race card is filled out properly.

There is no need to dwell further on the massacre of Macdonald at Bellevue House—historian and Macdonald expert Patrice Dutil has called it "a drive-by shooting"—but on the matter of historical figures and slavery Canadians can look south of the border and take a lesson from Mount Vernon in Virginia, which is the preserved estate of the aforementioned George Washington, first president of the United States. Washington's immense legacy includes his career as a politician, military general and businessman. But he was also a slaveowner with a workforce of hundreds of slaves on his vast property. Mount Vernon, which isn't run by any level of government and receives no tax dollars, doesn't whitewash anything from the man's past. On the grounds today is a slave memorial, cemetery and burial ground for enslaved and freed African-Americans who were connected to Mount Vernon. Note—when Washington died his will stipulated that those enslaved in his name be freed after the death of his widow.

No monument or tribute to Joseph Brant dares mention a word about his slaves. The Joseph Brant Museum in Burlington doesn't mention it and neither does the City of Brantford on its website or anywhere else. And why would it? Nor does any statue or plaque honouring Brant carry the word *controversial*. However, the Canadian Encyclopedia entry about Brant does refer to Sophia Pooley and Brant's slaves in a paragraph under the heading "Did You Know?"[95] And so do the Archives of Ontario under the heading 'Sophia Burthen Pooley—Part of the Family?' along with a photo of the 1856 book 'The Refugee' by Benjamin Drew.[96]

Brantford also happens to be where Canada's first residential school—the Mohawk Institute—opened in 1831. What started out as a day school for boys from the Six Nations began to accept boarding students that year, but it would be another half century before the federal residential school system, administered by the Canadian government and run by churches, got going. Exactly what transpired at those schools depends on where one draws the line between fact and fiction.

Sometimes that line is hard to define.

A good example illustrating what can happen when the latter—fiction—takes over from historical fact may be seen through an American example that involves a pillar of American culture. Baseball. And especially its origins.

Legend has it—as did the so-called historical record for a great many years—that baseball began with a man named Abner Doubleday in the town of Cooperstown, New York, and not only that, it happened in 1839. It was there and then that Mr. Doubleday is said to have drawn out the diagram of a baseball field, along with the rules of the game. Thus, we have baseball's creation myth which for the better part of a century was accepted as fact.

In 1939, exactly a hundred years after the proverbial virgin birth of the game, the National Baseball Hall of Fame and Museum opened its doors in Cooperstown, complete with the historic Doubleday Field—a real-life *Field of Dreams*—served up as bona fide American history. The biggest advocate of the story was none other than Franklin D. Roosevelt, President of the United States.

There was a great deal of ballyhoo across America leading up to the opening of the Hall of Fame in 1939. Said President Roosevelt in his proclamation: "General Doubleday was a distinguished soldier in the Civil War, but his part in giving us baseball shows again that peace has her victories no less renowned than war."[97] This was a few months before the outbreak of World War II. Abner Doubleday was indeed a military officer, a captain in the Union Army who gave the order to fire the first cannon in defense of Fort Sumter in North Carolina. That event set off the Civil War.

Linking him to baseball made for a good story.

On May 30, 1939—Memorial Day in the United States—24 members of the Doubleday family were on hand in Cooperstown to see a portrait of Abner Doubleday placed on the wall, right over the fireplace, on the first floor of the new National Baseball Hall of Fame and Museum. Two weeks later—on June 12—the US Congress and President Roosevelt commemorated the day as the official centennial of baseball.

But the tale about Doubleday and baseball wasn't true. So how did it begin?

In the early 1900s two schools of thought prevailed. Albert Spalding, a former pitcher who co-founded the Spalding sporting goods company, insisted that the game had been invented in America. It *had to be*. But another baseball pioneer, Henry Chadwick—he was born in England and came to the United States as a boy—said baseball had evolved over time from the old British game of rounders. In 1905 Spalding formed a commission to study the matter and since he was in charge the commission concluded that Abner Doubleday was the man.

A letter surfaced that had been prepared by another Abner—Abner Graves—relating the Cooperstown story and there was no questioning the character of this person. Graves would later shoot and kill his wife, which got him committed to an insane asylum, as those institutions were called then, and there he remained the rest of his life. But the whole Doubleday-Cooperstown saga, which for decades was reported in the media as historical fact and celebrated far and wide by Americans, not to mention occupants of the White House, started with Graves and his letter. As for the real Abner Doubleday, he died in 1893 after writing his memoirs which, curiously enough, contained not a word about baseball.

In 2011 Major League Baseball established the Baseball Origins Committee and the Doubleday story was debunked as myth once and for all. This may be a long way from the announcement of 'graves' being discovered at a residential school in Kamloops, BC, but one thing both episodes have in common is revising and *sensationalizing* history in order to meet a desired end. And do it with not a shred of evidence.

But that is what happened.

Notwithstanding the first residential school in Brantford in 1831, these federally-administered institutions endured from the 1890s to 1996 when the last one closed in Saskatchewan. It is believed that about 150,000 First Nation, Inuit and Métis children attended, and the year 1990 would serve as a pivotal turning point for how Canadians regarded the schools. In October that year, Barbara Frum of the CBC interviewed Chief Phil Fontaine from the Assembly of Manitoba Chiefs. In the interview he told her about the abuse he had experienced at a residential school—abuse of a physical, psychological and sexual nature. Understandably, the country was outraged and it wasn't long before a string of lawsuits got under way.

In 2005, when Paul Martin was Prime Minister, a settlement was negotiated with his Liberal government. Later, when Stephen Harper succeeded Martin as PM, the Conservative government of the day accepted that settlement and about $5 billion in compensation would be paid to some 80,000 claimants.

In 2007 Harper launched the Indian Residential Schools Settlement Agreement that would establish the Truth and Reconciliation Commission. The next year—on June 20, 2008—he issued his famous apology on behalf of the Government of

Canada to former residents of Indian Residential Schools. Said Harper in his statement: "This Commission presents a unique opportunity to educate all Canadians on the Indian Residential Schools System. It will be a positive step in forging a new relationship between Aboriginal peoples and other Canadians, a relationship based on the knowledge of our shared history, a respect for each other and a desire to move forward together with a renewed understanding that strong families, strong communities and vibrant cultures and traditions will contribute to a stronger Canada for all of us."

Fine words to be sure, but the end result has been something quite different from that lofty aspiration. In its report released in 2015 the Truth and Reconciliation Commission declared Canada to be "guilty of cultural genocide against Indigenous peoples" and came out with 94 recommendations.

In his initial apology Harper described the Indian Residential Schools as "a dark chapter in Canadian history," a sentiment largely accepted by the public. But everything changed, and changed drastically, on May 27, 2021. A Thursday. Rosanne Casimir, Chief of the Tk'emlúps te Secwépemc, or what had been known as the Kamloops Indian Band, issued a press release that began like this.

> It is with a heavy heart that Tk'emlúps te Secwé pemc Kukpi7 (Chief) Rosanne Casimir confirms an unthinkable loss that was spoken about but never documented by the Kamloops Indian Residential School. This past weekend, with the help of a ground penetrating radar specialist, the stark truth of the preliminary findings came to light—the confirmation of the remains of 215 children who were students of the Kamloops Indian Residential School.

The story immediately went viral around Canada and the world. The next day *The New York Times* reported on the "mass grave of Indigenous children" in Canada.[98] That night CTV News said: "The discovery of the mass grave is gripping the nation tonight." In Ottawa Prime Minister Justin Trudeau ordered the flag over Parliament Hill lowered to half-mast and by the following Monday flags were lowered on all federal buildings across the country from coast to coast. They would remain that way for months. Said the CBC: "After children's mass grave found, advocates say it's time to scan all residential school sites."[99]

By Tuesday, five days after the press release, Chief Casimir started changing her story, especially regarding *ground-penetrating radar*, a phrase quickly becoming familiar to the Canadian public. She spoke of the "initial horrific findings of what potentially could be, they are very preliminary ... there could very well be children beneath the surface."[100]

Three days after that she said it was not a mass grave, but "unmarked" and "undocumented" burial sites. But by this time it didn't matter what she was saying because the story had been hatched and kept growing and growing. It had become Canada's version of the Doubleday-Cooperstown yarn, parable, call it what you want, but with mass graves of children at residential schools widely accepted as fact, the consequences would be far more dramatic and far more severe than any story about the origins of baseball in the United States.

On July 4, 2021—five weeks after the Casimir press release—Trudeau staged what turned out to be a photo op. He was shown kneeling, and holding a small teddy bear, at what was reported to be the site of a former residential school in Cowessess First Nation, Saskatchewan. That photograph went viral around the world. In hindsight one may argue that this photo did more damage to Canada, the nation's history, and its international reputation than any other photo since Confederation. It not only opened the door to historical revisionism being accepted as fact, but ran a transport truck right through it, taking along the entire country for a wild, tumultuous ride.

That ride continues to this day.

Mass graves were said to have been discovered on the sites of former residential schools all over Canada with claims of missing and murdered children popping up everywhere. The country began a long and tortuous period of national paranoia and shame about its past. What's more, all this coming on the heels of the Black Lives Matter movement in the United States only added fuel to the fire.

Indeed, the flames became a funeral pyre and the corpse was Canada.

The immediate upshot was the vandalism and burning of dozens of churches across the country. The number of reported anti-Catholic hate crimes tripled. Statues and monuments of once-renowned historical figures were now considered legitimate targets. Incredibly, government officials largely went along with this mob rule and, in some cases, even condoned such actions.

It would be a massive understatement to say that the woke version of history—with all its misrepresented claims of settler-colonial-occupier-slave-trade-imperialism—did not receive a boost with the news of mass graves and murder of Indigenous children. In no small way the story contributed to the desecration and removal of statues meant to honour such figures as Macdonald, Ryerson, Cornwallis, Begbie and others. Not to mention defacing statues and monuments celebrating Winston Churchill, Queen Elizabeth II, and even Terry Fox whose statue in Ottawa—along with the War Memorial—was sprayed with paint during the freedom convoy in 2022.

All of a sudden, mob rule became the order of the day with nothing off limits. When you deface a war memorial and kick Terry Fox something is very much out of whack. It is even more out of whack when the authorities appear okay with it.

To this day there is not a shred of evidence to support the mass-grave story. No such graves have been found—not one—and while there have apparently been excavations at two former residential schools, no graves were found. What's more, as of this writing no excavations are planned. And why would they be? They would reveal no graves. Nevertheless, the Government of Canada has committed more than $320 million to help search the sites of residential schools and support survivors. It's all about looking for mass graves—that do not exist.

We have since learned some hard realities. Two in particular. First, that ground-penetrating radar may well detect ground disturbances due to irrigation ditches, water lines, utility lines or archaeological digs—but it doesn't detect human remains.

Second, that confirmed burials in cemeteries located on the sites of former residential schools were almost entirely due to infectious diseases.

Not murder.

This is not to make light of the very legitimate claims of abuse, including sexual abuse, that took place at many of those schools over a long time. It is not to make light of the fact that the lives of Indigenous People most definitely experienced an about-face with the arrival of Europeans. But what has been the outcome across Canada since Chief Rosanne Casimir's press release of May 27, 2021? The historical record of noted figures from the country's past have been rewritten and falsified to satisfy an ideology bent on their destruction; witness the 215 pairs of moccasins and shoes, representing the lives of dead and murdered children, placed at the base of the statue of Egerton Ryerson—a man who did *not* create residential schools.

Coming to grips with your nation's history is one thing, but revising that history and replacing it with fiction is something else. But where did this story about mass graves develop in the first place? Its roots go back further than the 2021 press release. The fires were stoked decades ago by a source no more credible than Abner Graves and his letter containing the elaborate tale of Abner Doubleday and Cooperstown which found its way to Spalding's commission looking at the origins of baseball.

Kevin Annett was a United Church minister who got defrocked

in 1997 after making wild claims about residential schools. Once of those claims was that Queen Elizabeth II and her husband Prince Philip had taken children from the Kamloops Residential School to a picnic and those kids were never seen again! This apparently happened in 1964. Never mind that there was no Royal Visit to Kamloops that year. Despite that, Annett spoke of such entities as the International Tribunal into Crimes of Church and State, and the International Common Law Court of Justice in Brussels, allegedly looking into all this.[101]

Annett has written books, articles and whatever to support his claims which one can find on various websites. One of those sites says he has been nominated for the Nobel Peace Prize—and more than once! For the record I checked with Nobel and inserted his name only to find "Your search returned 0 results." One of Annett's collaborators, a man named William Combes, said he had personally seen the body of a child being buried in the apple orchard when he was attending the school in Kamloops.[102]

One person who called out Kevin Annett and decried the mass-grave story as a hoax was Frances Widdowson, an associate professor—and a tenured professor at that—at Mount Royal University in Calgary. Widdowson earned her Hon. B. A. and M. A. in political science from the University of Victoria, and her PhD in political science from York University. She had worked as a policy analyst for the Government of the Northwest Territories, and joined the faculty of Mount Royal in 2008, obtaining tenure in 2011.

Widdowson was a staunch critic of the Black Lives Matter movement and rejected the conclusions of the Truth and Reconciliation Commission that the residential school system was 'genocidal.' She even spoke of the educational *benefits* of residential schools. Thus, she was no friend of the woke community. In fact, she was public enemy no. 1.

A book she co-authored with Albert Howard—*Disrobing the aboriginal industry: the deception behind indigenous cultural preservation*—was published by McGill-Queen's University Press back in 2008. The book got short-listed for the Donner Prize which is awarded to books "considered excellent in regard to the writing of Canadian public policy." It examined what the authors saw as the root causes of aboriginal problems and an industry that has "grown up around land claim settlements."[103]

Here are five takeaways from this book, and keep in mind it was published in 2008 and short-listed for a major book award.

1. The "evidence" from "oral histories" (authors' quotation marks) becomes more problematic when economic interests are involved since oral histories have been known to change when a claim is necessary to obtain access to valuable resources. Since aboriginal peoples did not have writing before contact, it is easy to change "oral histories" to support their claims for compensation and privileges. (Pg 44)
2. Oral testimonies masquerading as history have been used to establish that conceptions of ownership and sovereignty, and their associated "institutions," existed before contact with Europeans. (Pg 44)
3. Land claims constitute the most significant and costly of all aboriginal projects, and require the greatest amount of historical revision and legal justification from the Aboriginal Industry. (Pg 82)
4. Almost all aboriginal economic activity needs constant sheltering from competition through such mechanisms as tax breaks, interest-free loans and grants, and preferential contracts. (Pg 93)

5. Over 600 bands stretch across the entire Canadian land mass in isolated pockets that are completely dependent on federal funds. (Pg 115)

Widdowson also wrote a follow-up book called *Separate but Unequal: How Parallelist Ideology conceals Indigenous Dependency*, published by University of Ottawa Press in 2019. It criticized the view that Indigenous cultures and the wider Canadian society should exist separately from each other in a 'nation-to-nation' relationship.

It is worth noting what has happened to Frances Widdowson.

In December of 2021, after speaking out and going against the grain, she was effectively fired from her position at Mount Royal, which is rare indeed for a tenured faculty member. Said Widdowson to the CBC: "I was generally criticizing 'woke' ideas." She said that identity politics had become "totalitarian" and was "imposing itself on the university, and preventing people from openly discussing ideas."[104]

An arbitrator later found that her firing was not justified. What's more, Widdowson has been cancelled from the Canadian academia scene. In January, 2023 she was to speak at the University of Lethbridge—the topic 'How Woke-ism Threatens Academic Freedom'—but her lecture got cancelled after pushback by students and faculty. She appeared instead at a local public library. She is a prime example of what happens to free speech when radical *woke* ideology is allowed to permeate on the campuses of Canadian colleges and universities; there is only free speech when you tow the party line.

In political terms we call this fascism.

For what it's worth, Widdowson isn't the only voice harbouring such views. Joseph Quesnel is a writer and researcher in Nova Scotia with extensive experience on Indigenous issues. He holds an undergraduate degree in political science and history from McGill University and a master of journalism degree from Carleton University. This is from an essay Quesnel wrote for the book *The 1867 Project: Why Canada Should be Cherished—Not Cancelled*, published in 2023 by The Aristotle Foundation for Public Policy, a public policy think tank.

> The real division in the 21st century is not necessarily between "Indigenous" and "settlers" as many vested interests, too many academics, and some Indigenous ideologues claim. Instead, the division is between middle-class, pro-reform Indigenous leaders, grassroots Indigenous peoples, and businesspeople, versus the Indigenous political organizations and scholars who are overly invested in the status quo including reflexive, unproductive activism.
>
> That status quo includes an attachment to ongoing government-granted preferences including, ironically, for the continued isolation of Indigenous peoples, but this time justified with reference to protecting an assumed "pure" culture.[105]

The first time I ever read anything about the mass-grave story being something other than the truth was courtesy of Terry Glavin, a journalist with a long track record covering Indigenous matters, especially in British Columbia. An article he wrote appeared in *The National Post* in 2022 and he has since written many other articles about this. Glavin readily acknowledged that what transpired at residential schools was not glamourous. He said: "Many of the church-run, federally-administered institutions, whatever the good intentions of the religious orders that ran them, were dark and forbidding places that incubated disease, cultural dislocation, abuse and despair, for much of their history."[106]

But he also said there was no grain of truth behind the mass graves and other people said the same thing. One of the most prominent has been Tom Flanagan who is no stranger to the Indigenous file. Flanagan, once a top advisor to Stephen Harper, is Professor Emeritus of Political Science and Distinguished Fellow, at the School of Public Policy, University of Calgary. He taught political science at the university from 1968 to 2013, and is the author of books and articles on such subjects as Métis history, aboriginal rights and land claims. Flanagan has also been an expert witness in litigation over aboriginal and treaty land claims.

One of his books, co-authored with C. P. Champion, founder and publisher of *The Dorchester Review*, is *Grave Error: How the Media Misled Us (and the Truth about Residential Schools)*. It was published in 2023 by True North, a digital-media company and registered charity. The book is a bestseller on Amazon, which is the only place it's sold. Flanagan, who is a Senior Fellow of The Fraser Institute, a public policy think tank, told me his book has been "boycotted" by all legacy media in Canada except for *The National Post*. He said he had initially approached McGill-Queen's University Press to do the book, but they wouldn't touch it even though they had published five of his earlier books. Two of them involve Indigenous issues—*First Nations? Second Thoughts*, which won the Donner Prize for excellence in public policy, and *Beyond the Indian Act, Restoring Aboriginal Property Rights*, which he co-wrote with two other authors.

In February, 2024, Flanagan published a 'Commentary' piece for The Fraser Institute, summarizing *Grave Error*. It concluded with this.

> The claims about missing children, unmarked burials and "mass graves" reinforced a genocide scenario. Perhaps sensing the weakness of their evidence-free position, purveyors of the genocide narrative are beginning to double down, demanding that criticism of their ideology be made illegal.

For example, in 2022, Winnipeg NDP MP Leah Gazan, introduced a resolution declaring residential schools to be genocidal—the House of Commons gave unanimous consent.

So, there we are—a narrative about genocide in residential schools firmly established in the public domain while unbelievers are called heretics ("denialists") and threatened with criminal prosecution. But don't believe the hype, no matter how often the propositions are repeated. As the little boy said in Hans Christian Andersen's fairytale, "The Emperor has no clothes."

More recently, in December of 2024, The Fraser Institute published Tom Flanagan's piece *An Avalanche of Money: The Federal Government's Policies Toward First Nations*. It was not published as Commentary, but as a Study, and to say the findings are disturbing puts it mildly. Here are a few of them.

- From 2015 to 2025 the annual Indigenous budget almost tripled from roughly $11 billion to more than $32 billion, and despite this increase the lives and well-being of the First Nations community have not improved.
- Class actions have been settled without litigation, with estimated liabilities reaching $76 billion in 2023, while specific claims have been settled at a rate four times higher than by the previous Conservative government.
- Even though tens of billions of dollars are involved, the public is being told nothing about when and to whom class action payouts take place, and how the trust funds that result from specific claims settlements are used.
- First Nations have become relatively less financially independent and more dependent on government transfers, and far fewer First Nations are publishing audited

statements and we are now seeing the result of such non-enforcement.

But the single most startling thing I found from Flanagan's research was this.

> The federal government now spends more on Indigenous Peoples than it does on national defense.

It is to defy belief.

The late Carl Sagan was an American astronomer who popularized science for the masses. His 1978 book—THE DRAGONS OF EDEN: *Speculations on the Evolution of Human Intelligence*—won him the Pulitzer Prize. One thing he said in that book was this: "When we abandon the hunter/gatherer life, we abandon the childhood of our species."[107]

Here is something else Sagan said: "You can't convince a believer of anything; for their belief is not based on evidence, it's based on a deep-seated need to believe."[108]

We can apply both these observations to the plight of Canada's Indigenous community and how Canadians—dare I mention those considered woke—perceive that community. What are some of the things people believe?

That Indian Residential Schools constitute a cultural genocide, if not a complete genocide, against Indigenous People.

That all First Nations children attended these schools.

They were forcibly removed from their families.

The intent of the schools was to destroy their culture.

The institutions were run like prisons.

Untold numbers of children disappeared only to be murdered and buried in unmarked graves.

If you accept all that at face value you might as well subscribe to Abner Doubleday inventing the game of baseball in Cooperstown,

New York on a whim in 1839. Because the facts don't bear any of it out.

Greg Piasetzki is an intellectual property lawyer and a person with passionate interest in Canadian history. He is a citizen of the Métis Nation of Ontario and a contributor to *The National Post, The Dorchester Review, The Hub, The Aristotle Foundation for Public Policy* and others. Piasetzki has made a habit of digging into federal archives to learn more about residential schools. He points out that the federal government wanted to get rid of these schools in the early 1940s, but didn't because it wasn't prepared to abandon vulnerable Indigenous children.

"The devastating inter-generational effects of alcoholism and parental dysfunction on reserves had turned residential schools into a de facto native child welfare system," he says. "Had the government shut these schools down in the 1940s, as it very much wanted to, those children would have been left at grave risk of injury or death. There was, quite simply, no other place for them to go."

The numbered treaties signed between the federal government and various tribes required Ottawa to build and run schools *whenever the Indians of the reserve shall desire it*. That is according to Treaty 6 which was signed in 1876 by representatives of the Crown and leaders from the Cree, Assiniboine and Ojibwe. If we go back to the late 1800s when the federal government began to administer the schools, the problem at hand was how to help some 120,000 Indigenous people, who had been used to a hunter-gatherer lifestyle, cope with the demands of modern society. During the time of John A. Macdonald the schools were to be run on a voluntary basis.

States the Annual Report of Indian Affairs for the year 1898: "The Department's policy is as long as possible to refrain from compulsory measures and try the effect of moral suasion and an appeal to self-interest."

That report was issued seven years after the death of Macdonald. What else did Piasetzki, who has downloaded 70 *Indian Affairs Annual Reports* over the years, learn from poring through all these government archives?

In the 1920s federal legislation extended compulsory education to Native children, although the policy was rarely enforced. Most children attended for only a few years, with more than half the attendees of both day and residential schools dropping out after Grade 1. The system peaked in 1931 with 80 schools, but things changed during the Great Depression. Ottawa cut back on funding, many church-run buildings fell into disrepair, and it was difficult to find teachers. The result? The quality of instruction and care declined, as did most of everything in Canada at that time.

What with the post-war baby boom, the number of Indigenous students at the schools more than doubled from 16,000 in 1943 to 32,500 in 1954. According to those federal archives, a growing share of those students were "neglected children," "orphans and part-orphans," or children from "broken and problem homes."

A federal census of the Indian Schools taken in 1953 found that 43 per cent of the 10,012 Indigenous children in residential schools across Canada were listed as neglected or living in homes that were unfit because of parental indifference or over-crowding. The upshot was that Indian Residential Schools were forced to transform from educational institutions to "a sort of foster home which endeavour[s] to cater to the social and emotional needs of the child," that according to a 1966 departmental report. In that year 75 per cent of 9,778 residential students were welfare cases.

Since the last residential school closed in 1996, things have not improved for Indigenous children. According to the 2021 census, Native children under the age of 14 account for 53.8 per cent of children in care, while representing less than 8 per cent of children that age in Canada.

Says Piasetzki: "Indigenous youth continue to struggle with alcohol and drug use, unemployment, low educational attainment, and mental health problems at rates substantially above the rest of the country. The most obvious conclusion regarding the intractable persistence of these social issues is that jurisdiction is irrelevant. The residential school system was never the cause, but one of many attempted solutions."

In March of 2025 I attended a lecture in Toronto by the eminent British scholar Nigel Biggar who is Regius Professor Emeritus of Moral Theology at the University of Oxford. Biggar's bestselling book *Colonialism: A Moral Reckoning* was a staunch defense of British colonialism and this was the subject of his talk, but before he finished he waded into some domestic waters, namely, Canada's residential schools. His observations echoed those of Greg Piasetzki and were neatly summed up in an article he did for *The National Post*.

Biggar said there is no concrete evidence of hidden graves in Kamloops or anywhere else. "The claim that over 3,000 pupils were deliberately killed or died through culpable neglect—and that their deaths amount to an atrocity—is patently false, lacking any evidential basis whatever," wrote Biggar. He said the record falls a long, long way short of systematic "cultural genocide." He also took aim at the Truth and Reconciliation Commission, among others.

> Blame for the tyranny of a false public orthodoxy about the residential schools rests with representatives of the TRC and academics, who know full well that the data is being misrepresented and yet have failed to offer any correction. It lies with journalists and editors who have declined to ask questions. It lies with politicians who have tied their careers to the mendacious narrative. And, most of all, it lies with those who have—shockingly—persecuted skeptics and critics to the point of destroying their reputations and careers.[109]

The week after that lecture Biggar was supposed to speak at Regent College on the University of British Columbia campus. But that lecture got cancelled and he was accused of being a residential school apologist and "mass graves denier."[110]

While we can all agree that there was abusive behaviour and abusive conditions at these schools—how much depends on who you talk to—and that those responsible should be held to account, we must also accept the facts. There are no mass graves. There were no disappearing and murdered children. There was no forced attendance. And there was no genocide. But still, a great many people refuse to accept that and it doesn't matter how much evidence you present.

On top of all this Canadians are having to apologize to all and sundry—again and again and again—for the violent, racist history of this country that we currently *occupy*. Indeed, what is a *land acknowledgement* other than an apology to earlier inhabitants of what is now called Canada?

Today before every professional hockey game, baseball game, basketball game, football game—every professional sports event, not to mention cultural event, anywhere in the nation—we have a land acknowledgement. Companies have a land acknowledgement before board meetings and other kinds of meetings. On the websites of virtually any type of organization, be it public, private, or government or not-for-profit, words are expressed about land acknowledgement. It takes place at Sunday morning mass in churches. It takes place at the local charity. It takes place everywhere and has become seeped into the national consciousness.

If the Canadian government had jurisdiction over the holy city of Jerusalem a meeting might start like this.

> We humbly acknowledge that our operations at head office and at all other offices across the region are home to the traditional territories and lands of the Homo Sapiens who first appeared in the Galilee some 100,000 years ago and were later occupied by their descendants during the Stone

Age and Bronze Age. Only to be followed by the Canaanites and then the Assyrians and the Babylonian people who each came, in turn, after them. And then we have the Persians and the ancient Greeks and the Romans and the Christians of the Byzantine period as well as the Arabs and Crusaders and Turks of the Ottoman Empire and yes also the British who were here for a time as well although they had no business being there. We acknowledge them all for they were the earlier inhabitants of this land. We remain forever mindful and cognizant of their cultures and their languages. We strive to honour them and recognize their contributions and we dedicate ourselves to building fair, inclusive and sustainable relationships with all who live on these lands today.

Once that land acknowledgement is over—a great many people of assorted races and backgrounds have occupied Jerusalem over thousands of years—there would be no time left for the meeting! And what is true about all those people who have dwelt in Jerusalem during all this time is that none of those turnovers occurred without violence. Jerusalem—the holiest of cities—has a more violent and turbulent history than any city on the face of the earth.

But as far as I know, the State of Israel doesn't do land acknowledgements in Jerusalem.

The Federal Republic of Germany doesn't do them either and if any country has something to apologize for it would be Germany. But then Germany has apologized for its sorry role with the rise of the Nazis, setting off World War II, and the Holocaust. Since 1945 Germany has paid more than 80 billion euros—equal to about $120 billion (Cdn)—in reparations to survivors. Aside from the purview of far-right, neo-Nazis who continue to exist and who often deny what took place, Germany has come face to face with its history and become a successful, free, liberal democracy.

This is to its credit.

Do German companies today in Berlin, Hamburg and Munich begin their board meetings with an acknowledgement to all the Jews, not to mention gays and other transgendered, as well as gypsies, intellectuals, communists and what have you, who had their businesses shut down, their homes taken, and their lives lost due to happenings of the 1930s and 1940s?

No.

Do companies and charitable organizations in the United Kingdom launch their latest sales campaigns and fundraising drives with an acknowledgement to the Scots whose lives were destroyed by the English seven hundred years ago?

No.

To cite an example alluded to earlier in this book, how about an organization in Tyre, Phoenicia, which today is part of Lebanon? Does such an organization begin its Annual General Meeting with an acknowledgement to all the women who were raped and the children who were taken captive and thrown into slavery when Alexander defeated Darius in the historic siege of Tyre in 332 BC?

Of course not.

History is history and we can't erase it, but hopefully we can learn from it. But it's much harder to learn from it if you don't know the history to begin with and harder still if we allow what real and legitimate history we have to be rewritten and changed for political and ideological reasons.

History is something to accept and to go on from. But to forever apologize for what took place is to bury yourself and wallow in regret, shame and this deep sense of self-pity. In the greater scheme of things, I am hard-pressed to find any country with less to apologize for than Canada which is why people continue to come here from all over the world.

We should start asking ourselves what is the purpose and end result of land acknowledgements, especially considering how they are done here. If the purpose is to apologize, when does it end? If the purpose is to recognize and honour those who were here before us, what about all the non-Indigenous people who helped build this country? Should they not also be recognized and honoured?

How about an acknowledgement to John Graves Simcoe for enacting the first legislation in the British Commonwealth to bring about the end of slavery? Or to Egerton Ryerson for establishing the public education system? Better still, how about acknowledging John A. Macdonald who—more than any other single person—was responsible for creating this country that we now call home?

Doing a land acknowledgement that builds and strengthens the nation is one thing. But doing one that weakens it is another.

CHAPTER 12

A return to pride in country

IN 1997 I ATTENDED an extraordinary conference at the Israel Museum. It was a conference commemorating the 50th anniversary of the discovery of the Dead Sea Scrolls. Most of the attendees were archaeologists, along with historians and academics in related disciplines, and they all hailed from universities in Israel, the United States, and other countries including Canada. This was summer and what I remember most was the unbearable heat, the stark beauty of the desert, historic ruins everywhere you look, and Israeli Prime Minister Benjamin Netanyahu. Of course, he was much younger then but at the beginning of the conference an event with him speaking was held in the courtyard outside the main building of the museum which is in Jerusalem.

His talk took place in the evening and when all the invited guests were seated but before his arrival, four huge and very imposing men stationed themselves at each corner of the courtyard. As I say, this was outdoors in the open. Those four men were Netanyahu's security detail, the Israeli version of the Secret Service. Each one was about 6'4" and 230 pounds. Think of Dwayne Johnson, formerly known as The Rock, but times four. They had shaved heads and muscular arms crossed over their chests, and to say they looked grim would be an understatement.

I was sitting with a woman who was originally from Canada. She worked in public relations for the museum and I told her I'd like to interview one of those guys.

"You don't want to talk to *them*," was all she said.

A few days later I was in a taxi and my driver was taking me to a part of the city I hadn't seen yet. We passed these old buildings and I asked what they were.

"They are nothing," he said with a dismissive shrug. "They're not even five hundred years old."

To a Canadian these were remarkable words.

The next time I found myself in a taxi the driver took an interest in my being from Canada and in his broken English he asked me what it was like. I thought for a moment and came up with a comparison between his country and mine.

"Israel is a small country with a very big history," I said. "Canada is a big country with a small history."

Unfortunately, what little history we have we are hell-bent on destroying.

It seems that any history still taught in our schools—and it isn't much—stresses villainy and victimhood, and looks at the past through the prism of the present. There is a name for this phenomenon. We call it *presentism* and it's not without critics. David Wilson, a history professor at the University of Toronto, has warned about the perils of this decolonial approach to history.

"Decolonization goes wrong when it becomes an ideological weapon," he said.

The Toronto District School Board, Canada's largest school board, appears to be knee-deep in this sort of thing. It also suffers from a chronic condition of historical ignorance, which is shameful for an organization entrusted with educating our young. In early 2025 the TDSB came out with a report about renaming schools and the ones targeted right off the bat were Sir John A. Macdonald Collegiate Institute, Ryerson Community School, and Dundas Junior Public School. The names of these schools were to be changed because the names might act as "a potentially harmful microaggression."

Stated the report:

> Having to enter school buildings commemorating such individuals may even contribute to mental-health triggers which negatively impact students, staff or families' ability to effectively participate in the school environment.

What's more, the TDSB report recommended partnering with the City of Toronto "to support historical understanding of school names." That would be the same City of Toronto that displays blatant historical errors on huge neon signs in a public square that no longer has the name Dundas.

I suppose birds of a feather flock together, but all that's being celebrated here is a shoddy misrepresentation of history and the worst part is it's being shoved down the throats of our kids. This is irresponsible. But who is held to account?

No one.

The Ontario Ministry of Education later introduced legislation to prevent the TDSB from removing Macdonald's name from one of its high schools.

Observed noted journalist David Frum: "I'm proud of this country. It is blemished as every country's history, but less blemished than just about anybody's."

I confess that I am humbled by history and always have been. When I was in Bergen, Norway I walked through these wooden gates that were almost 1,000 years old. Vikings used to walk through them. Those very same gates. When my wife and I were in the Greek island of Rhodes we passed the spot where the Colossus of Rhodes stood in the third century BCE. It rose some 32 meters—more than a hundred feet—over the water. It was the same thing when we saw the Colosseum in Rome, the Palace of Versailles in France, and other historic sites we have visited.

The history just pours out of them and fills you up.

On that same trip to Norway I got to interview Helge Ingstad, the explorer who, along with his wife archaeologist Anne Stine, discovered the old Viking settlements at L'Anse aux Meadows in Newfoundland. He was 100 years old at the time and it may well have been the last interview he ever gave. Ingstad was a remarkable man on many fronts and is the only person I know of whose life spanned three centuries. He was born in 1899 and died in 2001. What's more, the gods must have been involved in this development because he was born on December 30, 1899. Nevertheless, when I saw him at his home outside Oslo he related the story about finding these settlements and how he and his wife managed to do this because they had based their travels on the old Norse sagas—*The Saga of the Greenlanders* and *The Saga of Eric the Red*—which go back to the 13th century. But those sagas tell the story of the original Viking travels to what is now Newfoundland—they had called it *Vinland*—from more than 1,000 years ago.

The upshot of all this was that scholars, archaeologists among them and from all over the world—but especially from Italy, Spain and Portugal—ridiculed them for having the temerity to suggest that Vikings had been to North America 500 years before Christopher Columbus. It was sacrilege. However, during a series of digs at L'Anse aux Meadows in the 1960s, the Ingstads found some 2,000 artifacts and there was no doubt.

In 1978 L'Anse aux Meadows was declared a UNESCO World Heritage Site. In Canada it was named a National Historic Site.

History isn't what you *want* it to be. It just is. But it's up to archaeologists, historians and the like to do the research, get the facts, and uncover the truth.

Indeed, studying history is about finding the truth.

At all these places I have mentioned there are statues, monuments and plaques that recognize individuals from the past who have made worthwhile contributions. At L'Anse aux Meadows there is a statue of Leif Erikson who is thought to be the first

European to set foot in North America. There is also a bust of two people—Helge Ingstad and his wife Anne Stine—with their names below. After all, they found the site and if not for them and their years of painstaking work we might never have learned that Vikings arrived on these shores more than 1,000 years ago.

For what it's worth, The Royal Norwegian Navy named one of its frigates after Ingstad and there is even an asteroid named after him. In Canada on the main campus of Memorial University in St. John's, Newfoundland, there is The Helge and Anne Stine Ingstad Building. Ingstad was also given an honourary doctorate from the same university. A small river in the Northwest Territories that flows into Great Slave Lake is called Ingstad Creek and in Alaska there is Ingstad Mountain.

There may well be people who are still upset about the Vikings usurping Columbus as the discoverers of the New World. It is true that the celebrated Italian explorer reached the Bahamas on October 12, 1492 and there is an old poem those of my generation learned as kids that begins with "In 1492 Columbus sailed the ocean blue." We were told this is the man who discovered America and today in the United States a national holiday—Columbus Day—commemorates him. Of course, when we are talking Columbus we can't forget about all the statues, streets and even cities that are named after him. But, with thanks to the Ingstads, we and the entire world learned that Columbus was not the first European in these parts since he came some 500 years after the Vikings.

Now if those who are uncomfortable with all this want to do something about it they could start a campaign to at least give Mr. Columbus equal billing. After all, the man did cross the Atlantic in his flagship, the Santa Maria, which was a humble merchant ship of only 18 meters or 60 feet in length, and with an average speed of about four knots. That isn't very big or fast. Such a campaign would mean erecting a statue of him right beside the one of Leif Erikson even though Columbus never got anywhere near Newfoundland. It would mean taking a new enlightened look at what the Ingstads did and that might even entail erecting a plaque beside the bust of them at L'Anse aux Meadows. On this new plaque we might see the word *controversial*.

Yes, I realize all this sounds ridiculous. And it is. But it's no more ridiculous than what has transpired in recent years in Canada when it comes to those who built this country. People who know nothing about our history, but believe what they want to believe because it gives them *comfort*, suddenly become experts. They organize and manage to hoodwink elected officials, not to mention the media, and before you know it our history has been revised.

There isn't a country in the world that doesn't want to observe its past. This is why a statue of Julius Caesar, who was no Emperor but a dictator, stands in the middle of the Roman Forum today. This is why a 170-ton statue of Abraham Lincoln looks out at you from inside the Lincoln Memorial in Washington, DC. And why statues of Winston Churchill are all over the British Commonwealth and beyond. It's why here in Canada we have statues of people like John A. Macdonald.

Is our history so shameful?

English writers such as the aforementioned Nigel Biggar with his book *Colonialism: A Moral Reckoning* and Douglas Murray, author of *The War on the West*, point out that those who are quick to condemn the British Empire and all it stands for are very selective about how they look at history. For example, consider the slave trade. The critics forget—or choose to ignore—that Britain was the leader in eradicating slavery. Says Murray:

"It is true that Britain engaged in the slave trade and that it took part in a trade in human beings that was appalling. But as we've seen, Britain also led the world in the abolition of that trade.

And Britain not only abolished that trade for itself but used its navy to seek to wipe out that trade in all parts of the world the navy could reach."[III]

By the same token those from the woke community in Canada are also selective, if not deceitful, about how they pick and choose from history in order to advance their agenda. And make no mistake. Their agenda is to tear down this country. The *modus operandi* follows a definite path and always begins with a conclusion.

John A. Macdonald is a racist who set out to starve the Indigenous Peoples.

Now that we have established this we can search for quotes or parts of quotes to prove that point and it doesn't matter if things are taken out of context.

Egerton Ryerson created Indian Residential Schools.

Henry Dundas prolonged the slave trade.

Edward Cornwallis set out to eliminate every Mik'maq man, woman and child he could find.

Matthew Begbie was a hanging judge who lynched six innocent Chilcotin chiefs.

None of this is true, of course, but that doesn't matter.

The next thing is to set up a committee of hand-picked 'experts' who are cut from the same cloth and who recommend the removal of statues, changing the names of streets and schools, and the same thing for mountains and what have you. After all, it is now abundantly clear that these characters from the past are nothing but evil white supremacists. Then, when learned voices who actually know a thing or two about those figures emerge to counter such unfounded claims, the next step is clear—condemn such individuals outright and *cancel* them. And if such voices then want to debate the issue in a public forum, there is only one course of action.

Retreat.

The irony here is that one would be hard-pressed to find any country in the world with a history as peaceful and orderly as Canada's.

We are unique because this nation did not arise from war or revolution. Instead, it came from an *idea*. We should celebrate that and celebrate those who made it happen. But doing so means wiping the slate clean of those who want no part of it and are only interested in demonizing this country and its history. Allowing such misinformed people to influence public policy—never mind our schools—is a fool's game that undermines us as a nation.

But Canada did serve in major conflicts and serve admirably. In the last century there were two world wars. In World War I, also known as the Great War, more than 650,000 Canadians and Newfoundlanders—Newfoundland didn't join confederation until 1949—served and more than 66,000 of them died with another 172,000 wounded. In World War II the numbers were 1.1 million who served with 42,000 killed and 55,000 wounded. There was also the Korean War which saw 26,000 Canadians taking part and more than 500 were killed in that one.

This is no small sacrifice.

My father served in the Canadian Army in World War II but didn't go abroad or see combat as he was stationed in Newfoundland. Of course, there was conscription back then. When my brother and I were growing up our Dad never talked much about his time in the army, but the wedding photograph of my parents does have him in military attire. We also have this old black-and-white snapshot of him when he was in training. With the ever-present cigarette hanging out of his mouth, there is a rifle in his hands and he appears ready to use it. Another thing I have in my possession is his old dog tag which is the identification tag worn by military personnel with their personal information on it. In case of casualty, they would then be accounted for. There on my father's dog tag is his serial number, the letters GNR for gunner, his first initial and last name, and finally his citizenship and religion.

HEB.CDN.

That's right. Hebrew Canadian.

It was a different time.

While I personally have no such experience with the military, working as a journalist has occasionally led to doing articles about the war. Many years ago I did a magazine profile of noted military man Richard Rohmer, who as of this writing is still going strong at more than 100. I remember him showing me his medals. What's noteworthy about Rohmer is that he was a young reconnaissance pilot during D-Day and saw the entire invasion of the Beaches of Normandy from the air. He told me about that.

Another time, earlier still when I was a newspaper reporter, I had an assignment to cover what would be the last reunion between members of the Canadian Armed Forces who liberated Belgium from Nazi Germany and the Belgians they liberated. This would have been the 30th anniversary of that event and the gathering took place at the Royal York Hotel in Toronto. The Belgians came to Canada specifically for this purpose and some of them were well advanced in years. But despite such a passage of time—three decades—the bond between those Canadian soldiers and the Belgian citizens they freed remained real and palpable. You could see it and feel it. I distinctly remember speaking to an older Belgian man who said, "Any German over the age of 50 is a murderer," and his eyes told me that he meant it.

This is all part of our history and it's important. But just how far can this nonsense—the *rewriting* of history—go? Well, let's see. In the United States they have four presidents carved into Mount Rushmore: George Washington, Thomas Jefferson, Abraham Lincoln and Teddy Roosevelt. The first two were slaveowners which was not unusual at the time if you happened to be a wealthy and powerful man. Should those two be replaced by two presidents who were not slaveowners? If the answer to that question is yes, two candidates might well be Richard Nixon and Donald Trump. We now would have four presidents on Mount Rushmore, none of them slaveowners, and perhaps the high-minded moralists of the 21st century would be satisfied. Indeed, this would give Mount Rushmore a very different look.

It's no different in Canada.

Imagine for a moment that someone proposed making a Mount Rushmore in this country and advanced the name of John A. Macdonald as the first candidate for the honour. Frankly, I can't think of another person who is more deserving to be there. But think what would happen. The uproar would be swift and severe with historical revisionists coming out of the woodwork, spreading lies and myths, and denouncing our first prime minister every chance they get. Of course, the media by and large would play along with it and be complicit in the skullduggery.

No doubt, there would be elected officials—at every level of government—only too happy to advance the program of the historical conspirators because their knowledge of history is just as deficient. The best example I can think of to illustrate this sad state of affairs took place in our own parliament in September, 2023.

Volodymyr Zelenskyy, President of Ukraine, was addressing the Canadian House of Commons when a special guest sitting in the gallery was introduced. Yaroslav Hunka, a 98-year-old resident of North Bay, Ontario, was called "a Ukrainian hero" and "a Canadian hero" by the Speaker of the House. Indeed, this Ukrainian man fought against the Red Army in World War II, and what with the Russian invasion of Ukraine in 2022, anyone who ever fought the Russians deserves an applause. And Hunka got one. Every member of the House of Commons stood up and clapped, but no one bothered to ask who the Russians were fighting in World War II.

The last time I checked it was Nazi Germany.

Hunka had served in the 14th Waffen-ss Grenadier Division, a unit comprised of ethnic Ukrainians under Nazi command. And so, Canada's House of Commons gave a standing ovation to a Nazi and our country became an international laughingstock.

Ignorance is not bliss. It is just ignorance. And when our elected officials play along with the game of historical revisionism it leaves behind bewildered members of the public scratching their heads and thinking there must be some truth to all this.

Even when there isn't.

If you repeat a lie often enough, people will believe it.

That statement has been attributed to Hitler's propagandist Joseph Goebbels and whether or not he actually said it doesn't matter. But it does apply to the narrative that is widely accepted as history in Canada today.

I mentioned earlier that I had met, on two occasions, the noted historian Sir Martin Gilbert. What if he was still alive and could undertake an assignment on behalf of this nation? It would be to concentrate on Canada's past and use all his skills as a brilliant scholar and researcher who leaves no stone unturned in his search for the truth.

We would ask him to learn all that he could about Indian Residential Schools and if there are warts to be found, so be it.

We would ask him to see what he can unearth about the wars in Nova Scotia, and why streets and public places in Toronto carried the name Dundas. And why a certain university had the name Ryerson. We would ask him to look into what really happened with the Chilcotin War in British Columbia. We would ask him to take a long, hard look at how and why this country of Canada got going in the first place because it seems to me this is a story worth telling and not telling it is irresponsible. What's more, telling it inaccurately is criminal.

It was a wise man who said the following words: "We are a great country, and shall become one of the greatest in the universe if we preserve it; we shall sink into insignificance and adversity if we suffer it to be broken."

His name was John A. Macdonald. We could use him today.

Endnotes

CHAPTER 3

1. Hughes, Coleman. *The End of Race Politics: Arguments for a Colorblind America*. Thesis, 2024. p. 36
2. Hughes, Coleman. *The End of Race Politics: Arguments for a Colorblind America*. Thesis, 2024. p. 106
3. Hughes, Coleman. *The End of Race Politics: Arguments for a Colorblind America*. Thesis, 2024. p.129
4. The New York Times, July 17, 2020
5. The Sacramento Bee, July 18, 1971
6. www.nytimes.com/2020/07/17/obituaries/nancy-green-aunt-jemima-overlooked.html
7. www.youtube.com/watch?v=RosCZkH5uTI
8. www.youtube.com/watch?v=oQySRYyjZjI
9. National Post, June 11, 2024
10. www.youtube.com/watch?v=oQySRYyjZjI
11. The Hub, March 7, 2024

CHAPTER 4

12. The Hub, December 15, 2023
13. Paul W. Bennett, *The State of the System: A Reality Check on Canada's Schools*, McGill-Queen's University Press, 2020) p. 148
14. www.nas.org/blogs/article/its_something_but_its_not_history_canadian_history_in_ontario_schools

CHAPTER 5

15. Richard Gwyn, *Nation Maker: Sir John A. Macdonald: His Life, Our Times, Vol.II*, Vintage Canada, 2012, p. 554

16. https://jamiebradburnwriting.wordpress.com/2021/04/21/sir-john-a-macdonalds-last-hurrah-the-1891-federal-election/

17. E. B. Biggar, *Anecdotal History of John A. Macdonald*, Publisher J. Lovell, Montreal, Chapter x

18. Richard Gwyn, *John A: The Man Who Made Us, Vol. 1*, Vintage Canada, p. 78

19. Richard Gwyn, *John A: The Man Who Made Us, Vol. 1*, Vintage Canada, p. 153

20. Richard Gwyn, *John A: The Man Who Made Us, Vol. 1*, Vintage Canada, p. 153

21. Richard Gwyn, *Nation Maker: Sir John A. Macdonald: His Life, Our Times, Vol. II*, Vintage Canada, p. 390

22. Richard Gwyn, *Nation Maker: Sir John A. Macdonald: His Life, Our Times, Vol. II*, Vintage Canada, p. 29

23. Richard Gwyn, *Nation Maker: Sir John A. Macdonald: His Life, Our Times, Vol. II*, Vintage Canada, p. 3

24. Richard Gwyn, *Nation Maker: Sir John A. Macdonald: His Life, Our Times, Vol. II*, Vintage Canada, p. 242

25. Alexander Morris, *The Treaties of Canada with the Indians of Manitoba and the NWT*, 1880, p. 274

26. Richard Gwyn, *Nation Maker: Sir John A. Macdonald: His Life, Our Times, Vol. II*, Vintage Canada, p. 420

27. Richard Gwyn, *Nation Maker: Sir John A. Macdonald: His Life, Our Times, Vol. II*, Vintage Canada, p. 592

28. E. B. Biggar, *Anecdotal Life of Sir John Macdonald*, John Lovell & Son, Montreal, 1891, p. 293

29. Douglas Murray, *The War on the West*, Broadside Books, 2022, p. 131

30. https://macleans.ca/news/canada/a-toast-to-sir-john-a-canadas-controversial-nation-builder/

31. https://macleans.ca/news/canada/a-toast-to-sir-john-a-canadas-controversial-nation-builder/

CHAPTER 6

32. https://globalnews.ca/news/7926605/ryerson-statue-university-removed-toronto/
33. www.bbc.com/news/world-us-canada-57381522
34. Donald B. Smith, *Egerton Ryerson and the Mississauga, 1826 to 1856, An Appeal for Further Study*, Volume 113, Number 2, Fall 2021, p. 226
35. Donald B. Smith, *Egerton Ryerson and the Mississauga, 1826 to 1856, An Appeal for Further Study*, Volume 113, Number 2, Fall 2021, p. 233
36. www.dorchesterreview.ca/blogs/news/the-imbecile-attack-on-egerton-ryerson?_pos=5&_sid=c9c291d6c&_ss=r
37. https://financialpost.com/opinion/lynn-mcdonald-the-historical-record-vindicates-egerton-ryerson
38. www.erudit.org/en/journals/onhistory/2021-v113-n2-onhistory06334/1081114ar/
39. www.erudit.org/en/journals/onhistory/2021-v113-n2-onhistory06334/1081114ar/

CHAPTER 7

40. www.blogto.com/city/2020/08/why-toronto-tkaronto/
41. https://americanindian.si.edu/nk360/manhattan/schaghen-letter/schaghen-letter.cshtml
42. www.sankofasquare.ca/
43. Parliamentary Register in London
44. https://macdonaldlaurier.ca/torontos-sankofa-square-the-terrible-folly-and-historic-injustice-of-erasing-the-legacy-of-abolitionist-henry-dundas-lynn-mcdonald-for-inside-policy/
45. www.opendemocracy.net/en/opendemocracyuk/henry-dundas-empire-and-genocide/

CHAPTER 8

46. https://archive.org/details/cihm_20153/page/n5/mode/2up
47. https://archive.org/details/cihm_20153/page/n5/mode/2up
48. https://archive.org/details/halifaxhistory00akinuoft/page/n7/mode/2up
49. https://archive.org/details/halifaxhistory00akinuoft/page/n7/mode/2up
50. www.fortressoflouisbourg.ca/
51. https://archive.org/details/ScalpingProclamation1749/page/n3/mode/2up
52. www.wpgfdn.org/centennial-essay/murray-sinclair-llb-msc-ipc/
53. www.thecanadianencyclopedia.ca/en/article/edward-cornwallis
54. https://activehistory.ca/wp-content/uploads/2011/07/Bennett-in-Chronicle-Herald.pdf
55. https://activehistory.ca/wp-content/uploads/2011/07/Bennett-in-Chronicle-Herald.pdf
56. www.cbc.ca/news/canada/nova-scotia/halifax-survey-edward-cornwallis-name-majority-cra-survey-1.4127871
57. https://wordsfest.ca/events/2020/monumental-problems
58. Daniel Paul, We Were Not the Savages, Fernwood Publishing, 2022, p. 183
59. Daniel Paul, *We Were Not the Savages*, Fernwood Publishing, 2022, p. 248
60. Daniel Paul, *We Were Not the Savages*, Fernwood Publishing, 2022, p. 205
61. Daniel Paul, *We Were Not the Savages*, Fernwood Publishing, 2022, p. 137
62. Daniel Paul, *We Were Not the Savages*, Fernwood Publishing, 2022, p. 29
63. https://activehistory.ca/wp-content/uploads/2011/07/Bennett-in-Chronicle-Herald.pdf
64. *National Post*, 'School drops Halifax founder's name over Mic'maq complaints,' July 5, 2011

65. John Shy, *The Oxford History of the British Empire: Volume II: The Eighteenth Century*, Chapter 14—The American Colonies in War and Revolution, 1748–1783

CHAPTER 9
66. www.nfb.ca/film/legendary-judge/
67. www.library.ubc.ca/archives/pdfs/bchf/bchq_1947_1.pdf, p. 1
68. www.library.ubc.ca/archives/pdfs/bchf/bchq_1947_1.pdf, p. 1
69. Adrien Gabriel Morice, *The History of the Northern Interior of British Columbia (formerly New Caledonia)*, (1660 to 1880,), p. 16
70. Hamar Foster, *Voicing Identity—Cultural Appropriation and Indigenous Issues*, Chapter 13—Sharp as a Knife: Judge Begbie and Reconciliation, p. 236
71. Chartres Brew (1864), "Letters to the Colonial Secretary of British Columbia, May 23, "Nobody Knows Him; Lhatŝ'aŝʔin and the Chilcotin War," https://canadianmysteries.ca/sites/klatsassin/home/indexen.html
72. www.timescolonist.com/opinion/mel-rothenburger-the-chilcotin-war-and-the-rewriting-of-history-4661043
73. David R. Williams, *The Man for a New Country*, Gray's Publishing Ltd., Sidney, British Columbia, 1977
74. Anthony Sarich (1993), *Report on the Cariboo-Chilcotin Justice Inquiry* (Province of British Columbia)
75. https://cpcml.ca/cpcmlarticle2210261033/
76. Peter Shawn Taylor, *The 1867 Project—Why Canada Should be Cherished, Not Cancelled*, Editor—Mark Milke, Chapter 10—A Crime Against Sir Matthew Begbie's Humanity, p. 126.
77. Peter Shawn Taylor, *The 1867 Project—Why Canada Should be Cherished, Not Cancelled*, Editor—Mark Milke, Chapter 10—A Crime Against Sir Matthew Begbie's Humanity, p. 126.
78. Tsilqot'in National Government (2016), "Tsilqot'in Nation Commends Law Society of BC for Removing Begbie Statue," NationTalk (June 3)

79. www.youtube.com/watch?v=aE9lhZU-Gb8
80. David R. Wiliams, *The Man for a New Country*, Gray's Publishing Ltd., Sidney, British Columbia, 1977, p. 275.
81. David R. Williams, *The Man for a New Country*, Gray's Publishing Ltd., Sidney, British Columbia, 1977, p. 1.

CHAPTER 10

82. www.nobelprize.org/prizes/literature/1953/summary/
83. https://dn790007.ca.archive.org/0/items/myafricanjourney00churuoft/myafricanjourney00churuoft.pdf
84. https://calgary.ctvnews.ca/protesters-crash-calgary-s-winston-churchill-monument-unveiling-1.6916827
85. https://globalnews.ca/news/7958911/edmonton-winston-churchill-statue-red-paint/?utm_medium=Twitter&utm_source=%40GlobalEdmonton
86. https://winstonchurchill.org/publications/finest-hour/finest-hour-160/leading-myths-churchill-advocated-the-first-use-of-lethal-gas/
87. https://winstonchurchill.org/publications/finest-hour/finest-hour-160/leading-myths-churchill-advocated-the-first-use-of-lethal-gas/
88. www.martingilbert.com/sir-martin-on-history/
89. www.martingilbert.com/sir-martin-on-history/
90. https://claremontreviewofbooks.com/an-interview-with-martin-gilbert/
91. https://winstonchurchill.org/publications/finest-hour/finest-hour-168/sir-martin-gilbert-in-his-own-words/
92. www.martingilbert.com/blog/churchill-forty-years-on/

93. www.martingilbert.com/blog/churchill-forty-years-on/
94. www.nationalchurchillmuseum.org/some-chicken-some-neck.html
95. www.thecanadianencyclopedia.ca/en/article/joseph-brant

CHAPTER 11
96. www.archives.gov.on.ca/en/explore/online/slavery/sophia_pooley.aspx
97. Dennis Corcoran, *Induction Day at Cooperstown*, McFarland and Company Inc., 2011, p. 17
98. www.nytimes.com/2021/05/28/world/canada/kamloops-mass-grave-residential-schools.html
99. https://nationalpost.com/opinion/terry-glavin-kamloops-first-nation-puts-even-more-distance-from-mass-grave-claim
100. https://nationalpost.com/opinion/terry-glavin-canada-slowly-acknowledging-there-never-was-a-mass-grave
101. https://republicofkanata.org/about-kevin-annett/
102. https://caid.ca/NoLonHid2010.pdf
103. www.amazon.ca/stores/Frances-Widdowson/author/B003NE9MQI?ref=ap_rdr&isDramIntegrated=true&shoppingPortalEnabled=true
104. www.cbc.ca/news/canada/calgary/frances-widdowson-mount-royal-university-fired-1.6303734
105. Joseph Quesnel, *The 1867 Project: Why Canada Should be Cherished—Not Cancelled*, published in 2023 by The Aristotle Foundation for Public Policy, p. 224
106. *National Post*, May 30, 2024
107. Carl Sagan, *THE DRAGONS OF EDEN: Speculations on the Evolution of Human Intelligence*, p. 91
108. www.peacetothepeople.com/quotes/carl-sagan

109. Residential Schools were no 'atrocity.' Just look at the evidence, *National Post*, April 2, 2025
110. www.catholicregister.org/item/1730-public-lecture-at-regent-college-canceled-amid-controversy

CHAPTER 12
111. Douglas Murray, *The War on the West*, Broadside Books, 2022, p. 120

Index

Academy of Music, 63, 64, 66
Act to Limit Slavery in Upper Canada, 121
African Ancestral Acknowledgement, 115
Africville, 42
Akins, Thomas B., 133
Alexander the Great, 139, 214
American Revolutionary War (War of Independence), 94, 117, 120, 121, 191
Antisemitism, 38, 40, 43
Ali, Ayaan Hirsi, 37–38, 40
Aliens Act of 1859, 159
Allies, 26, 181
Alphonse, Joe, 167
Annett, Kevin, 201–202
Annual Report of Indian Affairs, 209–210
Archives of British Columbia, 158
Archives of Ontario, 195
Aristotle Foundation for Public Policy, 205, 209
Asapo-Muxika (Crowfoot), 77
Assembly of Manitoba Chiefs, 197
Astaire, Fred, 179
Athabasca Glacier, 188
Aunt Jemima, 29, 32–33, 47
Auschwitz, 20, 26
BABE RUTH—A Superstar's Legacy, 30
Baden-Powell, Robert, 17
Bank Act of 1871, 77
Baseball Origins Committee, 197
Battle of Britain, 177
Beaches of Normandy, 27, 107, 225

Begbie, Matthew:
    Dakhel (Carrier) People, 160–161
    early days as a judge, 155–156
    gold discovered in Fraser Valley, 157
    legislation in BC, 159
    media coverage, 166–167
    murder trials, 163
    Native tribes, 160
    plaque in Quesnel, 164
    reputation, 59, 223
    Sir Matthew Begbie Elementary School, 160, 171
    statues, 168, 171, 172
    things named after him, 157
Begbie Summit, 157
Belarus, 10, 41, 116
Bell, Alexander Graham, 191
Bell Centre, 66
Bellevue House, 82–87, 137, 193
Bennett, Paul W., 50, 54, 145
Biggar, Emerson Bristol, 79
Biggar, Nigel, 211, 222
Black, Conrad, 185
Black History Month, 36
Black Lives Matter, 16–17, 32–33, 85, 91, 124, 125, 164, 181, 182, 200, 202
Bolt, Usain, 15, 16, 58
Book of Genesis, 25
Boy Scouts, 17
Bounty Proclamation of 1749, 141, 145, 146, 151
Brando, Marlon, 11, 37
Brant, Joseph, 191–194
Brewster, Willy, 162
BBC, 177

British Columbia, 27
(The) British Columbia Historical Quarterly, 158
British Columbia Legislature, 166
British North America Act, 85
British North American Exploring Expedition, 71
Bronfman, Charles, 49
(The) Bronzeville Historical Society, 33
Buffalo, 88, 183
CBC, 37, 93, 119, 125, 142, 144, 147, 150
CNN, 34, 36
Caesar, Julius, 222
Canada Day, 42
Canadian Army, 224
Canadian Bar Association, 170
(The) Canadian Encyclopedia, 195
Canadian History Report Card, 54
Canadian Pacific Railway, 64, 84
Canadian War Museum, 51
Cariboo-Chilcotin Justice Inquiry, 163, 165
Casimir, Rosanne, 198, 199, 201
Census of 1871, 75
Census of 2021, 76
Chadwick, Henry, 196
Champion, C. P., 206
Charlottetown Conference, 74
Chauvin, Derek, 16
Cherington, Tom, 112
Chilcotin War, 162, 227
Chinese Taipei, 24
Chinlac massacre, 160
Chinook, 156
Chow, Olivia, 112, 113, 114, 126, 129
Chretien, Jean, 67
(The) Chronicle-Herald, 144
Churchill Falls, 188
Churchill, Jennie Spencer, 175
Churchill, John, 175
Churchill, Randolph III, 181
Churchill Square, 182

Churchill, Winston, 26, 52, 107, 175, 176, 177, 179, 181, 182
Civil War, 11, 64, 72
Clark, Christy, 163, 168
Clark, Isabella, 70, 71, 83
College and university campuses, 27, 33
Colonialism, 42, 43, 108, 181, 211
Colonialism: A Moral Reckoning, 211, 222
Colony of British Columbia, 72
Colosseum, 219
Colossus of Rhodes, 219
Columbus, Christopher, 220, 221
Columbus Day, 221
Combes, William, 202
Common School Act, 95
Comprehensive School Act of 1871, 96
Confederation Day, 74
Cooper, Gary, 159, 172
Corbet, Mary Lazier, 80
Cornwallis, Edward:
    arrival in Nova Scotia, 134
    Cornwallis Junior High, 144
    Cornwallis: The Violent Birth of Halifax, 143
    early years, 135
    media reporting, 142, 144, 147, 148, 149, 150
    meeting Indigenous chiefs, 135
    renaming the park and street, 141, 146
    reputation, 59
    scalping proclamation, 138, 141, 143, 146, 150, 151, 152
    statue, 140, 141, 142, 143, 144, 146, 147, 148, 149, 150
CTV, 148, 166, 198
Cuba, 43
Czechs, 24
D-Day, 27, 107, 181, 189, 225
Dalhousie University, 148

Dallaire, Joanne, 98, 99, 127
Darius, 141, 142, 214
Darwin, Charles, 72, 177
Dartmouth Massacre, 137, 146
DEI, 36, 44, 45, 46, 118
De Mille, Nelson, 57
David and Goliath, 25
Dead Sea Scrolls, 217
Democratic party, 38
(The) Diary of a Young Girl, 43
Deveau, Leo J., 143, 144, 145, 149
Disraeli, Benjamin, 78
Disrobing the aboriginal industry: the deception behind indigenous cultural preservation, 203
(The) Dominion Institute, 49, 50, 51, 54
Donner Prize, 203, 206
(The) Dorchester Review, 206, 209
Doubleday, Abner, 195, 196–197, 199, 201, 208
Doubleday Field, 195
Douglas, James, 171
THE DRAGONS OF EDEN: Speculations on the Evolution of Human Intelligence, 208
Drew, Benjamin, 193, 194, 195
Duke University, 51
Dundas, Henry:
    lawyer, 121
    politician, 121, 122
    removing the name, 114, 120, 127
    reputation, 59, 125, 127
    slavery, 121, 123
Duke of Marlborough, 175
Dundas, Jennifer, 119, 125
Dundas, Linda, 119
Dutil, Patrice, 86, 87, 101, 102–103, 105, 106, 127, 128, 194
Eastwood, Clint, 159
Edinburgh University Student Association, 124

(The) 1867 Project: Why Canada Should Be Cherished—Not Cancelled, 165, 205
Ellis, Catherine, 98, 99, 127
(The) End of Race Politics: Arguments for a Colorblind America, 32
Erikson, Leif, 220, 222
Ethiopia, 38
Executions, 73, 169
Fascism, 204
Father Le Loutre's War, 135
(The) Final Solution, 26
Flanagan, Tom, 206, 207, 208
Floyd, George, 16, 17, 32, 33, 117, 119, 125, 125, 164, 182
Fontaine, Phil, 197
Ford, Henry, 178
Fort Sumter, 196
Fort Victoria, 161
Fortress Louisbourg, 135, 136, 137, 138, 143
Foster, Hamar, 168, 169, 170, 187
Fox, Terry, 200
Framework for History and Commemoration: National Historic Sites, 58, 85
Frank, Anne, 43
(The) Fraser Institute, 206, 207
Freeman, Alice (Faith Fenton), 65
Freeman, Morgan, 36–37
French and Indian War, 135
Friends of Egerton Ryerson, 104
Frum, Barbara, 197
Frum, David, 219
Fry, Michael, 124
Gay, Claudine, 34–35
(The) Gay Divorcee, 179
Gaza, 34, 40, 43, 108, 151
Genocide, 35, 40, 80, 81, 104, 125, 141, 144, 145, 147, 151, 180, 198, 206, 207, 208, 211, 212

Germany, 11, 13, 39, 40, 59, 81, 82, 213, 225, 226
Ghana, 120, 121, 123
Ghandi, Mahatma, 180
Gift of the Bambino, 29
Gilbert, Martin, 184–188, 227
Giles, Harry, 25–27
(The) Giles School, 22–23
Gilfillan, Rory, 54
Girl Guides, 17
Gladstone, William, 78
Glavin, Terry, 205
(The) Globe and Mail, 74
Godfrey, Paul, 111
Goebbels, Joseph, 227
Gogh, Theo van, 37
Gold Fields Act of 1859, 159
Googoo, Roderick, 148
Gradual Civilization Bill, 71, 72
Grammar, 21, 22, 25, 100
Granatstein, J. L., 51, 53, 54, 55
Grand Trunk Railway, 71
Grant, Ulysses S., 85
Grave Error: How the Media Misled Us (and the Truth about Residential Schools), 206
Graves, Abner, 196, 201
Graves at residential schools, 90, 99, 182, 197, 199, 200, 201, 205, 206, 208, 211, 212
Great Depression, 210
Green, Kenneth, 39
Green, Nancy, 32
Greene, Nancy, 32
Green party, 39
Grenier, John E., 152
Gretzky, Wayne, 191
Griffiths, Rudyard, 49
Gwyn, Richard, 70, 72, 74, 77, 78, 79, 85, 86
Halifax, 42
Halifax Regional Municipal council, 144
Halifax Regional School Board, 144
Hamas, 27, 33, 34, 38, 39, 40, 52, 108, 109, 127
Hamilton, 19
Hamilton-Wentworth District School Board, 19
Hamilton West-Ancaster Dundas, 19
Hanlan's Point, 30, 111
Hansard, 88
Harper, Stephen, 67, 197, 198, 206
Harvard University, 34–35
Hatt, Samuel, 193
Henry Dundas Committee of Ontario, 119, 126
Heritage Minutes, 50
Heritage Toronto, 112
Hilderman, Jane, 86
Hillier, Rick, 129
Historica Foundation, 49
(The) History of the Northern Interior of British Columbia (formerly New Caledonia), (1660 to 1880, 160
History of the Settlement of Halifax, 133
Hitler, Adolf, 15, 52, 59, 84, 145, 150, 179, 180, 227
Hitler Youth, 82
Holocaust, 26–27, 34, 57, 150, 151, 184, 185, 213
Holocaust Education Week, 27
Hong Kong, 24, 187
House of Commons, 20, 45, 123, 188, 189, 207, 226, 227
Howard, Albert, 203
(The) Hub, 34, 49, 209
Hughes, Coleman, 32
Humber College, 21, 22, 25
Hunka, Yaroslav, 226
Hunter, Andrew, 194
Hunter, Mitzie, 53
Huron-Wendat, 81
ILTV Israel, 38–40
India, 13
Indian Act, 42

Indian Residential Schools
   Settlement Agreement, 197
Infidel, 37
Ingstad, Helge, 220, 221, 222
International Education Association, 24
International Churchill Society, 177
Inuit, 197
Israel Museum, 217
Iroquois, 81, 115, 191
Islamophobia, 38, 42
Israel-Hamas War, 27, 38
It Was Dark There All the Time: Sophia Burthen and the Legacy of Slavery in Canada, 194
Jasper National Park, 188
Jefferson, Thomas, 225
Jerusalem, 27, 212, 213, 217
Jews, 10, 13, 17, 26, 35, 38, 39, 40, 42, 43, 81, 116, 145, 150, 151, 175, 184, 214
Johnson, Dwayne, 217
Jones, Peter, 97, 109
Joseph Brant Hospital, 192
Joseph Brant Memorial Statue, 191
Joseph Brant Museum, 192
Kamloops Indian Band, 198
Kamloops Residential School, 202
Kenya, 38
Khadintel, 161
King George II, 134
King George III, 192
King, Mackenzie, 64, 189
King, Martin Luther, 31
King's University College, 19
Klatsassin, 163, 167
Klatsassin Memorial Day, 167
Komagata Maru, 42
Korean War, 224
Koreans, 24
Labour party, 38
Laden, Osama bin, 33, 52
Lady Agnes, 64
L'Anse aux Meadows, 220, 222
Lakefield College, 54

Land acknowledgements, 114, 212, 213, 214, 215
Hector-Louis Langevin, 74
The Last Witness, 26, 57, 185
Laurier, Wilfrid, 63, 84
Law Society of British Columbia, 157, 166, 168, 169, 170
Law Society of Upper Canada, 69
Layton, Jack, 112
Lemon, Don, 36
Lewis, Avi, 38
Lewis, Stephen, 38
Liberation75, 27
Lincoln, Abraham, 64, 78, 222, 225
Lincoln Alexander School of Law, 108
Lochhead, Andrew, 113
Lord Carnarvon, 74
Luftwaffe, 177
Lutz, John, 166
MS St. Louis, 43
Macdonald, Hugh, 68
Macdonald, John A.:
   accused of being a racist and bigot, 16, 84, 87, 193, 223
   achievements, 76, 77, 78, 79, 85, 86, 87, 215
   birth, 67
   coming to Canada, 68
   daughter Mary, 78
   death, 79
   death of brother James, 68
   death of son John, 70
   elections, 64
   government administrator, 70, 72
   head tax on Chinese, 84
   Indigenous people, 77, 78, 87, 223
   lawyer, 69, 70, 85
   marriage to Isabella, 70–71
   politics and the politician, 63, 73–78
   popularity, 69

residential schools, 80, 81
running for office, 69
Sir John A. Macdonald Day, 80
Sir John A. Macdonald Fact Sheet, 87
Sir John A. Macdonald Parkway, 79
speaking, 65, 76
statues, 79, 85
student, 69
Toronto's Friends of Sir John A. Macdonald, 86
Macdonald-Laurier Institute, 43, 45, 122
MacDonald, Monica, 148
Maclean's magazine, 86
Major League Baseball, 197
(The) Man for a New Country, 146
(The) Man Who Shot Liberty Valance, 146
Maritime Museum of BC, 159
Martin, Paul, 197
Marxist-Leninist Party of Canada, 164
McKenna, Catherine, 58
Mackenzie, William Lyon, 73
McDonald, Lynn, 103, 104, 109, 122
McGill University, 127
McMaster University, 19, 80, 81
Melville Monument, 123
Memorial Day, 196
Memorial University, 46, 221
Mengele, Joseph, 26
Methuselah, 25
Métis, 114, 197, 206, 209
Mills, David, 88
Mi'kmaq, 131–153
Mohawk Institute, 195
Mohawk Warriors, 193
Moms Against Racism, 41, 43, 77, 187
Montreal's Cadre d'intervention en Reconnaissance, 128
Morice, Adrien Gabriel, 160–161
Mount Begbie, 157
Mount Columbia, 188
Mount Royal University, 202
Mount Rushmore, 225
Mount Vernon, 194
Mowat, Oliver, 69
Mulroney, Brian, 67
Munk Debates, 49
Murray, Douglas, 85, 222
My African Journey, 176–178
National Association of Scholars, 55
National Baseball Hall of Fame and Museum, 195, 196
National Film Board of Canada, 157
National Gallery of Canada, 192
National Park Service, 87
National Policy, 63
(The) National Post, 22, 103, 152, 205, 206, 209, 211
Netanyahu, Benjamin, 217
Netherlands, 37, 39
(The) New York Times, 33, 57, 76, 118, 198
New York Yankees, 30, 111
Newton, Isaac, 177
Newton, Melanie, 125–127, 148
Nigeria, 21
Nixon, Richard, 226
Noah, 25
Nobel Peace Prize, 202
Nobel Prize in Literature, 176
Northwest Mounted Police, 42, 77
On the Waterfront, 12, 37
Ontario Historical Society, 109
Ontario Human Rights Commission, 31
Ontario Ministry of Education, 22, 55, 219
Order of Canada, 23, 51, 167
Oregon Treaty, 161
Owens, Jesse, 15, 16, 58, 59, 73
Oxford University, 127
Palace of Versailles, 219
Palmer, Geoffrey, 124
Parents Advisory Council, 21, 24, 52

Parks Canada, 58, 82, 84, 85, 137, 193
Paul, Daniel, 141–145, 150
Peace and Friendship Park, 141
Pearl Harbor, 189
Peary, Robert, 178
Peel District School Board, 43
PepsiCo, 33
Pettit, Sydney G., 158
Phelps, Lisa, 148
Phillip, Aretha, 129
Piasetzki, Greg, 209–211
Pickford, Mary, 63
Poland, 10, 11, 20, 27, 41, 116, 187
Pooley, Robert, 193
Pooley, Sophia Burthen, 193–195
Por, Anna, 22
Pre-emption Act of 1860, 159
Presentism, 218
Prince Charles, 185
Princeton University, 36
Pro-Palestinian encampment, 39
(The) Protocols of the Elders of Zion, 151
Providence Grays, 30
Public school system, 22
Pulitzer Prize, 208
Quaker Oats, 33
Queen Elizabeth II, 17, 200, 202
Queen Victoria, 17, 71, 159
Quesnel, Joseph, 204
Ramsay, Mike, 45–46
Ramsey, Adam, 124
Recognition Review Community Advisory Committee, 120
Red Army, 226
(The) Refugee: or the Narratives of Fugitive Slaves in Canada, 193, 195
Remembrance Day, 27, 127, 128
Residential schools, 42, 80–81, 93, 99, 102–105, 124, 129, 180, 183, 193, 197–202, 205–211, 223, 227
Rideau Club of Ottawa, 13
Rogers, Ginger, 179
Rohmer, Richard, 225

Romania, 10, 41, 116
Roosevelt, Franklin Delano, 52–53, 189, 195, 196
Roosevelt, Teddy, 225
Rothenburger, Mel, 162
Rounders, 196
Royal Canadian Mint, 178
Royal Canadian Mounted Police, 77
Royal Canadian Yacht Club, 13
Royal Historical Society, 103, 122
Royal Military College, 51
Royal Norwegian Navy, 221
Royal York Hotel, 225
Russia and Russians, 21, 151, 186, 187, 226
Ruth, Babe, 29–30, 111, 112
Ryerson, Egerton:
    birth and early life, 94
    educator, 95–97, 102, 105, 215
    Indigenous people, 96–97
    minister, 95
    residential schools and training schools, 93, 97–98, 102–103, 223
    statue, 91–94, 107
    Ryerson University, 91, 93–94, 98, 101, 102, 103
    Superintendent of Education, 95
Sagan, Carl, 208
St. Andrew Square, 123
St. Lawrence Hall, 89
Saint Mary's University, 50
Sankofa Square, 114–117, 120, 123, 129
Saudi Arabia, 14, 38, 66
Savage, Mike, 149
Schaghen, Pieter, 117, 118
Scotiabank Arena, 66
Seneca College, 26
Seneca at York, 26
Shackleton, Ernest, 178
Shakespeare, William, 177
Shirer, William, 184
Shy, John, 152
Siksika Indian band, 77

Simcoe, John Graves, 56, 83, 121, 193, 215
Sinclair, Murray, 102, 139
Sir Winston Churchill Square, 188
Sir Winston Churchill Provincial Park, 188
Sir Winston Churchill Society of Calgary, 181
Smith, Danielle, 181
Smith, Donald B., 103, 109
60 Minutes, 36
Slaves and slavery, 42, 56, 71, 83, 117, 121, 121–123, 192–195
Snow, Dave, 43–44
Social Democrats, 39
South African apartheid, 40
Spalding, Albert, 196, 201
Stagg, Ron, 101, 106–107, 178
Stalin, Joseph, 52
Standing Strong Task Force, 98–100, 104–106, 109, 127
Stanford University, 36
Steiger, Rod, 11
Stefanik, Elise M., 34–35
Stevens, Tom, 30
Stewart, James, 146
Stine, Anne, 220, 221
Submission, 37
Sullivan, Sam, 167–168
Tattrie, Jon, 143
Taylor, Peter Shawn, 164–165
(The) Times of London, 76
(The) Truth North Times, 20
Thrillerfest, 57
Times Square, 117–119
Toronto Blue Jays, 30, 111
Toronto District School Board, 45, 218
Toronto French School, 22
Toronto Granite Club, 13
Toronto Metropolitan University, 105, 106, 108, 109, 113, 127
Toronto Public Library, 120

(The) Toronto Sun, 111, 112
Toronto's Guiding Principles for Commemoration, 128
Tory, John, 114
Town of York Historical Society, 88
Tower of London, 66
Treaty of Aix-la-Chapelle. 135, 137
Trudeau, Justin, 67, 163, 199
Trudeau, Pierre, 67
Trump, Donald, 226
Truth and Reconciliation Commission, 102, 104, 105, 139, 146, 164, 197, 198, 202, 211
Tupper, Charles, 65
UCLA, 34
Underground Railroad, 42, 107, 117, 121
UNESCO World Heritage Site, 220
United Empire Loyalists, 94, 117
University of British Columbia, 19, 211
University of Calgary, 109, 206
University of Cambridge, 158
University of Guelph, 43, 103, 105, 122
University of Lethbridge, 204
University of Manitoba, 119
University of Oxford, 211
University of Toronto, 39, 51, 96, 109, 115, 125, 127, 169, 184, 218
University of Victoria, 158, 166, 168, 170, 202
University of Western Ontario, 36, 184
Victoria Park Square, 191
Vikings, 219, 220, 221
Vinland, 220
Voicing Identity—Cultural Appropriation and Indigenous Issues, 169
Waddington, Alfred, 162
Wallace, Mike, 36
(The) War on the West, 85, 222

Washington, George, 192, 194, 225
Waterloo Region District School Board, 45
We Were Not the Savages, 141
West India Company, 117
Wherry, Aaron, 86
White privilege, 10, 17
White supremacy, 17, 30, 32, 42, 45, 46–47, 93, 113, 125, 144, 150
Wicki, Silvan, 15
Widdowson, Frances, 202, 204
Wilberforce, William, 122
Williams, David R., 171
Wilson, David, 218
Wilson, John, 131–133, 134, 139
Winston Churchill Range, 188
Woke, Wokers, woke history, 17, 18, 32, 36, 38, 40, 82, 88, 128, 136, 139, 149, 164, 200, 202, 208, 223

Women's Christian Temperance Movement, 65
World War I, 182, 224
World War II, 26, 42, 43, 53, 82, 83, 107, 145, 175, 179, 180, 184, 185, 186, 189, 196, 213, 224, 226
Wright, William and Orville, 178
(The) Writers' Union of Canada, 31
Wynne, Kathleen, 53
Yad Vashem, 27
Yonge-Dundas Square, 114, 120, 180
York University, 26, 51, 202
Zedong, Mao, 52
Zelenskyy, Volodymyr, 226

Acknowledgements

IT WAS MY AGENT Bill Hanna who suggested that I write a book about history and the importance of preserving it. I had been doing talks and presentations for book clubs, historical societies and other groups about this and it had become a sticky point with me. The fact is if you don't know the history, the chances of it being stolen right from under your nose are greater. That is exactly what we have been witnessing with the 'woke' version of history, which make no mistake, is revisionist history and it's been getting into overdrive to the point of indoctrination.

The initial intent for this book was to bring my personal experience into the equation and devote one section to what has happened to the legacy of our first prime minister, Sir John A. Macdonald, and balance that against historical fact before combining the stories of Egerton Ryerson, Henry Dundas (both of them Ontario-based) and Edward Cornwallis (Nova Scotia) into another section. Then it was suggested that I also include Judge Matthew Begbie (British Columbia). As things turned out, it became clear that each of those figures deserved a chapter of their own and SLEEPWOKING became a Canada-wide project.

As I delved into research on these notables from our past and explored other elements crucial to the book, I received help from many people. Patrice Dutil, respected professor, author and expert on history, is Canada's foremost mind on John A. Macdonald today. He was of invaluable assistance when it came not only to this man, but others as well. I also want to thank Lynn McDonald, Jennifer Dundas, Paul Bennett, Leo J. Deveau, Tom Flanagan, Hamar Foster, Rory Gilfillin, John Lutz, Mark Milke, Greg Piasetzki, Mike Ramsay, Mel Rothenburger, Dave Snow, Ron

Stagg, J. D. M. Stewart, and Sam Sullivan, the former mayor of Vancouver. A number of those people, in addition to my friend Julian Fantino and Don Cranston of the Canadian Institute for Historical Education, provided testimonials for the book and I want to thank each and every one of them for that.

Two individuals no longer with us—renowned historian Sir Martin Gilbert and noted Canadian educator Harry Giles—left a permanent stamp with me when I met and interviewed them years ago and should be included here as well.

From the production end, this book would not have been possible without the talent and keen insights from designer Jan Westendorp and the printer, Printing Legacy.

Finally, it's not easy sharing your life with someone when that person is also sharing all their waking hours, never mind nights, with historical figures from the past. I realize this made it a crowded household at times. Thank you, Dorothy, for putting up with me.

About the Author

JERRY AMERNIC HAS BEEN a newspaper reporter and columnist, feature writer for magazines, an editor and publisher, college instructor, and media consultant. He is the author of books of fiction and non-fiction. His first book—*Victims: The Orphans of Justice*—examined Canada's criminal justice system from the purview of victims of violent crime and led to the column *Justice For All* in The Toronto Sun. He also worked with Julian Fantino, former Toronto police chief and Commissioner of the Ontario Provincial Police, on his memoir DUTY—*The Life of a Cop*.

Jerry's novel *Gift of the Bambino* won rave reviews in Canada and the United States. It's about a young boy and his grandfather, and how they are bound by baseball and Babe Ruth. Jerry's extensive research into baseball's idol led to BABE RUTH—*A Superstar's Legacy*, a book that looked at this enduring legacy on many fronts over and above baseball. Ruth's grandson Tom Stevens wrote the Foreword. Jerry has done presentations for the National Baseball Hall of Fame and Museum in Cooperstown, New York and many other organizations.

His novel QUMRAN is a work of historical fiction with biblical themes, while *The Last Witness* is about the last living survivor of the Holocaust in a near-future world that doesn't know history. The importance of not losing sight of our history is a central theme with Jerry who often lectures on the dire state of historical knowledge in contemporary society. His latest book SLEEPWOKING tackles this head-on. Jerry has written for The Globe and Mail, The National Post, The Toronto Star, other newspapers, and media websites. He often speaks to book clubs, library clubs, historical societies, and other groups.

www.ingramcontent.com/pod-product-compliance
Lightning Source LLC
Chambersburg PA
CBHW020522080526
44583CB00013B/701